Mental Health and Wellbeing in Rural Regions

This book considers how rurality interacts with the mental health and well-being of individuals and communities in different regional settings. Through the use of international and comparative case studies, the book offers insight into the spatiality of mental health diagnoses, experiences, services provision and services access between and within rural areas. It is the first book to specifically address rural mental health geographies from an international perspective, and will be of interest to researchers and policymakers in rural studies, regional studies, health geography and rural mental health.

Sarah-Anne Munoz is Reader and Acting Head of Department in Rural Health and Wellbeing at the University of the Highlands and Islands, UK.

Steve F. Bain is Professor and Interim Dean of the College of Education and Human Performance at Texas A&M University-Kingsville, USA.

Routledge Advances in Regional Economics, Science and Policy

The Canada–U.S. Border in the 21st Century
Trade, Immigration and Security in the Age of Trump
John B. Sutcliffe and William P. Anderson

Economic Clusters and Globalization
Diversity and Resilience
Edited by Francisco Puig and Berrbizne Urzelai

Transnational Regions in Historical Perspective
Edited by Marten Boon, Hein A.M. Klemann and Ben Wubs

Urban Development in China under the Institution of Land Rights
Jieming Zhu

The Geography of Mobility, Wellbeing and Development in China
Understanding Transformations Through Big Data
Edited by Wenjie Wu and Yiming Wang

Traveling Expertise and Regional Development
Andreas Öjehag-Pettersson and Tomas Mitander

Governing Cities
Asia's Urban Transformation
Edited by Kris Hartley, Glen Kuecker, Michael Waschak, Jun Jie Woo, and Charles Chao Rong Phua

Mental Health and Wellbeing in Rural Regions
International Perspectives
Edited by Sarah-Anne Munoz and Steve F. Bain

For more information about this series, please visit www.routledge.com/series/RAIRESP

Mental Health and Wellbeing in Rural Regions

International Perspectives

Edited by Sarah-Anne Munoz and Steve F. Bain

Routledge
Taylor & Francis Group
LONDON AND NEW YORK

First published 2021
by Routledge
2 Park Square, Milton Park, Abingdon, Oxon OX14 4RN

and by Routledge
52 Vanderbilt Avenue, New York, NY 10017

Routledge is an imprint of the Taylor & Francis Group, an informa business

British Library Cataloguing-in-Publication Data
A catalogue record for this book is available from the British Library

Library of Congress Cataloging-in-Publication Data
Names: Muñoz, Sarah-Anne, editor. | Bain, Steve F., editor.
Title: Mental health and wellbeing in rural regions: international perspectives / edited by Sarah-Anne Munoz and Steve F. Bain.
Description: Abingdon, Oxon; New York, NY: Routledge, 2021. | Series: Routledge advances in regional economics, science and policy | Includes bibliographical references and index.
Identifiers: LCCN 2020015098 (print) | LCCN 2020015099 (ebook) |
Subjects: LCSH: Rural population—Mental health—Cross-cultural studies. | Rural mental health services—Cross-cultural studies.
Classification: LCC RA790.5 .M4183 2021 (print) |
LCC RA790.5 (ebook) | DDC 362.209173/4—dc23
LC record available at https://lccn.loc.gov/2020015098
LC ebook record available at https://lccn.loc.gov/2020015099

ISBN: 978-1-138-34344-3 (hbk)
ISBN: 978-0-429-43913-1 (ebk)

Typeset in Bembo
by codeMantra

This book is dedicated to all rural residents past, present, and future and to all those who serve these amazing communities

For Mr. A., who inspires me like no other
- Sarah-Anne

To my family and friends who have encouraged me...
To Maria for being you...
Thank you!
- Steve

Contents

List of figures ix
List of tables x
List of contributors xi

Introduction: mental health and wellbeing in rural regions of the Global North 1
STEVE F. BAIN AND SARAH-ANNE MUNOZ

1 **Adversity and resilience: rural mental health in Australia** 8
HAZEL DALTON AND DAVID PERKINS

2 **Mental health and wellbeing among migrants in rural areas of the Global North: evidence from the literature** 26
JOHANNE JEAN-PIERRE AND LINAMAR CAMPOS-FLORES

3 **Muddying the therapeutic geographies of mental healthcare: carescapes of psychiatric transition in the Scottish Highlands** 40
CHRISTOPHER PHILO AND HESTER PARR

4 **Care farming, therapeutic landscapes, and rurality in the UK** 57
RICHARD GORMAN

5 **Non-clinical wellbeing interventions in rural regions** 75
SARAH MORTON AND SARA BRADLEY

6 **Delivering effective treatment in rural regions** 94
JAMES IKONOMOPOULOS, YA-WEN MELISSA LIANG, KAREN FURGERSON, AND KRISTOPHER GARZA

7 **Wildlife: exploring the potential of an innovative digital narrative approach to improve mental health interventions for adolescents in indigenous rural populations of low- to middle-income countries** 116
MARK GRINDLE AND JOHANNES H. DE KOCK

8 **Rurality: social forces, stress, and mental health** 133
ROBERT VILLA AND EVA MOYA

9 **Rural mental health and global ethical perspectives** 150
STEVE F. BAIN AND SARAH-ANNE MUNOZ

10 **Towards a research agenda for global rural mental health** 165
SARAH-ANNE MUNOZ AND STEVE F. BAIN

Index 171

Figures

1.1 Nine guiding principles of Aboriginal and Torres Strait Islander social and emotional wellbeing (as outlined in Gayaa Dhuwi) 11
1.2 Suicide rates (A) by regional of usual residence, Australia, 2017; (B) by region, 2013–2017, Australia 12
1.3 Key issues for the Australian healthcare system (from "Shifting the Dial") 14
3.1 "Organic" fusing ("muddying") of tree and wall at asylum 52
5.1 Individual, social and material model 80
7.1 Comparison of mental health care workers per 100,000 population and government mental health expenditure per capita by region 118
8.1 Rurality: clinical/activist paradigm 138

Tables

2.1 The corpus 28
2.2 Document type references 28
5.1 ISM model used to interpret information collected from case study sites 80
7.1 Comparative mental health human resources: selected countries' national averages per 100,000 population 127
7.2 SA's mental health workforce compared to that of LMICs and other high MICs per 100,000 population 127
7.3 South Africa's rural population sizes, health facilities, and selected mental health human resources and rates per 100,000 population 128

Contributors

Steve F. Bain is a Professor of Counseling Education and Interim Dean of the College of Education and Human Performance at Texas A&M University-Kingsville, USA. He is a Licensed Professional Counselor Intern Supervisor and a National Certified Counselor (NCC). His research interests include rural mental health counselling, global rural mental health collaborations, contemporary leadership issues, graduate student success, and self-injurers. Dr Bain has extensive experience working with rural communities as they seek to address the mental health challenges so pervasive with rural and remote populations.

Sara Bradley is a Research Fellow in Rural Health and Wellbeing at the University of the Highlands and Islands. She has extensive experience of carrying out qualitative and evaluative work in rural health contexts. Her research interests include social prescribing and the use of the outdoors, green exercise and non-pharmaceutical interventions to promote health and mental wellbeing.

Linamar Campos-Flores holds a Master's Degree in Intercultural Mediation (Université de Sherbrooke) and is a PhD candidate in Human Geography at Université de Montréal. She was awarded the FRQSC scholarship for her research project on the Seasonal Agricultural Workers Program which hires Latin-American men and women to work in the Canadian fields and greenhouses. One of her interests is the emotional dimension in the study of social phenomena through the lenses of Emotional Geographies. She also explores the overlap of intersectionality and post-colonial perspectives.

Hazel Dalton is the Research Leader and Senior Research Fellow (Executive) at the University of Newcastle's Centre for Rural and Remote Mental Health, based in Orange, New South Wales, Australia. She manages research across mental health promotion (including the Rural Adversity Mental Health Program), innovation in mental health service provision (including integrated care), and rural suicide prevention.

Johannes H. De Kock is a Research Fellow in Digital Health at the University of the Highlands and Islands, UK. He is also a practising chartered clinical psychologist with a special interest in adolescent and young adult mental health.

Karen Furgerson is an Associate Professor and School Counseling Coordinator in the Department of Educational Leadership and Counseling at Texas A&M University, Kingsville, USA.

Kristopher Garza is an Associate Professor and Clinical Mental Health Counseling Coordinator in the Department of Educational Leadership and Counseling at Texas A&M University, Kingsville, USA.

Richard Gorman is a Postdoctoral Research Fellow in Geography at the University of Exeter, UK. He is a cultural geographer with particular interests in health and the more-than-human. His research takes an interdisciplinary approach to understand situated practices of health, care, and medicine. He is specifically interested in how health intersects with people's cultural, ethical, and emotional relationships with animals and opens up complex policy interfaces relating human and animal care.

Mark Grindle is a Senior Lecturer in Digital Health at the University of the Highlands and Islands, UK.

James Ikonomopoulos is an Assistant Professor in the Department of Educational Leadership and Counseling at Texas A&M University, Kingsville, USA.

Johanne Jean-Pierre, PhD, is an Assistant Professor in the School of Child and Youth Care at Ryerson University. She holds a PhD in Sociology from McMaster University and conducts bilingual research projects in the fields of sociology of education and child and youth studies. Her current research program explores postsecondary trajectories and experiences, alternative school discipline practices, and child and youth care pedagogy. Her research focuses on the social-cultural dynamics that can inform promising policies and practices to work with refugee and immigrant youth, African Canadian communities, and linguistic minorities such as Francophone minority communities. In 2019, she co-edited a bilingual special issue of the *Canadian Journal of Sociology* (volume 44, no. 4) titled "African Canadians, Gender and Sexuality".

Ya-Wen Melissa Liang is an Assistant Professor in the Department of Educational Leadership and Counseling at Texas A&M University, Kingsville, USA.

Sarah Morton is a design engineer and ethnographer at the Centre for Clinical Brain Sciences, University of Edinburgh. Her research covers a broad range of interests including improving outcomes post-stroke, reducing sedentary behaviour, pain management, end of life care, virtual reality (VR) greenspaces for therapeutic benefit, and how greenspace can be used to address mood-related issues and improve quality of life. She manages co-design projects to develop digital and non-digital interventions for use in clinical, healthcare, and community settings.

Eva Moya is a graduate of the Texas A&M University-Kingsville Clinical/Activist MSW program. She has over 20 years' experience working with Children Youth and Families in the rural US-Mexico Border in Texas. Eva has a Bachelor's Degree in Social Work from the University of Texas Pan American (now UTRGV) and obtained her Master's Degree in Education with a major in Guidance and Counseling. She has over 15 years' experience with social services. The bulk of her social work experience comes from the Texas Department of Family and Protective Services in South Texas both as a family-based safety services worker and as an investigator.

Sarah-Anne Munoz is a Reader in Rural Health and Wellbeing at the University of the Highlands and Islands, Scotland, UK where she is the Acting Head of the Division of Rural Health and Wellbeing. She is a Health Geographer with research interests in rural mental health, rural health services, citizen participation, and non-pharmaceutical interventions. Her expertise is in qualitative research and participatory methods. She leads a team of social scientists at UHI who conduct research on community engagement and co-production in rural health. She also has a longstanding research interest in the role of the outdoors and natural landscape in the promotion of health and wellbeing.

Hester Parr is a Professor in the School of Geographical and Earth Sciences at the University of Glasgow, UK. She has wide-ranging research interests spanning questions of health, mental health, nature-encounters, political activisms, collaborative methods, emotional geographies, and creative geohumanities. She routinely works with community organisations and research partners to deliver a "geography that matters". Her previous research has investigated the relationship between mental health and place by focusing on how "mentally ill identities" are defined by reference to streets, institutions, cities, regions, virtualities, natures, and mobilities.

David Perkins is the Director and Professor of Rural Health Research at the University of Newcastle's Centre for Rural and Remote Mental Health, based in Orange, New South Wales, Australia. He has extensive research experience in mental health services, rural suicide prevention, public health, rural health, and primary healthcare. David's career spans senior management and health service research roles in both the UK and Australia.

Christopher Philo is a Professor of Geography at the University of Glasgow, UK. His ongoing research interests concern the historical, cultural, and rural geographies of mental ill health. His historical research on "madness" and asylums was brought together in his 2004 publication *A Geographical History of Institutional Provision for the Insane from Medieval Times to the 1860s in England and Wales: The Space Reserved for Insanity*. He is an editor of the journal *Progress in Human Geography*.

Robert Villa is an Associate Professor and Clinical/Activist MSW Program Director in the Department of Social Work at the Texas A&M University, Kingsville, USA, and responsible for *Council on Social Work Education Accreditation* of the program. He developed the Rurality Paradigm for use with the diverse populations along the US-Mexico border *Colonias*. He was formerly Director of the Social Work Department at United Arab Emirates University, Al Ain, where he developed both the Bachelor of Social Work and the Master of Social Work Programs. Both programs received favourable reviews by the International Association of Schools of Social Work. Dr Villa earned his PhD at University of Utah Graduate School of Social Work and Master of Social Work from New Mexico Highlands University. He has ten years of experience working with the rural villages and communities in the United Arab Emirates. He has over 30 years of experience working and organising in rural New Mexico and South Texas. He has over 25 years of academic experience as faculty member, Director, Associate Dean, and Dean.

Introduction

Mental health and wellbeing in rural regions of the Global North

Steve F. Bain and Sarah-Anne Munoz

In the early years of the twenty-first century, we have seen a shift in the public discourse surrounding mental health. Celebrities and public figures are increasingly speaking openly about their own mental ill health and strategies for maintaining mental wellbeing. In 2019, the editors of this book met Davey, an impassioned young social entrepreneur who spoke about how, eight years ago, he decided to make his first podcast talking about his mental ill health and personal experience of suicidal ideation – because he felt that such an open account by a young man *had never been publicly given before.* We now live in a context within the UK and, to a greater or lesser extent, other countries within the Global North where mental ill health and/or wellbeing is openly discussed routinely by celebrities, within public health messages, within the press, other media and, to some extent, within general day-to-day conversation.

Whilst it is undoubtedly positive that mental ill health is now more openly on the public agenda, it would be disingenuous to suggest that this means mental health stigma is a thing of the past. Work such as that by Bowen, Kinderman and Cooke (2019) and Ohlsson (2018) shows that while public discourses may have shifted from the openly stigmatising language of the (recent) past, the way in which mental ill health is discussed in some public realms still holds the power of 'othering'. Bowen et al.'s (2019) analysis of British tabloids, for example, demonstrates an association between discussions of schizophrenia and violence. Orphanidou and Kadianaki's (2018) work also demonstrates how media discourse of mental ill health can play a role in constructions of an individualistic blame culture that places an onus on people to self-manage their way out of a depression for which they are positioned as personally responsible. And in the Australia context, the work of Kenez, O'Halloran and Liamputtong (2015) shows that within the press, there is still proportionally a greater representation of mental illness than there is of mental wellbeing. However, Ma's (2017) review of media portrayals of mental ill health interestingly finds that 'mental illnesses in direct-to-consumer advertisements and social media tend to be more objective and informative' when compared to portrayals in other media formats. Ma's (2017) review recognises that the media can be 'used strategically' to challenge negative and normative perceptions of mental illness. This takes our thoughts back to people such as Davey and his passion for sharing his own lived experience through 'new' media channels such as podcasts and Twitter in order to break down stigma.

Despite this rising and shifting public profile for mental health, it would also be misleading to suggest that our mental health is improving as a result of public awareness. Mental ill health is, to the contrary, often portrayed as one of the biggest public health concerns of the modern age. Increases in depression have been seen in the Global North as the impacts of governmental austerity and the 2008 financial crises have played out in the everyday lives of citizens (Orphanidou & Kadianaki, 2018).

We're more open about, and aware of, mental ill health than ever before; anti-stigma initiatives are more high profile than they have ever been; employers are increasingly aware of, and adaptive to, mental health problems. But, at the same time, levels of prescriptions of anti-depressants are higher than ever in the UK (and elsewhere); more people are using counsellors; mental ill health is proclaimed as a public health crisis and suicide is the top cause of death amongst young men. Mental health and wellbeing are an ever-changing landscape of contradictions such as these that this book aims to explore, critique and inform.

Mental health

One of the most commonly used definitions of mental health comes from the World Health Organization (WHO) that defines it as:

> a state of well-being in which the individual realizes his or her own abilities, can cope with the normal stresses of life, can work productively and fruitfully, and is able to make a contribution to his or her community.
>
> (WHO, 2004)

Thus, the concept of mental health encompasses much more than the presence or absence of mental ill health or disease. In this book, we adopt such a holistic and encompassing definition of mental health. Some of our chapters do focus on the provision of services to those experiencing mental ill health in rural areas but our consideration goes further than this and towards what could be termed an examination of overall wellbeing within rural regions.

Mental illness or ill health, however, is situated as a global threat with the potential for wide-ranging impacts (e.g. social, economic and political) that can be linked to geographies of poverty and affluence in a myriad of ways.

Mental health and wellbeing in rural regions

The geographies of human health and illness disregard political boundaries. In recent years, this has been well documented and studied in relation to the spread of infectious disease and its relationship with international travel.

Our mental health, however, has more rarely been considered in such global contexts. This book is one of the first texts to engage critically with the concept of global mental health. We argue that it is possible, and necessary, to look across international contexts in order to pursue equity in mental health outcomes and services access. In particular, this book considers global mental health in the context of rural regions, within the Global North.

With just under half of the world's population living in rural and remote regions, this book, therefore, brings an important contribution to the global mental health and mental health literature in general. While the rustic charm of rural life is often considered idyllic, many rural communities remain chronically under-resourced, under-funded and under-researched. Through this book, we seek to offer a myriad of views and perspectives on mental health in rural areas in order to facilitate greater awareness of the mental health needs of rural communities, as well as their wellbeing assets and the ways in which these are mobilised and utilised in order to promote mental wellbeing and cope with mental ill health.

Definitions of rural, however, vary internationally, and even within countries. In much the same way as our book takes a holistic definition of health, we also take a wide definition of rurality. Within this book, rural areas are considered to be those that are either formally (e.g. through governmental geographical definitions) or socio-culturally (e.g. through accepted norms) considered to not be urban, metropolitan or city. Within each of the book's chapters, the authors present their own understandings of 'rural' that are critically examined through the use of international case studies, but all broadly come under this 'non-urban' banner.

Although there is a paucity of research and scholarship on rurality, rural regions and mental health, some previous work has considered the topic. Much work has focused on the rural as idyll or wilderness as therapeutic or restorative environment. Much less work has considered the rural as a working or lived-in landscape. Work that has considered this has tended to focus on the experiences of agricultural workers and mental ill health and suicide within this population. The chapters within this book focus mainly on the contextual situations and perspectives of what we term 'rural residents' – those with permanent or semi-permanent living and/or working ties to rural areas. These residents can face layerings of isolation, service access challenges and increased social visibility that compound inequalities. This book attempts to unravel some of the interconnections between these different layers of disadvantage.

Each chapter within this book is written from the vantage of researchers and/or healthcare professionals working within the rural and regional areas of different countries. This prismatic view represents a clarion call to approach global aspects of rural mental health from a robust and dynamically multicultural perspective. An international perspective allows us to see the connections, and differences, between rural regions in several countries. In this book, such an approach allows us to compare rural mental health conditions and challenges in the hope of providing a collective series of solutions for those living in rural and remote regions of the world.

As editors, we wish to acknowledge this book is only the beginning of an integrated and collaborative approach to the improvement of mental health in rural and remote regions worldwide. Across the globe, rural populations and peoples are forced to deal with unprecedented change. This impacts the economic, cultural, social, educational and political disposition of those living in rural and remote regions. Such change often outpaces the community resources needed to sustain and bolster these populations, especially those needed to sustain mental wellbeing. This brings us towards conclusions on how rurality interacts with mental health as well as how good mental health can be supported within rural regions and across rural borders.

At the same time, however, we are acutely aware of the geographical limitations of this book – most of our chapters represent accounts and understandings of rural and remote mental health largely within the Anglophone, postcolonial world (the United Kingdom, Canada, the United States, Australia and South Africa). While this limits our understanding of rural mental health within other contexts, the countries considered within this book do have similar, and often shared, histories of industrialisation, de-industrialisation, colonisation and migration. This allows us to consider economic, social and cultural similarities and whether, and if so how, these impact rural mental health. Mental health within rural areas of the Global South is an important topic that merits further investigation and Grindle and De Kock's contribution to this book (Chapter 6) paves the way for future, innovative work in this regard.

This book was conceived by researchers who believe that it is important to consider and understand the unique characteristics of rural regions in relation to mental health. Rural populations have, and continue be, important to countries worldwide. Rural communities are known for their resilience and are the genesis of the foundational mettle that has formed urban strength. Countries who neglect the overall wellbeing of their rural peoples often experience detrimental impacts to their own social, economic and environmental mainstays. We use evidence largely drawn from rural Australia, Canada, the United Kingdom, South Africa and the United States to consider the different ways in which rurality interacts with mental health.

Summary of the book

This book considers how rurality interacts with the mental health and wellbeing of individuals and communities in different rural and regional settings. The book considers rural mental health geographies from an international comparative perspective, critically examines how rural mental health is measured and defined, and explores the spatial (in)equities associated with rural mental health (their drivers and potential mitigators). The results, we hope, will make a unique contribution to the conceptualisation and empirical examination of global rural mental health.

In Chapter 1, Dalton and Perkins examine the diverse Australian rural context and the epidemiology of rural mental health, paying particular attention to the social and emotional wellbeing of Aboriginal Australians. Through this lens, the chapter introduces us to a key theme in global rural mental health – that of interactions with the land, landscape and environment. Rural Australia encompasses a broad range of distinctive communities, with attendant environmental, economic and social challenges of drought, flood and fire. Tensions in land and water use between and within industries and communities contribute to particular stressors for rural dwellers. This introduces us to the notion of contextually appropriate mental health services.

Jean-Pierre and Campos-Flores move on in Chapter 2 to discuss the mental health of migrants within rural and regional areas. The results of a literature review undertaken on international migrants and mental health are outlined in this chapter. Emerging issues and trends in relation to theoretical framings, methodological approaches and empirical findings as well as the identification of gaps and suggestions for further research are highlighted. The chapter sets the findings and conclusions from the authors' literature review in the broader context of recent efforts to reconceptualise migrant wellbeing in relation to the social determinants of health; including the work by the UN and the WHO on international migration. The authors emphasise that in order to understand and develop effective interventions for migrant wellbeing in rural context, there must be a recognition of the transversal and dynamic nature of migrant wellbeing and related policies stretching beyond destination societies' perspectives. Additionally, disciplinary and policy silos must seek to include rural migrants' own perspectives if beneficial change is to occur.

We are then introduced in Chapter 3, by Philo and Parr, to the topic of inpatient facilities in rural areas. This chapter picks up the topic alluded to in Chapter 1, of links between rural mental health and land, landscape and environment. Philo and Parr's chapter presents a detailed case study of 'Old Craigs' and 'New Craigs' in Inverness (Scotland) – the 'old' Inverness District Lunatic Asylum (closed in the early 2000s) and the New Craigs inpatient hospital built in land adjacent to the old asylum site. Through consideration of this case study, the authors show how various writers and therapists have proclaimed the importance of 'natural' (rural, scenic, countryside) settings as conducive to the recovery of mental wellness for people enduring periods of mental ill health. Such proclamations have a deep historical lineage that is explored in this chapter. Philo and Parr demonstrate that there is much merit in reconsidering what kinds of 'therapeutic landscapes' were being created and how they have since been experienced by patients resident in such institutions. They also demonstrate the need to consider whether more modern versions of therapeutic landscapes designed for mental health inpatients, associated with updated discourses about model psychiatric facilities, are necessarily improvements on what went before. The authors argue that a thoroughly 'muddied' therapeutic landscape in the grounds of the Old

Craigs, organically blended into its rural surroundings over many years, may have now been lost, replaced by a new facility largely devoid of grounds or connections into real earth. These themes are developed as a fresh perspective for work on the rural geographies of mental healthcare, with relevance to both facilities and individual bodies and psychologies.

Gorman picks up on the themes considered by Philo and Parr by looking at the 'modern' phenomenon of care farming in Chapter 4. Gorman considers this 'intervention' that attempts to facilitate mental wellbeing, recovery and therapeutic experience through the use of agricultural practice. This considers the muddied landscapes of Philo and Parr from the position of 'outsiders' to the rural region, coming in to consume these landscapes and lifescapes as therapy. Drawing on a non-representational approach, Gorman's chapter explores how new wellbeing capacities are produced from mutual entanglements between humans and animals on rural care farms.

In Chapter 5, Morton and Bradley widen the view on non-pharmaceutical interventions in rural areas by considering how those dwelling within rural landscapes and communities (rather than visiting them in order to consume rurality) interact with non-pharmaceutical interventions. They do so by considering two case studies from rural Scotland – a nature on prescription programme and an outdoor cycling programme. The case studies are used in order to illustrate and discuss how services can utilise natural capital in rural areas but also issues relating to accessibility, challenges, successes, costs, benefits and barriers.

In Chapter 6, Ikonomopoulos, Liang, Furgerson and Garza turn to consider the delivery of effective treatments in rural areas for people living with mental ill health, including depressive disorders and suicidal ideation. The chapter considers the use of various treatment programs, theories and therapeutic techniques within the rural context and highlights how therapists working within these areas must be attuned to, and cognizant of, the needs of rural communities.

In Chapter 7, Grindle and De Kock introduce us to an innovative digital narrative approach to improving the mental health of adolescents within the indigenous rural populations of low- to middle-income countries. This is the one contributing chapter to this volume that takes us beyond the Global North and in doing so it brings a particularly valuable contribution to the volume. Interestingly, Grindle and De Kock's approach again links rural mental health with notions of landscape and nature – stressing the apparent human connections that can be made around such aspects of rurality across national boundaries, and social and cultural norms. In their chapter, the authors present a case study from South Africa that employed a digital narrative approach (DNA) to online and blended behaviour change interventions and therapies. They successfully demonstrate the ways in which rurality and mental health interact to create great opportunity for the deployment of innovative mental healthcare in rural LMICs. They argue that DNA is one approach to addressing the global implications of rural mental health.

Villa and Moya take us to the realm of social work and introduce our final geographical area of concern in Chapter 8 through discussions of the border regions of South Texas, USA. They introduce us to the conceptualisation of social workers as clinical activists who understand the structural inequalities inherent in social and economic policies that negatively impact quality of life and wellbeing in rural and regional areas.

In the final two chapters of the book, our lens zooms out once more and we consider firstly the potential benefits of a global ethics code for rural mental health in Chapter 9 (Bain and Munoz) and a research agenda for rural mental health in Chapter 10 (Munoz and Bain). We conclude by summarising the possible links between rurality and mental health outcomes and services access. We highlight the variety of ways in which our chapter authors have illustrated that rurality interacts with mental health in terms of, for example, experience of remoteness, distance, community cohesion, landscape and culturally appropriate service provision. We suggest international determinants of rural mental health that could form the basis of a research strategy for this area such as rural socio-economic crises, interactions with landscape, constructions of belonging, industrial and agricultural change, and place attachment.

References

Bowen, M., Kinderman, P., and Cooke, A. (2019). Stigma: A linguistic analysis of the UK red-top tabloids press' representation of schizophrenia. *Perspectives in Public Health, 139*(3), 147–152.

Kenez, S., O'Halloran, P., and Liamputtong, P. (2015). The portrayal of mental health in Australian daily newspapers. *Australian and New Zealand Journal of Public Health, 39*(6), 513–517.

Ma, Z. (2017). How the media cover mental illnesses: A review. *Health Education, 117*(1), 90–109.

Ohlsson, R. (2018). Public discourse on mental health and psychiatry: Representations in Swedish newspapers. *Health, 22*(3), 298–314.

Orphanidou, M., & Kadianaki, I. (2018). Between medicalisation and normalisation: Antithetical representations of depression in the Greek-Cypriot press in times of financial crisis. *Health (London, England: 1997).* Advance online publication. https://doi.org/10.1177/1363459318804579

World Health Organization. (2004). *Promoting mental health: Concepts, emerging evidence, practice.* Geneva: World Health Organization.

1 Adversity and resilience

Rural mental health in Australia

Hazel Dalton and David Perkins

Introduction: Australia and its rural population

Australia occupies a vast continent of almost 7.7 million km^2 (Geoscience Australia, 2019). Its population in 2018 was estimated to be 24.77 million; the 2011 census figure was 21.5 million (Australian Bureau of Statistics, 2018a). The population density would be approximately 3.2 persons per square kilometre if two-thirds of the population did not live in cities, mostly located on the coast. Five of the capital cities have populations of more than 1 million people and range from Sydney with 4.7 million to Adelaide with 1.3 million. Collectively, they account for approximately 15 million people (Australian Bureau of Statistics, 2018a).

In considering the Australian context and its people, it is important to acknowledge the Indigenous Australian population. Aboriginal people have occupied mainland Australia continuously for 50,000–60,000 years and likely represent one of the oldest continuous populations outside Africa (Rasmussen et al., 2011). White or European settlement is usually seen as commencing with invasion and colonisation and the arrival at Sydney Cove of James Cook and then Arthur Philip in 1788, a mere 230 years ago. In 2018, it was estimated that there were about 797,000 Aboriginal and Torres Strait Islander people in Australia of whom 80% live in cities. This is a 17.4% increase in population since 2011. Notably, Aboriginal people are younger than the non-Indigenous population, with a median age of 21 while the corresponding age for non-Indigenous people was 38 (Australian Bureau of Statistics, 2018b).

The definition of rural is contentious. It usually depends on answers to the question: who wants to know and why? Living in rural Australia is often understood by city residents as some form of hardship and so an equitable basis is needed for the government to assist recruitment, retention of public sector employees or to justify hardship allowances or incentives. Answering the question of "what is rural?" is largely outside the scope of this chapter; but the most popular classification indices are the Accessibility and Remoteness Index of Australia (ARIA) and the so-called modified Monash approach. The ARIA classifies rural communities into the following categories: inner and outer regional, remote, and very remote based on distance to communities defined as service centres. Thus, very remote communities have the longest road distances to service centres, while inner-regional communities are usually defined as service centres (Australian Bureau of Statistics, 2016; Department of Health, 2015).

We understand "rural" as places, usually distant from larger communities which are characterised by a shortage of specialists, whether in health, education, commerce or any other sector. Australian remote communities may have a shortage of generalists such as general medical practitioners, teachers, and other professionals, and they are often served by visiting fly-in or drive-in non-resident services such as the Royal Flying Doctors Service (RFDS).

However, Australian rural communities are diverse. A common saying in Australia is that "when you've seen one rural town, you've seen one rural town". That diversity might be understood in terms of the economic *raison d'etre* such as farming, fishing, mining, tourism, transport, or winemaking. A recent paper by McGrail et al. (2017) examined the association between the supply of primary care workforce and the amenity or attractiveness of rural places in the United States and Australia, finding significant associations with the following factors: proximity to a local hospital, increased house prices and affluence, age and education of population (United States), and coastal location (Australia) (McGrail et al., 2017). It follows that the comparisons of rural and metropolitan communities, whether through stereotypes of rural health and illness, economic productivity, population structure, and other factors, are likely to be misleading and oversimplified. A number of authors have challenged the rural deficits approach, suggesting a more nuanced model which recognises rural strengths (Bourke, Humphreys, Wakerman, & Taylor, 2010) or environmental, economic, and social capital (Bourke et al., 2010). The Forum for the Future, a leading international sustainability non-profit organisation, has identified five types of capital: natural, human, social, manufactured, and financial all of which will vary by location and need to be taken into consideration within the remote and rural context (Forum for the Future, n.d.)

An influential study by Smith, Humphreys, and Wilson (2008) examined epidemiological evidence about the health disadvantage of rural populations in the global north (Smith et al., 2008). After controlling for some major risks such as socio-economic disadvantage, ethnicity, poor service availability, environmental risks, and personal risk-taking, they found that rural location does not always translate into health disadvantage. They argue that focusing on rural distance and access difficulties without also addressing poverty, discrimination, inequality, and inequities of resource allocation must result in sub-optimal interventions. On a positive note, Wilkins (2015) reports that living in towns with less than 1,000 residents in non-urban areas has a positive effect on satisfaction with life. They found that characteristics such as neighbours helping each other out and doing things together appeared to be very important.

Australia: rural mental health

Evidence about mental illness in rural Australia has been hard to collect because of the distances involved. Two national surveys of mental health and wellbeing were conducted in Australia in 1997 (Australian Bureau of Statistics, 1998) and 2007 (Australian Bureau of Statistics, 2008). They focused on high-prevalence conditions: affective (mood) disorders, anxiety, and substance use disorders. The authors recognise that these surveys under-represented rural and particularly remote communities since collecting information and conducting interviews in such locations is expensive compared to metropolitan locations. A team led by Kelly (2010) attempted to fill this gap by surveying in rural and remote New South Wales (Kelly et al., 2010). The prevalence of mental health problems is similar in major cities (17%), inner-regional (19%), outer-regional, and remote areas (19%) (Australian Institute of Health and Welfare, 2017). These averages mask a considerable variation due to social and other determinants. The Equally Well movement has highlighted the fact that people with mental illnesses have higher death rates from preventable physical illnesses and these rates increase with remoteness (Roberts, 2017). This builds on a ground-breaking research conducted in Scotland (Barnett et al., 2012).

Aboriginal and Torres Strait Islanders appear to have a higher prevalence of mental health problems and worse outcomes, in part due to poor access to generalist and specialist health service (Nasir et al., 2018). A further consideration regarding the mental health of Aboriginal and Torres Strait Islander people is that they have a broader understanding of health in comparison to the biomedical model accepted by most non-Indigenous Australians. On 27th of August 2015, following widespread consultation, the National Aboriginal and Torres Strait Islander Leadership and Mental Health entity (NATSILMH) launched the Gayaa Dhuwi (Proud Spirit) declaration (NATSILMH, 2015). This statement concerns the challenges in addressing mental health problems facing Aboriginal and Torres Strait Islanders peoples. It builds on the key principles of social and emotional wellbeing first documented in the 1989 National Aboriginal Health Strategy (NAHSWP, 1989). The declaration aims "to achieve the highest attainable standard of mental health and suicide prevention outcomes for Aboriginal and Torres Strait Islander Peoples". Nine principles of social and emotional wellbeing are appended to the declaration which calls for the combination of Aboriginal and Torres Strait Islander concepts of social and emotional wellbeing, mental health, and healing combined with (Western) clinical perspectives as key to achieving the best possible outcomes (see Figure 1.1).

While it is inaccurate to assume that all people who self-harm or die by suicide have a mental illness, many certainly do (Australian Bureau of Statistics, 2018c). Indeed, the Australian Bureau of Statistics released co-morbidity data for the first time in 2017. These data showed that there were comorbid factors for 80% of suicides, including mood disorders, drug and alcohol disorders, anxiety, and the presence of alcohol and other drugs in the blood. There

1. Aboriginal and Torres Strait Islander health is viewed in a holistic context, that encompasses mental health and physical, cultural and spiritual health. Land and sea* is central to wellbeing. Crucially, it must be understood that when the harmony of these interrelations is disrupted, Aboriginal and Torres Strait Islander ill-health will persist.
2. Self-determination is central to the provision of Aboriginal and Torres Strait Islander health services.**
3. Culturally valid understandings must shape the provision of services and must guide assessment, care and management of Aboriginal and Torres Strait Islander peoples' health problems generally, and mental health problems, in particular.
4. It must be recognised that the experiences of trauma and loss, present since European invasion, are a direct outcome of the disruption to cultural wellbeing. Trauma and loss of this magnitude continues to have inter-generational effects.
5. The human rights of Aboriginal and Torres Strait Islander peoples must be recognised and respected. Failure to respect these human rights constitutes continuous disruption to mental health, (versus mental ill-health). Human rights relevant to mental illness must be specifically addressed.
6. Racism, stigma, environmental adversity and social disadvantage constitute ongoing stressors and have negative impacts on Aboriginal and Torres Strait Islander peoples' mental health and wellbeing.
7. The centrality of Aboriginal and Torres Strait Islander family and kinship must be recognised as well as the broader concepts of family and the bonds of reciprocal affection, responsibility and sharing.
8. There is no single Aboriginal or Torres Strait Islander culture or group, but numerous groupings, languages, kinships, and tribes, as well as ways of living. Furthermore, Aboriginal and Torres Strait Islander peoples may currently live in urban, rural or remote settings, in traditional or other lifestyles, and frequently move between these ways of living.
9. It must be recognised that Aboriginal and Torres Strait Islander peoples have great strengths, creativity and endurance and a deep understanding of the relationships between human beings and their environment.

* The original principle referred only to land. Contemporary understandings of this principle include 'sea' with land in acknowledgement of the importance of the connections to the sea to some Aboriginal and Torres Strait Islander peoples.
** These are now known as Aboriginal Community Controlled Health Organisations

Figure 1.1 Nine guiding principles of Aboriginal and Torres Strait Islander social and emotional wellbeing (as outlined in Gayaa Dhuwi).

is a clear and enduring difference in the rate of deaths by suicide between those who live in cities and those in rural and remote areas. The figures released in 2018 (see Figure 1.1) show that in all Australian states and territories, the rate of deaths by suicide in rural locations is higher than that in the capital cities, and this difference in rates appears to be a consistent feature (Australian Bureau of Statistics, 2018c). Between 2001 and 2010, the majority (absolute not percentage) of suicides among Aboriginal and Torres Strait Islanders took place outside capital cities (Australian Bureau of Statistics, 2012). A long-term review of Aboriginal deaths by suicide suggests that until the 1960s, they were rare events; however, they have been increasing in recent decades, accelerating after the 1980s (Hunter & Milroy, 2006). The consistency of the rural suicide figures suggests that different preventative strategies may be needed to those which appear to have had a positive effect in some cities (Campo & Tayton, 2015; van Dijk et al., 2013) (Figure 1.2).

Rural and remote residents experience similar personal traumas to urban residents such as accidents, domestic violence, bereavement, unemployment, and sickness. For instance, domestic violence is more prevalent in rural areas, with fewer support services, and may result in homelessness, loss of employment, poverty, and physical and mental illnesses, among other factors which pose a serious risk to mental health (Campo & Tayton, 2015). If these traumas are prolonged or repeated, they may contribute to poor mental health. They also experience "rapid onset" environmental adversities such as fire or flood as well as chronic events such as the "Millennium Drought" in New South Wales which started in 2001 and continued until 2009 (van Dijk et al., 2013).

Research has identified a number of mental health problems associated with drought including drought-related worry/distress (Stain et al., 2011) which is normally understood to include financial and business worries and concerns and cares about social and family life. Austin et al. (2018) identified both "personal drought-related stress" and "community drought-related stress" with particular reference to farmers (Austin et al., 2018; Brew, Inder,

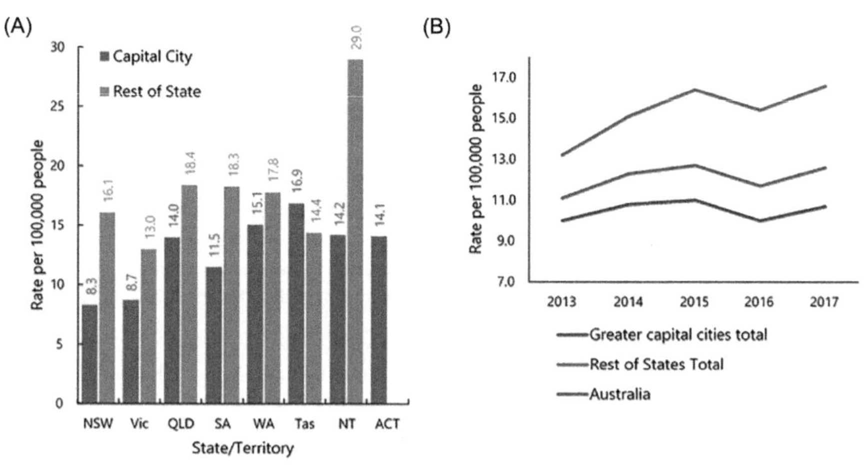

Figure 1.2 Suicide rates (A) by regional of usual residence, Australia, 2017; (B) by region, 2013–2017, Australia.

Allen, Thomas, & Kelly, 2016). The need for both individual and community psychological preparedness for drought has been recognised for some time (Morrissey & Reser, 2007; Sartore, Hoolahan, Tonna, Kelly, & Stain, 2005).

Drought is not the only form of rural adversity known to have an impact on mental health and wellbeing. Australia is prone to bushfires which can have severe and enduring consequences. Research which followed the South Australian bushfires in 1983 found that after 12 months, 42% of survivors who participated in the research met the criteria for a psychiatric disorder, mainly anxiety, depression, or post-traumatic stress disorder (McFarlane, 1986). After 20 months, much of this morbidity continued (McFarlane, Clayer, & Bookless, 1997). Following the 2003 Canberra bushfires, young children were found to suffer ongoing distress. Clearly, drought and bushfires can be related, and both may have an impact on environmental degradation and may pose challenges to water security (Australian Institute of Health and Welfare, 2018).

Floods are also part of the rural landscape and are known to be associated with poor mental health (Fernandez, Black et al., 2015). Indeed, the impacts of environmental changes on people have been described by Albrecht as the phenomenon of "solastalgia", which is defined as "distress that is produced by environmental change impacting on people while they are directly connected to their home environment" (Albrecht et al., 2007). An instructive analysis by Deloitte Access Economics (2016) examined the social and economic impacts of major Australian natural disasters and distinguished tangible, indirect tangible, and intangible costs with reference to the Newcastle earthquake in 1989, the Queensland floods in 2010/2011, and the Black Saturday bushfires in 2009 (Economics, 2016; Muller, 2010). Tangible costs are incurred as a direct result of the event and have a market value or cost such as damage to property which may also be remedied if the necessary resources such as insurance payouts are available. Indirect tangible costs are the flow-on effects of the event which cannot be directly attributed to the event or costed, such as disruption to businesses and networks. Intangible costs cannot be easily measured including death and injury, impacts on health and wellbeing (including psychological distress), and community connectedness. Indeed, the incorporation of the intangible costs of these events implies a true cost that was 50% higher than previous estimates.

Rural mental health service models in Australia

The provision of mental health services in Australia has shifted from institutions to the community since the second half of the twentieth century. However, as a former New South Wales Mental Health Commissioner observed: "We jettisoned one mental health system built around institutions, and patched together another out of hospital wards, hardworking community teams and non-government service providers, medication and wishful thinking" (Mendoza et al., 2013). From a policy standpoint, mental health reform has shifted to include a more holistic view of recovery as illustrated by the National Mental Health Commission strategy entitled "Contributing lives, thriving communities" (National Mental Health Commission, 2014) and aspired to equitable outcomes including better physical care for those with enduring mental illness (Roberts, 2017). A new focus on prevention and early intervention with regional planning and accountability is described in the Fifth National Mental Health and Suicide Prevention Plan (Department of Health, 2017). While the policy reforms and changes of direction have been positive, it should be noted that Australian mental health services are underfunded relative to the disease burden (7.8% of the health spending relative to 12% of the disease burden, according to AIHW), again demonstrating systemic inequality.

The Productivity Commission is the Australian Government's independent research and advisory body on a range of economic, social, and environmental issues affecting the welfare of Australians (Productivity Commission, 2017). In a recent enquiry entitled "Shifting the Dial" (2017), it made a number of key observations about the Australian healthcare system. While the health system performs well on a number of international indicators, there is room for significant improvement. It notes, for instance, that the proportion of years in ill health as a percentage of life expectancy is 13.2%, third last ahead of only Turkey and the United States. Key issues from the report are summarised in Figure 1.3.

While this critique is system-wide and not specific to rural or remote contexts, it describes rural mental health and wellbeing services accurately.

The most recent strategies to address this fragmentation are the introduction of Local Health Networks (LHN) in 2011 and Primary Health Networks (PHN) in 2015. LHNs are state organisations designed to coordinate and manage the activities of state-funded hospital and community services, while PHNs coordinate the Commonwealth-funded and -subsidised primary care services

1. **The system has structural impediments and is not patient-centred. It focuses on episodic treatment and medical procedures.**
2. **Services are fragmented and there is a particular gap between primary and acute care characterized by poor communication.**
3. **Data collection is haphazard.**
4. **The roles and relationships of, and between, public and private healthcare and the health insurance system are not clear.**
5. **There is scope to improve quality and safety by addressing ineffective interventions, hospital-acquired infection and investing in prevention and health promotion.**

Figure 1.3 Key issues for the Australian healthcare system (from "Shifting the Dial").

provided in the community. PHNs have been charged with developing regional mental health and suicide prevention plans for their communities in partnership with LHNs, focusing on primary and community-based services in the first instance and working towards fully integrated comprehensive regional plans by 2022. These plans address the Productivity Commission criticisms which are echoed in the 2017 Fifth National Mental Health and Suicide Prevention Plan (Department of Health, 2017; Productivity Commission, 2017).

PHNs are expected to adopt a stepped care approach (Department of Health, 2016) to mental health services in which patients receive appropriate care for their needs and the intensity of that care is escalated or reduced depending on its effectiveness. For non-emergency mental health services, the general medical practitioner acts as the gatekeeper through the production of an annual mental health plan which is needed to access subsidised and limited (i.e. the treatments are rationed), "evidence-based" psychological services. Access to further services requires a general medical practitioner review and an extended plan. Controversially, these services are only available to patients with a "clinically diagnosable" mental illness such as anxiety and depression, and so providing early intervention or preventive services is problematic.

There are new low-intensity mental health service types that do not require such a mental health treatment plan, including new digital mental health apps, programs and e-clinics, as well as services such as NewAccess in some areas, which offer psychosocial therapies by trained paraprofessionals (Dalton, Read, Handley, & Perkins, 2017). These are, however, new offerings in a complex service landscape which are less familiar to both general medical practitioners and the community.

In primary care, general medical practices provide a limited range of services, which are often restricted to general medical practitioner services and practice-nurse care. Allied health services are provided in the community by private practitioners such as psychologists or state-based community health services.

While considering the health service system in Australia, a particular distinction should be drawn for Aboriginal healthcare, which is provided by Aboriginal Community Controlled Health Services. These are primary healthcare services initiated and operated by the local Aboriginal community to deliver holistic, comprehensive, and culturally appropriate healthcare to the community which controls it, through a locally elected Board of Management (National Aboriginal Community Controlled Health Organisation [NACCHO], 2018).

Aboriginal Medical Services, as they are usually called, are federally funded and community controlled. They provide culturally appropriate, multidisciplinary primary care and are spread widely across Australia. They do not operate on a fee-for-service basis and so are not restricted by the rigid Medical Benefits Schedule or by their patients' ability to pay. They operate in parallel to non-Aboriginal services and refer to state specialist health services as needed.

The National Aboriginal Community Controlled Health Organisation (NACCHO) is the national advocacy organisation representing 143 Aboriginal Community Controlled Health Services. Community controlled means that the health service is an incorporated Aboriginal organisation, initiated by and based in a local Aboriginal community and governed by a body elected by the local Aboriginal community. In keeping with addressing the holistic Aboriginal concept of health, social, and emotional wellbeing (NAHSWP, 1989), Aboriginal Medical Services deliver holistic and culturally appropriate services to their communities. Organisations that are government controlled or offer a disease-based model of care are excluded from NACCHO membership.

Holistically and culturally appropriate care is understood as Aboriginal health:

> Aboriginal health means not just the physical well-being of an individual but refers to the social, emotional and cultural well-being of the whole Community in which each individual is able to achieve their full potential as a human being thereby bringing about the total well-being of their Community. It is a whole of life view and includes the cyclical concept of life-death-life.
>
> (NACCHO, 2020)

With the service landscape mapped out, we consider the differences between metropolitan and rural service provision. To deliver services rurally as they are in metropolitan areas is neither feasible from a funding or workforce perspective, given the vast distances and the sparsely distributed population. Indeed, mental health service usage data shows that rural and remote Australians access services at lower rates than their metropolitan peers, with psychologist access at half the rate and general medical practitioner mental healthcare visits at less than half (National Rural Health Alliance, 2017). The number of practising mental health professionals including psychologists, mental health nurses, and particularly psychiatrists decreases with remoteness. Thus, in considering the differences from metropolitan services, as one travels more remotely, there is first a loss of access to specialists and in very remote areas, to generalists.

Small and dispersed populations pose challenges for service provision whether by public, private, or voluntary sector providers. Demand for specialist care is not sufficient to satisfy providers who need adequate numbers of patients and a range of specialist support disciplines. Even where numbers are sufficient, specialists often resist becoming a sole provider with high on-call requirements and poor access to professional colleagues and career development opportunities. While the market may not justify private sector resident specialists, public and voluntary sector employers also find it difficult to recruit and retain medical, allied, and specialist administrative staff. While most rural populations with reasonable amenity can recruit generalist staff such as general medical practitioners, nurses, and managers, the same cannot be said for remote areas. In these cases, care may be provided by nurse-led services supplemented by visiting medical services and increasingly by telehealth solutions.

In order to improve access to services, an array of alternative service models have emerged. Some of these services have been co-designed locally, while others have been driven by pragmatic attempts to fill service gaps by Local Health Districts or other employers. Such service models include drive-in, drive-out (DIDO) and fly-in, fly-out (FIFO) models such as the iconic RFDS, hub and spoke models, and e-mental health and telehealth services.

Perhaps the best-known visiting service in Australia is the RFDS which provides primary care services by FIFO clinics in remote locations and aeromedical retrieval services for remote residents (Langford, 1994). The range and depth of services are increasingly being enhanced through telehealth solutions, increasing the use of allied health practitioners and responses to particular needs such as that of rural women who wish to consult female medical officers. The RFDS employs highly skilled clinical staff since they have to care for a wide range of presentations and need broader experience and skills than is the case in larger population centres where the scope of practice is narrower. Even so, remote communities may only be able to access routine medical care during RFDS monthly visits, and the alternative may be a long drive to a larger community.

Australia has a long history of visiting psychiatrists and other medical specialists, largely paid by state health services or others on a sessional basis. The challenges of integrating resident health services with visiting specialists are not insignificant. For rural and remote residents who need a combination of medical and multidisciplinary healthcare, it may be difficult to navigate a complex system. Visiting specialist services are often recruited on an *ad hominem* basis, and visits subject to interruption by bad weather events when flights are delayed or cancelled. Such events have a disproportionate impact within a pattern of monthly or less frequent visits. Visiting psychiatrists may arrive to find a busy clinic such that their time is swallowed up by patient assessments and their connections with the resident health system are limited. Between visits, they may be hard to contact since they are working for another employer or running a metropolitan specialist practice. There are good examples of integrated specialist services which combine specialist visits with telehealth and other support. One example is described by Perkins et al. (2006) where funding arrangements were adjusted to improve the integration of rural and remote resident services and visiting psychiatrists. In essence, the role of visiting psychiatrist was re-balanced from advising on the best course of action for particular patients to providing support to local providers as requested and needed. This might mean providing education, supervision, and support to a rural general medical practitioner, nurse, or Aboriginal mental health worker, conducting a caseload review or undertaking a secondary consultation with a local general medical practitioner.

This approach is described as follows:

> The local resident mental health team, general practitioners and other providers are supported by specialist mental health and counselling staff and visiting psychiatrists.
>
> (Perkins et al., 2006, p. 107)

While the idea of a specialist support or consultancy role is not unique, it represents a shift in balance from visiting experts to local resident leaders and service providers designed to strengthen rural and remote services.

In another community, the state-funded community mental health service, visiting psychiatrists, and federally funded general medical practitioners have overcome structural and cultural challenges to develop a leading rural service in a rural town with no resident psychiatrist or local mental health beds (Perkins et al., 2010; Fitzpatrick et al., 2018; Fitzpatrick, Perkins, Luland, Brown, & Corvan, 2017; Perkins et al., 2010).

While innovative models go some way to addressing service gaps, there are underlying issues facing the development and retention of the rural mental health workforce. As Cosgrave, Hussain, and Maple (2015) observe, staff retention is difficult (most particularly in small remote towns) and the decision to stay or leave is complex and multifactorial (Cosgrave et al., 2015). Indeed, for early career rural mental health workers, job satisfaction, support, and other professional factors affect their decision to stay early on as they establish themselves in the role. However, once settled, it is personal factors, including life-stage and social connectivity within the town, that have a real impact on the ongoing likelihood of remaining (Cosgrave, Maple, & Hussain, 2018a). For Aboriginal mental health workers, this is further complicated by a lack of awareness and community acceptance of their professional role, disciplinary differences and inequality, and culturally specific challenges that adversely impact on the professional and personal life of the worker (Cosgrave, Maple, & Hussain, 2018b). This might include communities that do not recognise boundaries between professional role and personal life.

A 2014 review into the rural and remote mental health workforce suggested the need to focus on the primary care setting, enhancing the skills of general medical practitioners and bolstering the community mental health service capacity (especially in nursing) and emphasising mental health promotion and early intervention when illness arises (Ridoutt, Pilbeam, & Perkins, 2014).

The Mental Health Emergency Care-Rural Access Program (MHEC-RAP) is a telepsychiatry service which provides mental health specialist support to providers in rural and remote areas through triage assessments and clinical advice (Saurman, Johnston, Hindman, Kirby, & Lyle, 2014). Over time, the program not only fulfilled its goal of supporting services on the ground in rural and remote areas but in rural and remote emergency departments.

This support has been shown to have changed both perspective and practice (Saurman, Kirby, & Lyle, 2015). This form of telehealth support supplements local services from a distance bringing specialist assessment and clinical advice closer to the patient's home. Patient travel for assessment and treatment is minimised, thereby reducing emotional stress and saving time and money for both consumer and health service.

Improving access to mental health services in rural communities also requires improved mental health literacy and knowledge of the existing services. Among a sample of Australian Rural Mental Health Study participants who exhibited moderate to high mental distress which implied a diagnosable mental illness, a third did not think they had a mental health problem (Handley, Lewin, Perkins, & Kelly, 2018).This is likely to mean that some rural residents who could benefit from services may not seek help.

In rural New South Wales, the Rural Adversity Mental Health Program (RAMHP) deploys coordinators in rural and remote communities to address access problems for rural residents (Rural Adversity Mental Health Program, n.d.). They link people with mental health services and improve mental health literacy via training and provision of information. Moreover, they work to reduce stigma and open up conversations about mental health in rural areas through mental health promotion activities. Notably, the program has sought to increase its reach and provide communication tools such as podcast series with trusted rural broadcasters and the Glovebox Guide to Mental Health (produced in partnership with the leading national rural newspaper). The guide contains stories of rural Australians' experience of recovery from mental illness coupled with evidence-based mental health advice and pathways to appropriate services.

Some Australian rural communities have tackled mental health literacy, stigma, and concerns over elevated suicide rates in a collaborative, strengths-based manner through Community Wellbeing Collaboratives (CWC). In the Clarence Valley in Northern New South Wales, a series of suicides caused fear and distress. With external support, the community worked together, listened to community perspectives, and gathered objective data to review their options. This community-owned collaboration involved state health and education services, local government, and private businesses. Their solution was to form a CWC named "Our Healthy Clarence" and to co-fund a community-based coordinator (Our Healthy Clarence, n.d.). In two years, the group has secured funds to address service gaps, increased community mental health literacy through training, and sponsored an active youth network. The local schools network has redesigned their processes to respond to student issues in real time and across school boundaries.

In other communities, the wellbeing agenda has spread beyond health to address social and economic determinants, but has retained a strengths-based focus. In the Upper Hunter Valley in New South Wales, two hours drive north of Sydney, the Muswellbrook CREATE Change coalition is addressing an economic transition from a coal-fired power generation and open-cut mining to a diversified economic base. It comprises a partnership of local stakeholders including the University of Newcastle, The Hunter New England Local Health District and key government departments such as the New South Wales Government Department of Premier and Cabinet which are collaborating to pursue social wellbeing and economic prosperity monitoring progress using a collective impact approach. Initiatives include water and land remediation, improving access to tertiary education and supporting Aboriginal students to complete school and obtain their higher school certificate. This is coupled with a broad-based community wellbeing initiative, Muswellbrook Healthy and Well, which equips the community to improve its physical and psychological wellbeing through educational and community development interventions (Muswellbrook Healthy and Well, n.d.).

Australia is not the only country with vast geographical distances, sparse rural populations, hostile natural environments, and distinctive rural mental health challenges. Similar problems arise in North America, Canada, Scandinavia, and elsewhere due to environmental, economic, and social phenomena. The mapping of mental health service systems by Carulla and colleagues demonstrates that rural and remote service structures differ from urban structures, but they also differ from each other (Fernandez et al., 2017; Fernandez, Salinas-Perez et al., 2015; Gutiérrez-Colosía et al., 2017; Sadeniemi et al., 2018). The observed differences between rural settings provide an opportunity for critical comparative research to understand particular settings but to examine the comparative effectiveness and efficiency of different services. For instance, what is the mixture of rural mental health service types and approaches and what can we deduce about their comparative efficiency and sustainability.

The use of information and communications technology (ICT) is frequently suggested as a solution to service provision in rural and remote settings, and while there is no shortage of online, app-based, and teleconference solutions, there are far fewer consistent services in which these technologies are embedded and normalised, or leveraged to effectively support the local service provision. There is still a lot to learn from implementation science, particularly when services are attempting to address environmental and social determinants and to prevent mental ill health.

Methodologies for evaluating population mental health initiatives are often unconvincing since the various forms of controlled trials may fail to take proper account of context or merely show us that we are unable to control or account for factors that turn out to be important. Building on approaches such as realistic evaluation and collective impact offers some hope, but they are not short-term solutions. Achieving better outcomes requires collaborative and perhaps co-designed solutions which require up-front investments before yielding benefits.

Finally, rural mental health services may require a different workforce of peer workers, allied and primary health staff with a wider range of expertise, a broad scope of practice, and different ways of working.

Conclusions

Rural Australia is a vital part of the national psyche and contributes to an economy which depends heavily on primary industries such as mining, farming, fisheries, forestry, and tourism. Subject to challenging demographic, environmental, and climatic challenges, people with broadly similar epidemiology can have very different and often poorer health outcomes than city dwellers. For Aboriginal people, the experience of colonisation and non-Indigenous rule has been very damaging to the wellbeing of individuals and communities. The Australian health system comprised of state specialist services and Federal reimbursement of defined medical expenses works tolerably well, if inefficiently, in large populations but not in the bush.

The response to poor health and wellbeing outcomes for rural people has been the flourishing of a wide range of local initiatives which attempt to reproduce smaller, mini-metro, city models of care in regional centres but depend heavily on primary care supplemented by visiting specialists in smaller rural communities. Rural Aboriginal and Torres Strait Islander people, whose health and wellbeing is most seriously compromised, have developed a parallel, community-controlled, primary care system in an attempt to reduce the "gap" in social and emotional wellbeing.

It is not difficult to find examples of excellent rural service responses to the challenges outlined above, but it would be hard to argue that they are consistently good or coherent. Recent governments are placing their hopes in the development of regional service planning and collaboration between state LHNs and Federal PHNs. One thing is clear: there are no easy solutions to providing consistent and high-quality care to residents of rural and remote communities in Australia.

References

Albrecht, G., Sartore, G. M., Connor, L., Higginbotham, N., Freeman, S., Kelly, B., … Pollard, G. (2007). Solastalgia: The distress caused by environmental change. *Australasian Psychiatry, 15*(sup1), S95–S98.

Austin, E. K., Handley, T., Kiem, A. S., Rich, J. L., Lewin, T. J., Askland, H. H., … Kelly, B. J. (2018). Drought-related stress among farmers: Findings from the Australian rural mental health study. *Medical Journal of Australia, 209*(4), 159–165.

Australian Bureau of Statistics. (1998). *4326.0- Mental health and wellbeing: Profile of adults, Australia, 1997.* D.o. Health, (Ed.). Canberra: Australian Government.

Australian Bureau of Statistics. (2008). *4326.0- National survey of mental health and wellbeing: Summary of results, 2007,* D.o. Health, (Ed.). Canberra: Australian Government.

Australian Bureau of Statistics. (2012). *3309_0 Suicides Australia, 2010.* Retrieved from http://www.abs.gov.au/ausstats/abs@.nsf/Products/3309.0~2010~Chapter~Summary?OpenDocument.

Australian Bureau of Statistics. (2016). *The Australian Statistical Geography Standard (ASGS) remoteness structure.* Retrieved March, 15, 2018 from http://www.abs.gov.au/websitedbs/d3310114.nsf/home/remoteness+structure.

Australian Bureau of Statistics. (2018a). *3101.0- Australian demographic statistics, Jun 2018.* 2018 LATEST ISSUE Released at 11:30 AM (CANBERRA TIME). Retrieved December 20, 2018, from http://www.abs.gov.au/AUSSTATS/abs@.nsf/mf/3101.0.

Australian Bureau of Statistics. (2018b). *3238.0.55.001- Estimates of Aboriginal and Torres Strait Islander Australians, June 2016* 2018 LATEST ISSUE Released at 11:30 AM (CANBERRA TIME). Retrieved August 31, 2018, from http://www.abs.gov.au/ausstats/abs@.nsf/mf/3238.0.55.001.

Australian Bureau of Statistics. (2018c). *3303.0- Causes of death, Australia, 2017,* A.B.o. Statistics, (Ed.). Canberra: Australian Government.

Australian Institute of Health and Welfare. (2017). *Rural & remote health*, AIHW, Editor. Canberra: Australian Government.

Australian Institute of Health and Welfare. (2018). *4.1 Impacts of the natural environment on health.* Australia's health, series no. 16. AUS 221 2018. Retrieved February 22, 2019, from https://www.aihw.gov.au/getmedia/cfd6abd4-32fb-4995-835f-5e94dac7a827/aihw-aus-221-chapter-4-1.pdf.aspx.

Barnett, K., Mercer, S. W., Norbury, M., Watt, G., Wyke, S., & Guthrie, B. (2012). Epidemiology of multimorbidity and implications for health care, research, and medical education: A cross-sectional study. *The Lancet, 380*(9836), 37–43.

Bourke, L., Humphreys, J. S., Wakerman, J., & Taylor, J. (2010). From 'problem-describing' to 'problem-solving': Challenging the 'deficit' view of remote and rural health. *Australian Journal of Rural Health, 18*(5), 205–209.

Brew, B., Inder, K., Allen, J., Thomas, M., & Kelly, B. (2016). The health and wellbeing of Australian farmers: A longitudinal cohort study. *BMC Public Health, 16*(1), 988.

Campo, M., & Tayton, S. (2015). *Domestic and family violence in regional, rural and remote communities.* Melbourne: Australian Institute of Family Studies.

Cosgrave, C., Hussain, R., & Maple, M. (2015). Retention challenge facing Australia's rural community mental health services: Service managers' perspectives. *Australian Journal of Rural Health, 23*(5), 272–276.

Cosgrave, C., Maple, M., & Hussain, R. (2018a). An explanation of turnover intention among early-career nursing and allied health professionals working in rural and remote Australia-findings from a grounded theory study. *Rural & Remote Health, 18*(3), 4511.

Cosgrave, C., Maple, M., & Hussain, R. (2018b). Factors affecting job satisfaction of Aboriginal mental health workers working in community mental health in rural and remote New South Wales. *Australian Health Review, 41*(6), 707–711.

Dalton, H., Read, D., Handley, T., & Perkins, D. (2017). Low intensity mental health services a rapid review. *Orange, New South Wales, Australia: University of Newcastle*, 54.

Department of Health. (2015). *Modified Monash model.* Retrieved June 12, 2018, from http://www.health.gov.au/internet/main/publishing.nsf/Content/modified-monash-model.

Department of Health. (2016). *PHN primary mental health care flexible funding pool implementation guidance: Stepped care.* D.o. Health, (Ed.). Canberra: Australian Government.

Department of Health. (2017). *The fifth national mental health and suicide prevention plan.* D.o. Health, (Ed.). Canberra: Australian Government.

Economics, D. A. (2016). *The economic cost of the social impact of natural disasters.* Sydney: Australian Business Roundtable for Disaster Resilience & Safer Communities, 116.

Fernandez, A., Black, J., Jones, M., Wilson, L., Salvador-Carulla, L., Astell-Burt, T., & Black, D. (2015). Flooding and mental health: A systematic mapping review. *PLoS One*, *10*(4), e0119929.

Fernandez, A., Gillespie, J. A., Smith-Merry, J., Feng, X., Astell-Burt, T., Maas, C., & Salvador-Carulla, L. (2017). Integrated mental health atlas of the Western Sydney Local Health District: Gaps and recommendations. *Australian Health Review*, *41*(1), 38–44.

Fernandez, A., Salinas-Perez, J. A., Gutierrez-Colosia, M. R., Prat-Pubill, B., Serrano-Blanco, A., Molina, C., … Salvador-Carulla, L. (2015). Use of an integrated atlas of mental health care for evidence informed policy in Catalonia (Spain). *Epidemiology and Psychiatric Sciences*, *24*(6), 512–524.

Fitzpatrick, S. J., Perkins, D., Handley, T., Brown, D., Luland, T., & Corvan, E. (2018). Coordinating mental and physical health care in rural Australia: An integrated model for primary care settings. *International Journal of Integrated Care*, *18*(2), 19.

Fitzpatrick, S. J., Perkins, D., Luland, T., Brown, D., & Corvan, E. (2017). The effect of context in rural mental health care: Understanding integrated services in a small town. *Health & Place*, *45*, 70–76.

Forum for the Future. (n.d.) *The five capitals.* Retrieved February 23, 2019 from https://www.forumforthefuture.org/the-five-capitals.

Geoscience Australia. (2019). Area of Australia – States and Territories. Retrieved February 19, 2019, from https://www.ga.gov.au/scientific-topics/national-location-information/dimensions/area-of-australia-states-and-territories

Gutiérrez-Colosía, M. R., Salvador-Carulla, L., Salinas-Perez, J. A., Garcia-Alonso, C. R., Cid, J., Salazzari, D., … Kalseth, J. (2017). Standard comparison of local mental health care systems in eight European countries. *Epidemiology and Psychiatric Sciences*, *28*(2), 1–14.

Handley, T. E., Lewin, T. J., Perkins, D., & Kelly, B. (2018). Self-recognition of mental health problems in a rural Australian sample. *Australian Journal of Rural Health*, *26*(3), 173–180.

Hunter, E., & Milroy, H. (2006). Aboriginal and Torres Strait Islander suicide in context. *Archives of Suicide Research*, *10*(2), 141–157.

Kelly, B. J., Stain, H. J., Coleman, C., Perkins, D., Fragar, L., Fuller, J., … Beard, J. R. (2010). Mental health and well-being within rural communities: The Australian *Rural Mental Health Study. Australian Journal of Rural Health*, *18*(1), 16–24.

Langford, S. A. (1994). The royal flying doctor service of Australia: Its foundation and early development. *Medical Journal of Australia*, *161*(1), 91–94.

McFarlane, A. C. (1986). Posttraumatic morbidity of a disaster: A study of cases presenting for psychiatric treatment. *Journal of Nervous and Mental Disease*, *174*(1), 4–14.

McFarlane, A. C., Clayer, J. R., & Bookless, C. L. (1997). Psychiatric morbidity following a natural disaster: An Australian bushfire. *Social Psychiatry and Psychiatric Epidemiology*, *32*(5), 261–268.

McGrail, M. R., Wingrove, P. M., Petterson, S. M., Humphreys, J. S., Russell, D. J., & Bazemore, A. W. (2017). Measuring the attractiveness of rural communities in accounting for differences of rural primary care workforce supply. *Rural & Remote Health*, *17*(2), 3925.

Mendoza, J., Elson, A., Gilbert, Y., Bresnan, A., Rosenberg, S., Long, P., … Hopkins, J. (2013). *Obsessive hope disorder: Reflections on 30 years of mental health reform in Australia and visions for the future.* Sippy Downs: BJN Graphic Design. [ConNetica Consulting].

Morrissey, S. A., & Reser, J. P. (2007). Natural disasters, climate change and mental health considerations for rural Australia. *Australian Journal of Rural Health, 15*(2), 120–125.

Muller, D. (2010). Ethics and trauma: Lessons from media coverage of Black Saturday. *Australian Journal of Rural Health, 18*(1), 5–10.

Muswellbrook Healthy and Well. (n.d.). Retrieved February 22, 2019, from http://muswellbrookhealthyandwell.org.au/home/.

NACCHO. (2020). Retrieved February 6, 2020, from https://www.naccho.org.au/.

Nasir, B. F., Toombs, M. R., Kondalsamy-Chennakesavan, S., Kisely, S., Gill, N. S., Black, E., … Nicholson, G. C. (2018). Common mental disorders among Indigenous people living in regional, remote and metropolitan Australia: A cross-sectional study. *BMJ Open, 8*(6), e020196.

National Aboriginal and Torres Strait Islander Leadership in Mental Health (NATSILMH). (2015). *Gayaa Dhuwi (Proud Spirit) declaration.*

National Aboriginal Community Controlled Health Organisation (NACCHO). (2018). Retrieved February 22, 2019, from https://www.naccho.org.au/.

National Aboriginal Health Strategy Working Party (NAHSWP). (1989). *A national Aboriginal health strategy.* Canberra: Australian Government.

National Mental Health Commission. (2014). *The national review of mental health programmes and services.* Sydney: NMHC.

National Rural Health Alliance. (2017). *Mental Health in Rural and Remote Australia.* Canberra: National Rural Health Alliance.

Our Healthy Clarence. (n.d.). Retrieved February 22, 2019, from https://www.ourhealthyclarence.org.au/.

Perkins, D., Hamilton, M., Saurman, E., Luland, T., Alpren, C., & Lyle, D. (2010). GP Clinic: Promoting access to primary health care for mental health service clients. *Australian Journal of Rural Health, 18*(6), 217–222.

Perkins, D. A., Roberts, R., Sanders, T., & Rosen, A. (2006). Far West Area Health Service mental health integration project: Model for rural Australia? *Australian Journal of Rural Health, 14*(3), 105–110.

Productivity Commission. (2017). *Shifting the dial: 5 year productivity review* in *Report No. 84.* Canberra.

Rasmussen, M., Guo, X., Wang, Y., Lohmueller, K. E., Rasmussen, S., Albrechtsen, A., … Kivisild, T. (2011). An Aboriginal Australian genome reveals separate human dispersals into Asia. *Science, 334*(6052), 94–98.

Ridoutt, L., Pilbeam, V., & Perkins, D. (2014). *Final report on workforce requirements in support of the 2014 National Review of Mental Health Programs and Services, National Mental Health Commission.*

Roberts, R. (2017). Equally well: Physical health and mental illness. *Australian Journal of Rural Health, 25*(6), 324–325.

Rural Adversity Mental Health Program. (n.d.) Retrieved February 22, 2019, from http://www.ramhp.com.au/.

Sadeniemi, M., Almeda, N., Salinas-Pérez, J., Gutiérrez-Colosía, M., García-Alonso, C., Ala-Nikkola, T., … Salvador-Carulla, L. (2018). A comparison of mental health care systems in Northern and Southern Europe: A service mapping study. *International Journal of Environmental Research and Public Health, 15*(6), 1133.

Sartore, G., Hoolahan, B., Tonna, A., Kelly, B., & Stain, H. (2005). Wisdom from the drought: Recommendations from a consultative conference. *Australian Journal of Rural Health, 13*(5), 315–320.

Saurman, E., Johnston, J., Hindman, J., Kirby, S., & Lyle, D. (2014). A transferable telepsychiatry model for improving access to emergency mental health care. *Journal of Telemedicine and Telecare*, *20*(7), 391–399.

Saurman, E., Kirby, S. E., & Lyle, D. (2015). No longer "flying blind": How access has changed emergency mental health care in rural and remote emergency departments, a qualitative study. *BMC Health Services Research*, *15*(1), 156.

Smith, K. B., Humphreys, J. S., & Wilson, M. G. (2008). Addressing the health disadvantage of rural populations: How does epidemiological evidence inform rural health policies and research? *Australian Journal of Rural Health*, *16*(2), 56–66.

Stain, H. J., Kelly, B., Carr, V. J., Lewin, T. J., Fitzgerald, M., & Fragar, L. (2011). The psychological impact of chronic environmental adversity: Responding to prolonged drought. *Social Science & Medicine*, *73*(11), 1593–1599.

van Dijk, A. I., Beck, H. E., Crosbie, R. S., de Jeu, R. A., Liu, Y. Y., Podger, G. M., … Viney, N. R. (2013). The millennium drought in southeast Australia (2001–2009): Natural and human causes and implications for water resources, ecosystems, economy, and society. *Water Resources Research*, *49*(2), 1040–1057.

Wilkins, R. (2015). *The household, income and labour dynamics in Australia survey: Selected findings from waves 1 to 12*. Melbourne: Melbourne Institute of Applied Economic and Social Research, The University of Melbourne.

2 Mental health and wellbeing among migrants in rural areas of the Global North

Evidence from the literature

Johanne Jean-Pierre and Linamar Campos-Flores

Introduction

Scholars of migration within the Global North have tended to focus on the integration of migrants primarily in urban settings, and to neglect any consideration of migrant wellbeing in rural areas. This research gap echoes the lack of rural studies within mental health literature and can be attributed to a privileging of the economic contributions of migrants, the persistence of disciplinary silos in migration studies, and a lack of attention to the increasingly diverse settlement patterns of migrants. This chapter presents a literature review of research relating to mental health and wellbeing among migrants in rural areas of the Global North. It bridges the gap between migration studies and mental health studies, and identifies emerging issues, trends, and gaps in research. It also identifies areas for further research and interventions, specifically the need to embed place sensitivity beyond the urban when considering the wellbeing of migrants, particularly their mental health.

Research about rural issues is usually limited to a small number of scholars, and it is challenging to find studies that consider multiple aspects of rural context, mental health, and migration. Most research on migration is utilitarian, incorporating questions specific to certain disciplines, and focusing on the economic contribution of migrants and their physical health. Studies in rural settings are often conducted as an afterthought, with data juxtaposed to urban-focused results with little critical contextualization of rural realities. This chapter, however, explores the overarching themes and research gaps in the scarce literature about the mental health of migrants in rural areas of the Global North. This is an important topic because, as noted in the introduction to this book, the World Health Organization stipulates that mental health is a global priority (WHO, 2018). This examination of mental health and wellbeing among migrants in rural settings of the Global North will help inform efforts to improve mental health among this population.

In this chapter, we use the term "migrants" to describe voluntary and involuntary documented and undocumented persons with various migration trajectories. In other words, we do not define migrants solely as asylum seekers, undocumented immigrants, or refugees – we also include permanent residents, international students, migrants with work permits, and legal immigrants. We also use the widely accepted 1946 World Health Organization definition of health: "a state of complete physical, mental, and social wellbeing not merely the absence of disease" (WHO, 1997, p. 1). We will examine the social determinants of health that may affect migrants, including income and social status, social support networks, education, employment and working conditions, social and physical environments, biology and genetic endowment, personal health behaviours and coping skills, healthy child development, access to health services, gender, and culture (Beverly & Reuter, 2005). These determinants vary widely among migrants due to the voluntary or involuntary nature of departure from their country of origin and the conditions of the migration process (Bhugra, 2004). When we discuss the Global North, we are referring to regions that are industrialized and/or former colonial powers, including the United Kingdom, Canada, the United States, Australia, New Zealand, and some countries in the European Union. Finally, we define rural and small-town regions as places "outside the main commuting zone of 10,000 or more" (Bollman & Clemenson, 2008, p. 9).

One challenge which emerged whilst conducting the review for this chapter was the lack of accurate and reliable data regarding international migrants. Various characteristics, for example, are used to refer to them (country of birth, foreign born, citizenship status, etc.), and there is a lack of available data on gender, ethnicity, and socio-economic status (Anderson & Blinder, 2015). Studies of the health and mental health of migrants have overwhelmingly been conducted in urban settings (Bhugra & Jones, 2001); have mainly included asylum seekers, refugees, and minority ethnic groups (Carta, Bernal, Hardoy, & Haro-Abad, 2005; Claassen, Ascoli, Berhe, & Priebe, 2005; Fazel, Wheeler, & Danesh, 2005); or have focused specifically on how the different phases of migration affect the social determinants of health (Davies, Borland, Blake, & West, 2011).

Methodological approach

A comprehensive examination of mental health and wellbeing in rural regions must incorporate all residents, including migrants. We conducted two literature reviews to identify key themes and gaps in the literature on the mental health and wellbeing of migrants in rural contexts. These reviews covered academic, peer-reviewed, and grey literature published in English and French, primarily in the European Union and Canada, with additional sources from Australia, New Zealand, and the United States. We used established search engines and databases to search for articles published between 1996 and 2016 with the following keywords: migration, migrants, asylum seekers, and refugees, coupled with the following terms: wellbeing, emotions, health, mental health, rural, rurality, rural services, social determinants of health, occupational health and hazards, and discrimination. We initially found 82 sources and retained 78 sources based on their relevance (see Tables 2.1 and 2.2). We excluded sources that did not address wellbeing and/or mental health

Table 2.1 The corpus

Document type	*Number*	*Region*
Peer-reviewed conceptual and review articles	26	Australia, Canada, Europe, US
Peer-reviewed empirical articles	31	Australia, Canada, Europe, New Zealand, US
Professional articles	5	Canada
Public reports	12	Canada, Europe, New Zealand
Book chapter	1	Canada
Books	3	Europe, US
Total	**78**	

Table 2.2 Document type references

Peer-reviewed conceptual and review articles N=26	*Region*
Achotegui (2008)	Europe (Spain)
Arcury, Estrada, and Quandt (2010)	US
Aronowitz (1984)	US
Bhugra and Jones (2001)	Europe (UK)
Bhugra (2004)	Europe (UK)
Bhugra et al. (2011)	Europe (UK)
Boyd and Parr (2008)	Europe (UK)
Carta, Bernal, Hardoy, and Haro-Abad (2005)	Europe (Spain)
Claassen, Ascoli, Berhe, and Priebe (2005)	Europe (UK)
Dabrowska and Campos-Flores (2018)	Canada
Davies, Borland, Blake, and West (2011)	Europe (Switzerland)
Dealberto (2007)	Canada
Fazel, Wheeler, and Danesh (2005)	Europe (UK)
Garnham and Bryant (2013)	Australia
Gerrard, Kulig, and Nowatzki (2004)	Canada
Hansen and Donohoe (2003)	US
Islam and Oremus (2014)	Canada
Jackson et al. (2007)	Australia
Keating, Swindle, and Fletcher (2011)	Canada
Kirmayer et al. (2011)	Canada
Lindert, Schouler-Ocak, Heinz, and Priebe (2008)	Europe
Mobed, Gold, and Schenker (2002)	US
Philo, Parr, and Burns (2003)	Europe (UK)
Preibisch and Hennebry (2011)	Canada
Scambler (2009)	Europe (UK)
Zimmerman, Kiss, and Hossain (2001)	Europe (UK)
Peer-reviewed empirical articles N=31	
Agudelo-Suárez et al. (2009)	Europe (Spain)
Arcury, Mora, and Quandt (2015)	US
Ariza-Montes, Lopez-Martin, and Navajas (2013)	Europe (Spain)
Beer and Lewis (2006)	New Zealand
Beverly and Reutter (2005)	Canada
Castaneda et al. (2015)	Europe (Finland)

Peer-reviewed conceptual and review articles N=26	*Region*
Curtis, Setia, and Quesnel-Vallee (2009)	Canada
Domnich, Panatto, Gasparini, and Amicizia (2012)	Europe (Italy)
Grzywacz, Quandt, and Chen (2010)	US
Henderson and Taylor (2003)	US
Hernández-Quevedo and Jiménez-Rubio (2009)	Europe (Spain)
Hennebry, McLaughlin, and Preibisch (2016)	Canada
Kelly et al. (2011)	Australia
McDonald and Kennedy (2004)	Canada
Merwin, Hinton, Dembling, and Stern (2003)	US
Montgomery et al. (2008)	Canada
Moreau, Rousseau, and Mekki-Berrada (1999)	Canada
Neufeld, Hirdes, Perlman, and Rabinowitz (2015)	Canada
O'Neil, George, Koehn, and Shepard (2013)	Canada
Parr and Philo (2003)	Europe (UK)
Parr, Philo, and Burns (2004)	Europe (UK)
Philo and Parr (2004)	Europe (UK)
Preibisch and Otero (2014)	Canada
Pysklywec, McLaughlin, Tew, and Haines (2011)	Canada
Riva, Bambra, Curtis, and Gauvin (2010)	Europe (UK)
Russell and Humphreys (2016)	Australia
Smith et al. (2006)	Canada
Snipes, Cooper, and Shipp (2017)	US
Starkes, Poulin, and Kisely (2005)	Canada
Steel, Liddell, Bateman-Steel, and Zwi (2011)	Australia
Toh and Quinlan (2009)	Australia
Professional articles N=5	
Battaglini and Rousseau (2012)	Canada
Coulombe and Vinet (2015)	Canada
Dongier, Kiolet, and Ledoux (2007)	Canada
Kirmayer (2012)	Canada
Rousseau, Hassan, Moreau, Jamil, and Lashley (2010)	Canada
Public reports and briefs N=12	
Ali (2002)	Canada
Anderson and Blinder (2015)	Europe (UK)
Beiser (1988)	Canada
Bollman and Clemenson (2008)	Canada
De Lima, Punch, and Whitehead (2012)	Europe (UK)
Hannigan, O'Donnell, O'Keeffe, and MacFarlane (2016)	Europe (Denmark)
McLaughlin, Hennebry, Cole, and Williams (2014)	Canada
Pong et al. (2000)	Canada
Stringer (2016)	New Zealand
Vartia-Väänänen et al. (2007)	Europe
World Health Organization (1997)	Europe
World Health Organization (2018)	Europe
Book chapter N=1	
Rousseau and Drapeau (2002)	Canada
Books N=3	
Bhugra and Gupta (2011)	Europe (UK)
De Lima (2016)	Europe (UK)
Gronseth (2012)	US

issues or that only focused on non-migrant residents. We included sources pertaining to temporary labour migration if they addressed health, mental health, or wellbeing. Relevant documents were analyzed to identify emergent themes and gaps related to international migration with a focus on wellbeing and mental health. Through an interpretive approach and a thematic analysis, we identified three main themes in the articles: (1) the wellbeing and mental health of migrants in primarily urban contexts, (2) health and mental health in rural contexts, and (3) labour migration and mental health issues. The following sections explore these themes, as well as research gaps that could be addressed in future research.

Thematic analysis

General links between wellbeing, mental health, and migration

This section summarizes the general information about migrants, wellbeing, and health. This section draws on evidence that has been gathered from primarily urban contexts, but the various stressors associated with different categories of migrants and different migration stages may also be relevant to rural contexts. Migration itself does not cause mental health disorders or poor mental wellbeing. Rather, it is the conditions of departure from the country of birth, the migration trajectories followed, and the settlement experiences of individuals that affect the health of migrants. Those who migrate may experience various stressors including stigmatization, discrimination, racialization, and family separation. Stress can be defined as the outcomes of physical, emotional, financial, or other threats to an individual's wellbeing, which can have substantial negative effects on health (Gerrard, Kulig, & Nowatzki, 2004). Migrants may face stressors during each stage of their migration journey from their country of origin to their host country (Beiser, 1988). In the country of birth, for example, human rights violations, environmental factors, biological characteristics, epidemics, and political circumstances can threaten physical and mental health, as can unsafe transportation, epidemics, and victimization during the migration process (Zimmerman, Kiss, & Hossain, 2001).

In contrast to asylum seekers and undocumented migrants, groups such as international students, migrants with work visas, and those moving with the intention to become permanent residents tend to be less affected by pre-migration and travel stressors. In fact, scholars have documented the "healthy migrant effect", whereby migrants – with the exception of asylum seekers and refugees – tend to be healthier than native-born populations upon arrival, and then their health tends to deteriorate to the native-born health level over time (Battaglini & Rousseau, 2012; Coulombe & Vinet, 2015; Domnich, Panatto, Gasparini, & Amicizia, 2012; Islam & Oresmus, 2014; Kirmayer, 2012; McDonald & Kennedy, 2004). After arrival in the host country, the health and wellbeing of all migrants is affected by factors such as employment, income/poverty, stigma and discrimination, access to co-ethnic social networks, and family support (Bhugra & Gupta, 2011; De Lima, 2016). However, undocumented and irregular migrants are particularly vulnerable because they may have limited access to healthcare in the host country (Davies et al., 2011). Additionally, the different definitions and criteria used for "migrant" in health system policies also affect access to healthcare, which could lead to, or aggravate, mental health issues for some individuals (Hannigan, O'Donnell, O'Keeffe, & MacFarlane, 2016). Finally, migrants who are intercepted and detained (Steel, Liddell, Bateman Steel, & Zwi, 2011; Zimmerman et al., 2001), and those who return to their country of origin, may experience negative health effects (Davies et al., 2011).

Overall, as a result of compounding stressors from the country of birth, migration travel conditions, and experiences in the host country, asylum seekers and refugees are more likely to experience mental health disorders compared to the general population or other categories of migrants (Achotegui, 2008; Ali, 2002; Bhugra, 2004; Bhugra et al., 2011; Fazel et al., 2005; Kirmayer et al., 2011; Lindert, Schouler-Ocak, Heinz, & Priebe, 2008; Moreau, Rousseau & Mekki-Berrada, 1999). Unusually high rates of schizophrenia and psychosis have been documented among asylum seekers and refugees (Castaneda et al., 2015; Dealberto, 2007; Smith et al., 2006). Yet despite the challenges that they face in the pre-migration, transit, and post-migration contexts, and the resulting health effects, migrants can demonstrate great creativity and agency (Gronseth, 2012) as they develop their own coping mechanisms (Bhugra, 2004). They may rely on social support, religious rituals, and spirituality to cope with mental health issues (Bhugra, 2004), and their narratives also point to stories of collective, familial, or individual success after migration challenges (Gronseth, 2012).

Migrant mental health in rural contexts

Rural communities differ from urban settings, so it cannot be assumed that the migration experience in these areas is like that experienced in cities. Despite common perceptions about idyllic rural life, research has shown that rural communities are not necessarily cohesive, slow-paced, or inherently caring (Boyd & Parr, 2008; Philo & Parr, 2004; Pong et al., 2000).

Rural communities differ from urban communities in terms of availability of health-related resources. They may be lacking economies of scale, health and social services, and affordable transport, and may also experience environmental adversity (Kelly et al., 2011) as Dalton and Perkins highlight within the Australian context in Chapter 1 of this book. All of these factors can lead to psychological distress for rural dwellers (Curtis, Setia, & Quesnel-Vallee, 2009). Rural communities may also have more pronounced gender segregation (Beverly & Reuter, 2005), more challenges related to aging (Keating, Swindle, & Fletcher, 2011), and higher suicide rates (Neufeld, Hirdes, Perlman, & Rabinowitz, 2015). Rural inhabitants have access to fewer hospital facilities (Henderson & Taylor, 2003), and are less likely to receive any form of treatment from primary or specialty healthcare practitioners

(Garnham & Bryant, 2013; Jackson et al., 2007; O'Neil, George, Koehn, & Shepard, 2013; Philo, Parr, & Burns, 2003; Pong et al., 2000; Russell & Humphreys, 2016; Starkes, Poulin, & Kisely, 2005).

Stigma can also act as a barrier to help-seeking, and rural communities may have more stigma related to mental illness compared to urban communities, which may discourage individuals from seeking assistance (Boyd & Parr, 2008; O'Neil et al., 2013; Parr & Philo, 2003; Parr, Philo, & Burns, 2004; Philo & Parr, 2004). Scholars have observed the "paradox of proximity" in rural settings: people know each other well despite being separated by great distances (Parr & Philo, 2003; Parr et al., 2004; Philo et al., 2003). This may exacerbate the fear of stigma, and rural residents may prefer to seek treatment far from their community to ensure that they maintain confidentiality (Boyd & Parr, 2008).

Agricultural labour migration and mental health issues

Few scholars have focused on migrants living in rural contexts, but a considerable body of research has explored the health and wellbeing of low-skilled migrants working as temporary labourers in rural areas. Seasonal agricultural labour migration in Canada, the United States, Australia, New Zealand, and the European Union has been associated with significant mental health issues and physical injuries, given the risk of exploitation and abuse (Arcury, Estrada, & Quandt, 2010; Beer & Lewis, 2006; Grzywacz, Quandt, & Chen, 2010; Hennebry, McLaughlin, & Preibisch, 2016; McLaughlin, Hennebry, Cole, & Williams, 2014; Preibisch & Hennebry, 2011; Preibisch & Otero, 2014; Pysklywec, McLaughlin, Tew & Haines, 2011; Snipes, Cooper, & Shipp, 2017; Stringer, 2016; Toh & Quinlan, 2009).

Migrant workers often enter a host country bound to an employer-tied work visa or permit, and employers have discretion in terms of recognizing and addressing security hazards and granting or denying access to medical care. In addition to injuries caused by workplace accidents, pesticide-related illnesses and musculoskeletal and hearing disorders have been documented among agricultural migrants (Arcury, Mora, & Quandt, 2015; Hennebry et al., 2016; McLaughlin et al., 2014; Mobed, Gold, & Schenker, 2002; Preibisch & Otero, 2014; Stringer, 2016). Many researchers have found that seasonal farmworkers have high levels of work-related stress, anxiety, depression, suicide, and other mental health issues that are closely related to their poor working conditions (Ariza-Montes, Lopez-Martin, & Navajas, 2013; Dabrowska & Campos-Flores, 2018; Grzywacz et al., 2010; Hansen & Donohoe, 2003; Hennebry et al., 2016; McLaughlin et al., 2014; Stringer, 2016). Most authors agree on two points: first, temporary farm workers are among those most at risk for physical injuries and psychosocial and mental health issues; and second, the rates, degrees, and effects of their mental health challenges (both in the host country and upon their return to the country of birth) are under-studied.

Gaps and future directions

Our literature review revealed various research gaps that have been identified and need to be addressed; we have classified these into four main categories:

First, different categories of migrants should be included in different research fields and areas. Researchers focusing on health and wellbeing should recruit different categories of international migrants, including undocumented and documented, first- and second-generation immigrants, asylum seekers and refugees, temporary workers, international students, and permanent residents (Claassen et al., 2005). Studies also tend to overlook immigrant children (Aronowitz, 1984; De Lima, Punch, & Whitehead, 2012) and migrants from developed countries (Smith et al., 2006). Researchers exploring the prevalence of mental health disorders should include migrants to broaden the scope of multicultural health research (Carta et al., 2005), including research exploring the effectiveness of treatments for drug addiction (Lindert et al., 2008). Additionally, migratory status, working conditions, and health issues should be incorporated into health-related research and not treated as separate themes (Vartia-Väänänen et al., 2007).

Second, the effects of discrimination, stigma, and exclusion on migrant health and wellbeing should be further explored. Several scholars have reported that discrimination and racism are main factors affecting the equilibrium and mental health of newcomers (Dongier, Kiolet, & Ledoux, 2007; Kirmayer, 2012; Rousseau & Drapeau, 2002; Rousseau, Hassan, Moreau, Jamil, & Lashley, 2010), and some have argued that stigma should be treated as a form of oppression with a clear emphasis on the power differential between stigmatizer and stigmatized (Scambler, 2009). Although it is challenging to measure discrimination as a risk factor for mental health, this issue clearly needs more investigation (Agudelo-Suarez et al., 2009). The intersectionality of geography, gender, and other contextual determinants is also important to explore when focusing on marginalization in rural and remote areas (Beverly & Reutter, 2005). The dynamics of social stigma and social exclusion in the rural context should be explored from a social geographic perspective, because these have strong influences on mental health (Boyd & Parr, 2008).

Third, initiatives and interventions intended to improve migrants' access to mental healthcare in rural contexts should be assessed. Access to mental healthcare remains a challenge for migrants in rural and urban areas due to several barriers: migrant status, culture, language, socio-economic status, and physical accessibility due to transportation issues (Hernandez-Quevedo & Jimenez-Rubio, 2009). More research is needed to explore the complex factors influencing the distribution of hospitals available in urban and rural areas (Henderson & Taylor, 2003), as well as best practices and policies to improve access to mental healthcare in rural and remote areas (Merwin, Hinton, Dembling, & Stern, 2003). It is also important to assess the role and work of interpreters in mental healthcare (Carta et al., 2005). When developing interventions, it is important to assess primary care strategies that can improve the mental health of migrants (Kirmayer et al., 2011), and to ensure that initiatives can increase resiliency to promote mental health in rural areas (Gerrard et al., 2004).

Fourth, a rural-specific approach is needed. Researchers investigating mental health should stop treating rural and remote contexts as a periphery of urban reality (Pong et al., 2000). It is also important to move beyond simple comparisons of urban and rural contexts (Boyd & Parr, 2008), and toward assessments of mental healthcare needs, access, formal and informal interventions, and collective initiatives in rural and remote areas in their own right. Areas for further research include suicide among elderly rural residents (Neufeld et al., 2015) and older male farmers (Garnham & Bryant, 2013), housing as a mental healthcare intervention in northern and rural areas (Montgomery et al., 2008), and the relationship between mental health and different types of occupations in rural areas (Riva, Bambra, Curtis, & Gauvin, 2010).

Conclusions

This chapter has summarized the main themes and research gaps in the literature related to migrant wellbeing and mental health in rural communities. However, we firstly considered the general links between migration and health and wellbeing; with recognition that most of what we know about migrants is derived from city-based studies. We then moved on to consider the characteristics of rural life that can affect migrants living in this context; for example, rural and remote regions may have fewer economic opportunities and more challenges related to access to healthcare facilities and practitioners, and more visible stigma related to mental illness. We also highlighted the particular case of agricultural migrant workers who may experience more physical and mental health challenges and are often vulnerable to exploitation and occupational injuries. In future research, scholars investigating migrant wellbeing and mental health in rural areas should include different categories of migrants for comparative purposes. They should also investigate the effects of discrimination and stigma in these populations. Finally, they should evaluate programs and initiatives implemented to promote mental health and wellbeing among migrants in rural areas to identify best practice.

Migrants in rural and urban areas share a common characteristic: their experiences of migration are heterogeneous. Therefore, it is crucial that health practitioners avoid generalizing migration as pathology (Carta et al., 2005) and instead treat it as a circumstantial factor. We know little about the experiences of migrants in rural areas, and the available literature mainly focuses on agricultural seasonal workers who often have a temporary working visa. Their experiences do not necessarily reflect those of rural international students, permanent residents, or refugees and asylum seekers. In future research, it will be important to explore issues such as how migrants experience mental health issues, search for healthcare, and cope with the various challenges they experience in rural contexts based on their migration status.

Other areas for future research include how race, class, gender, disability, and migration status shape mental health and wellbeing among children, youth, and adults in rural regions. These are just a few of the many questions that should be investigated in order to deepen our understanding of mental health and wellbeing in rural areas.

Acknowledgements

This research was supported by the Social Sciences and Humanities Research Council (SSHRC) and the Rural Policy Learning Commons Partnership (RPLC). The authors would like to acknowledge and thank Dr Philomena de Lima for the invitation to write this chapter and for her continued support.

References

Achotegui, J. (2008). Immigrants living in extreme situation: Immigrant syndrome with chronic and multiple stress (the Ulysses syndrome). *Avances en Salud Mental Relacional/Advances in Relational Mental Health*, 7(1), 1–22.

Agudelo-Suárez, A., Gil-González, D., Ronda-Pérez, E., Porthé, V., Paramio-Pérez, G., García, Ana M., & Garí, A. (2009). Discrimination, work and health in immigrant populations in Spain. *Social Science & Medicine*, *68*(10), 1866–1874.

Ali, J. (2002). *La Santé Mentale des Immigrants au Canada, Supplément aux Rapports sur la santé* (Publication 82–003–13). Ottawa: Statistics Canada. Retrieved from https://www150.statcan.gc.ca/n1/fr/catalogue/82-003-S20020016336.

Anderson, B., & Blinder, S. (2015). *Who counts as a migrant? Definitions and their consequences*. Oxford: The Migration Observatory at the University of Oxford. Retrieved from http://preview.tinyurl.com/n6yl2ag

Arcury, T., Estrada, J., & Quandt, S. (2010). Overcoming language and literacy barriers in safety and health training of agricultural workers. *Journal of Agromedicine*, *15*(3), 235–248.

Arcury, T., Mora, D., & Quandt, S. (2015). "...You earn money by suffering pain": Beliefs about carpal tunnel syndrome among Latino poultry processing workers. *Journal of Immigrant and Minority Health*, *17*(3), 791–801.

Ariza-Montes, J., Lopez-Martin, M., & Navajas, V. (2013). Native-immigrant working conditions in the European labor market. *La Pensée*, *75*(10), 39–44.

Aronowitz, M. (1984). The social and emotional adjustment of immigrant children. *International Migration Review*, *18*(2), 237–257.

Battaglini, A., & Rousseau, C. (2012). Adapter les services sociaux et de santé à la diversité culturelle: Un défi pour les institutions. *Le Point en Administration de la Santé et des Services Sociaux*, *8*(1), 18–22.

Beer, C., & Lewis, N. (2006). Labouring in the vineyards of Marlborough: Experiences, meanings and policy. *Journal of Wine Research*, *17*(2), 95–106.

Beiser, M. (1988). *Puis... la Porte s'est Ouverte. Problèmes de Santé Mentale des Immigrants et des Réfugiés au Canada: Rapport du Groupe Chargé d'Étudier les Problèmes de Santé Mentale des Immigrants et des Réfugiés au Canada*. Ottawa: Gouvernement du Canada.

Beverly, D., & Reutter, L. (2005). Women's health in northern British Columbia: The role of geography and gender. *Canadian Journal of Rural Medicine*, *10*(4), 241–253.

Bhugra, D. (2004). Migration and mental health. *Acta Psychiatrica Scandinavica, 109*(4), 243–258.

Bhugra, D., & Gupta, S. (Eds.). (2011). *Migration and mental health*. Cambridge: Cambridge University Press.

Bhugra, D., Gupta, S., Bhui, K., Craig, T., Dogra, N., Ingleby, J. D., ... Tribe, R. (2011). WPA guidance on mental health and mental health care in migrants. *World Psychiatry, 10*(1), 2–10.

Bhugra, D., & Jones, P. (2001). Migration and mental illness. *Advances in Psychiatric Treatment*, 7(3), 216–223.

Bollman, R. D., & Clemenson, H. A. (2008). Structure and change in Canada's rural demography: An update to 2006. *Rural and Small Town Canada Analysis Bulletin*, 7(7). Catalogue no. 21–006-XIE. Ottawa: Statistics Canada.

Boyd, C., & Parr, H. (2008). Social geography and rural mental health research. *Rural and Remote Health, 8*(1), 804. Retrieved from http://www.rrh.org.au/articles/subviewnew.asp?ArticleID=804

Carta, M. G., Bernal, M., Hardoy, M. C., & Haro-Abad, J. M. (2005). Migration and mental health in Europe (the state of the mental health in Europe working group: Appendix I). *Clinical Practice and Epidemiology in Mental Health, 1*(13). doi:10.1186/1745-0179-1-13.

Castaneda, A. E., Rask, S., Koponen, P., Suvisaari, J., Koskinen, S., Härkänen, T., ... Jasinskaja-Lahti, I. (2015). The association between discrimination and psychological and social well-being: A population-based study of Russian, Somali and Kurdish migrants in Finland. *Psychology and Developing Societies, 27*(2), 270–292.

Claassen, D., Ascoli, M., Berhe, T., & Priebe, S. (2005). Research on mental disorders and their care in immigrant populations: A review of publications from Germany, Italy and the UK. *European Psychiatry, 20*(8), 540–549.

Coulombe, V., & Vinet, D. (2015). Comment rendre les services de santé mentale plus aux besoins des personnes issues de l'immigration? *Le Partenaire, 24*(1), 22–24.

Curtis, S., Setia, M. S., & Quesnel-Vallee, A. (2009). Socio-geographic mobility and health status: A longitudinal analysis using the National Population Health Survey of Canada. *Social Science & Medicine, 69*(12), 1845–1853.

Dabrowska, E., & Campos-Flores, L. (2018). Distress or resilience? Examining socio-spatial relations impacting the wellbeing and emotional health of seasonal agricultural workers in rural Canada. *European Journal of Public Health, 28*(S1), cky048.208. doi:10.1093/eurpub/cky048.208.

Davies, A. A., Borland, R. M., Blake, C., & West, H. E. (2011). The dynamics of health and return migration. *PLOS Medicine, 8*(6), e1001046. doi:10.1371/journal.pmed.1001046.

Dealberto, M. J. (2007). Why are immigrants at increased risk for psychosis? Vitamin D insufficiency, epigenetic mechanisms, or both? *Medical Hypotheses, 68*(2), 259–267.

De Lima, P. (2016). *International migration: The well-being of migrants*. Edinburgh: Dunedin Academic Press Ltd.

De Lima, P., Punch, S., & Whitehead, A. (2012). *Exploring children's experiences of migration: Movement and family relationships*. Edinburgh: Centre for Research on Families and Relationships. Retrieved from http://hdl.handle.net/1842/6555.

Domnich, A., Panatto, D., Gasparini, R., & Amicizia, D. (2012). The "healthy immigrant" effect: Does it exist in Europe today? *Italian Journal of Public Health, 9*(3), e7532.

Dongier, P., Kiolet, M., & Ledoux, I. (2007). La santé mentale des immigrants: La médicine en contexte multiculturel-II. *Le Médecin du Québec*, *42*(3), 33–39.

Fazel, M., Wheeler, J., & Danesh, J. (2005). Prevalence of serious mental disorder in 7000 refugees resettled in Western countries: A systematic review. *The Lancet*, *365*(9467), 1309–1314.

Garnham, B., & Bryant, L. (2013). Problematising the suicides of older male farmers: Subjective, social and cultural considerations. *European Society for Rural Sociology*, *54*(2), 227–240.

Gerrard, N., Kulig, J., & Nowatzki, N. (2004). What doesn't kill you makes you stronger: Determinants of stress resiliency in rural people of Saskatchewan, Canada. *The Journal of Rural Health*, *20*(1), 59–66.

Gronseth, A. S. (2012). *Being human, being migrant: Senses of self and well-being.* New York: Berghahn Books.

Grzywacz, J. G., Quandt S., & Chen H. (2010). Depressive symptoms among Latino farmworkers across the agricultural season: Individual and contextual influences. *Cultural Diversity & Ethnic Minority Psychology*, *16*(3), 335–343.

Hannigan, A., O'Donnell, P., O'Keeffe, M., & MacFarlane, A. (2016). *How do variations in definitions of "migrant" and their application influence the access of migrants to health care services? Health Evidence Network Synthesis Report 46.* Copenhagen: World Health Organization.

Hansen, E., & Donohoe, M. (2003). Health issues of migrant and seasonal farmworkers. *Journal of Health Care for the Poor and Underserved*, *14*(2), 153–164.

Henderson, J. W., & Taylor, B. A. (2003). Rural isolation and the availability of hospital services. *Journal of Rural Studies*, *19*(3), 363–372.

Hennebry, J., McLaughlin J., & Preibisch K. (2016). Out of the loop: (In)access to health care for migrant workers in Canada. *Journal of International Migration and Integration*, *17*(2), 521–538.

Hernández-Quevedo, C., & Jiménez-Rubio, D. (2009). A comparison of the health status and health care utilization patterns between foreigners and the national population in Spain: New evidence from the Spanish National Health Survey. *Social Science & Medicine*, *69*(3), 370–378.

Islam, F., & Oremus, M. (2014). Mixed methods immigrant mental health research in Canada: A systematic review. *Journal of Immigrant and Minority Health*, *16*(6), 1284–1289.

Jackson, H., Judd, F., Komiti, A., Fraser, C., Murray, G., Robins, G., … Wearing, A. (2007). Mental health problems in rural contexts: What are the barriers to seeking help from professional providers? *Australian Psychologists*, *42*(2), 147–160.

Keating, N., Swindle, J., & Fletcher, S. (2011). Aging in rural Canada: A retrospective and review. *Canadian Journal of Aging/La Revue Canadienne du vieillissement*, *30*(3), 323–338.

Kelly, B. J., Lewin, T. J., Stain, H. J., Coleman, C., Fitzgerald, M., Perkins, D., … Beard, J. R. (2011). Determinants of mental health and well-being within rural and remote communities. *Social Psychiatry and Psychiatric Epidemiology*, *46*(12), 1331–1342.

Kirmayer, L. J., (2012). La santé mentale chez les immigrants et les réfugiés. *Quintessence: L'Accès au Savoir en Santé Mentale Populationnelle*, *4*(7), 1–2.

Kirmayer, L. J., Narasiah, L., Munoz, M., Rashid, M., Ryder, A. G., Guzder, J., … Pottie, K. (2011). Common mental health problems in immigrants and refugees: General approach in primary care. *Canadian Medical Association Journal*, *183*(12), 959–967.

Lindert, J., Schouler-Ocak, M., Heinz, A., & Priebe, S. (2008). Mental health, health care utilization of migrants in Europe. *European Psychiatry, 23*(S1), 14–20.

McDonald, T., & Kennedy, S. (2004). Insights into the "healthy immigrant effect:" Health status and health service use of immigrants to Canada. *Social Science & Medicine, 59*(8), 1613–1627.

McLaughlin, J., Hennebry J., Cole D., & Williams, G. (2014). *The migrant farmworker health journey: Identifying issues and considering change across borders.* Waterloo: International Migration Research Centre. Policy Points, Issue VI.

Merwin, E., Hinton, I., Dembling, B., & Stern, S. (2003). Shortages of rural mental health professionals. *Archives of Psychiatric Nursing, 17*(1), 42–51.

Mobed, K., Gold, E., & Schenker, M. (2002). Occupational health problems among migrant and seasonal farm workers. *West Journal Medicine, 157*(3), 367–373.

Montgomery, P., Forchuk, C., Duncan, C., Rose, D., Bailey, P. H., & Veluri, R. (2008). Supported housing programs for persons with serious mental illness in rural northern communities: A mixed method evaluation. *BMC Health Services Research, 8*(156). doi:10.1186/1472–6963–8–156.

Moreau, S., Rousseau, C., & Mekki-Berrada, A. (1999). Politiques d'immigration et santé mentale des réfugiés: Profil et impact des séparations familiales. *Nouvelles pratiques sociales, 12*(1), 177–196.

Neufeld, E., Hirdes, J. P., Perlman, C. M., & Rabinowitz, T. (2015). A longitudinal examination of rural status and suicide risk. *Health Management Forum, 28*(4), 129–133.

O'Neil, L., George, S., Koehn, C., & Shepard, B. (2013). Informal and formal mental health: Preliminary qualitative findings. *International Journal of Circumpolar Health, 72*(1). doi:10.3402/ijch.v72i0.21203.

Parr, H., & Philo, C. (2003). Rural mental health and social geographies of caring. *Social and Cultural Geography, 4*(4), 471–488.

Parr, H., Philo, C., & Burns, N. (2004). Social geographies of rural mental health: Experiencing inclusions and exclusions. *Transactions of the Institute of British Geographers, 29*(4), 401–419.

Philo, C., & Parr, H. (2004). "They shut them out the road": Migration, mental health and the Scottish Highlands. *Scottish Geographical Journal, 120*(1–2), 47–40.

Philo, C., Parr, H., & Burns, N. (2003). Rural madness: A geographical reading and critique of the rural mental health literature. *Journal of Rural Studies, 19*(3), 259–281.

Pong, R. W., Atkinson, A. M., Irvine, A., MacLeod, M., Minore, B., Pegoraro, A., … Tesson, G. (2000). *Rural health research in the Canadian Institutes of Health Research.* Vancouver: Centre for Rural Health Research.

Preibisch, K., & Hennebry, J. (2011). Temporary migration, chronic effects: The health of international migrant workers in Canada. *Canadian Medical Association Journal, 183*(9), 1033–1038.

Preibisch, K., & Otero, G. (2014). Does citizenship status matter in Canadian agriculture? Workplace health and safety for migrant and immigrant laborers. *Rural Sociology, 79*(2), 174–199.

Pysklywec, M., McLaughlin, J., Tew, M., & Haines, T. (2011). Doctors within borders: Meeting the health care needs of migrant farm workers in Canada. *Canadian Medical Association Journal, 183*(9), 1039–1042.

Riva, M., Bambra, C., Curtis, S., & Gauvin, L. (2010). Collective resources or local social inequalities? Examining the social determinants of mental health in rural areas. *European Journal of Public Health, 21*(2), 197–203.

Rousseau, C., & Drapeau, A. (2002). Santé mentale. In Institut de la Statistique (Ed.), *Santé et Bien-être, Immigrants Récents au Québec: Une Adaptation Réciproque? Étude Auprès des Communautés Culturelles 1998–1999* (211–245). Montréal: Les Publications du Québec.

Rousseau, C., Hassan, G., Moreau, N., Jamil, U., & Lashley, M. (2010). Du global au local: Repenser les relations entre l'environnement social et la santé mentale des immigrants et des réfugiés. *Thèmes Canadiens/Canadian Issues, Summer*, 88–92.

Russell, D. J., & Humphreys, J. S. (2016). Meeting the primary healthcare needs of small rural communities. Lessons for health service planners. *Rural and Remote Health, 16*(1), 3695. Retrieved from www.rrh.org.au/articles/showarticlenew.asp?ArticleID=3695

Scambler, G. (2009). Health-related stigma. *Sociology of Health and Illness, 31*(3), 441–455.

Smith, G. N., Boydell, J., Murray, R. M., Flynn, S., McKay, K., Sherwood, M., & Honer, W. G. (2006). The incidence of schizophrenia in European immigrants to Canada. *Schizophrenia Research, 87*(1–3), 205–211.

Snipes, S., Cooper, S., & Shipp, E. (2017). "The only thing I wish I could change is that they treat us like people and not like animals": Injury and discrimination among Latino farmworkers. *Journal of Agromedicine, 22*(1), 36–46.

Starkes, J. M., Poulin, C. C., & Kisely, S. R. (2005). Unmet need for the treatment of depression in Atlantic Canada. *Canadian Journal of Psychiatry, 50*(10), 580–590.

Steel, Z., Liddell, B. J., Bateman-Steel, C. R., & Zwi, A. B. (2011). Global protection and the health impact of migration interception. *PLOS Medicine, 8*(6), e100138. doi:10.1371/journal.pmed.1001038.

Stringer, C. (2016). *Worker exploitation in New Zealand: A troubling landscape [Report prepared for the Human Trafficking Research Coalition*]. Auckland: The University of Auckland.

Toh, S., & Quinlan, M. (2009). Safeguarding the global contingent workforce? Guestworkers in Australia. *International Journal of Manpower, 30*(5), 453–471.

Vartia-Väänänen, M., Pahkin, K., Kuhn, K, Schieder, A., Flaspöler, E., & Hauke, A. … Roskams, N. (2007). *Literature study on migrant workers*. Bilbao: European Agency for Safety and Health at Work. Retrieved from https://osha.europa.eu/en/publications/literature_reviews/migrant_workers/view

World Health Organization. (2018). *Guidelines for the management of physical health conditions in adults with severe mental disorders*. Geneva: World Health Organization Division of Mental Health and Prevention of Substance Abuse. Retrieved from https://apps.who.int/iris/bitstream/handle/10665/275718/9789241550383-eng.pdf?ua=1

World Health Organization. Division of Mental Health and Prevention of Substance Abuse. (1997). *WHOQOL: Measuring quality of life*. World Health Organization. Retrieved from http://www.who.int/iris/handle/10665/63482

Zimmerman, C., Kiss, L., & Hossain, M. (2001). Migration and health: A framework for 21st century policy-making. *PLOS Medicine, 8*(5), e1001034. doi:10.1371/journal.pmed.1001034.

3 Muddying the therapeutic geographies of mental healthcare

Carescapes of psychiatric transition in the Scottish Highlands

Christopher Philo and Hester Parr

Prelude: the valley, the asylum and mental healthcare

> I first became aware of all these worlds – new worlds in the valley, at home, inside myself – only after we'd moved to Cobble Hill, and I don't think that was coincidence. Looking back over the years, I can see that the valley had as much to do with it as anyone or anything else. That I'm able to stand here now and reflect on those ten years of my life with some measure of sanity, at least for the moment, is due in large part to the valley's influence, to the way this particular landscape seemed to pull me in and hold me close while the contours of land and water and air imprinted themselves on me, taught me things I'd need to know if I was going to change.
>
> (Osborne, 2001, pp. 4–5)

Terry Osborne, a teacher on the Environmental Studies Programme at Dartmouth College, North America, is here reflecting on ten years when he teetered on the edge of sanity, reconciling himself to a deep depression inside. During these years, he lived in a rural farming and wilderness landscape around his house on Cobble Hill, near the Connecticut River snaking along the boundary between the states of Vermont and New Hampshire. His experiences prompted his book *Sightlines: The View of a Valley through the Voice of Depression* (Osborne, 2001). Even the book cover suggests an expansive scene reflective of both his internal and external landscape. Through intimate experience with the valley's rock, soil, water, air, trees, and slopes, Osborne was enabled to learn about – even come to terms with, but "cure" is too loaded a word – his mental ill health. This was no straightforward process, no simple application of pure nature's supposedly soothing balm, but rather a mirroring: a recognition of how the forces at work in the valley landscape, both ones of nature and of human demands tearing at nature, were mirroring the juxtapositions coursing through his own psyche. These were "paradoxes" in play here, within both the Connecticut River Valley and Osborne's own self, and it is a version of these paradoxes – between nature and culture; between the old and the new – that we will inspect at the close of this chapter with respect to mental healthcare.

Mental healthcare provisions have been undergoing massive transformation over the last half-century in Britain and beyond, embracing many different elements, practices, and spaces. Central to this transition has been the progressive running down and closure of the old, sizeable long-stay residential institutions, the "lunatic asylums" dating chiefly to the nineteenth and early twentieth centuries, subsequently renamed mental or psychiatric hospitals. This "deinstitutionalisation" has brought forth a more dispersed assemblage of smaller facilities and arrangements, some entailing inpatient care and some with obvious nodes in mental health or resource centres, drop-ins, supported accommodation, therapeutic activities, and the like, running alongside a more amorphous "care in the community" sustaining mentally unwell individuals in their own homes and neighbourhoods. In another vocabulary, accenting the spatial facets of this transition, the shift has been from "asylum geographies" to "post-asylum geographies" (Philo, 2000). At a meta-level, it has also comprised a shift – certainly in the envisioning and representation of what is occurring, and often on the ground as well – from the countryside to the city, from the rural to the urban. Most of the old asylums grew up as *rural* phenomena, but, in some measure precisely because of their siting away from the supposedly "normal" locations of human inhabitation and busy-ness, they became subject to fierce condemnation and hence targeted for closure. The prevailing belief has been that the locus of mental healthcare should return to well-populated locations and, by implication, to the *urban* arena, thereby – if never quite expressed in this manner – de-ruralising the whole mental health sector.[1]

Various problematics core to this collection are signalled by these opening remarks, to do with both the therapeutic possibilities of rural areas with respect to mental ill health and the design, implementation, and sustaining of (inter-sectoral) rural mental healthcare services. What we wish to address in this chapter, however, is the specific process of closing the old asylums and opening new psychiatric inpatient facilities, a process often requiring a "physical" relocation of people – patients, clinicians, nurses, support staff, and others, also impacting carers – from one site to another. Such relocations have been occurring in large numbers throughout Britain and elsewhere since at least the 1980s, and a few are still ongoing, but they arguably remain a shadowy, little-known occurrence, only lightly tackled by scholars interested in the so-called "afterlives" of the asylum (e.g. Moon, Kearns, & Joseph, 2015). In many cases, the relocation has been from the countryside to the city, from institutions in clearly rural (or perhaps now suburban) settings to facilities sited on essentially urban campuses, within the city or town fabric, and likely with less extensive grounds surrounding them. The new facilities have often been trumpeted as state-of-the-art buildings embodying the latest practice-and-design principles, architecturally, technologically, and logistically (Burns, 1998), and often as offering a careful balance between clinical and more broadly therapeutic features (Gesler, Bell, Curtis, Hubbard, & Francis, 2004). They have been presented as "modern", with clean, bright, and sleek lines and furnishings, and by implication at one with the dynamic efficiencies and aesthetics of the contemporary metropolis (Högström & Philo, forthcoming a). Commonly too, they have been understood *against* what they are not, the now routinely cursed old asylums, with their grubbier, darker, and "dumpier"[2] spaces, supposedly "pre-modern" throwbacks to an archaic countryside.

In what follows, we wish to "muddy the waters" of this narrative of psychiatric transition from the old rural asylum to the new urban inpatient facility, complicating the latent progressivism that sees continual improvement in mental healthcare, forever sweeping aside the idiocies of past regimes. At the same time, we will take seriously matters of "mud", as in the organic properties of soil, dirt, grass, trees, and duckponds that were elemental features of many old asylum landscapes, and which have tended not to travel to – indeed, not to be welcomed in – the shiny, purified, and ordered worlds of new inpatient facilities. While much has been said about the value of "green spaces" within the latter, as potentially therapeutic additions in the shape of courtyards, potted plants, grass verges, and the like, these fugitive bits of nature – these tiny morsels of what might be conceived as "rurality" – hardly amount to the acres of gardens, fields, and rustic environs cradling the older asylums. The simple point of our chapter is hence to muddy what we suppose is actually a too scrubbed up, too sanitised, ideal of new inpatient facilities, one that from other research we know can strike some, even when recognising advances in how the new structures offer privacy, dignity, and safety, as overly clinical and even sterile (Högström & Philo, forthcoming a, b). It is to wonder about whether we should allow back in (some of) the dirt and disorder that the brave new vision wants to expel; to reintroduce the countryside asylum into the city facility; to trample mud on its spick-and-span floors.

Ruralising and de-ruralising mental healthcare

For all the claims about the novel therapeutic possibilities accompanying the appearance of the new inpatient facilities, claims that Sarah Curtis and co-workers explore within the frame of Wil Gesler's 'therapeutic landscapes' concept (Gesler, 1992, 1993; Gesler et al., 2004), there is nothing remotely new about efforts to harness landscape properties – the environments in and around buildings – when pursuing therapeutic advances in mental healthcare. Reflecting Gesler's typology, it is easy to identify a long history of efforts to mobilise "physical" properties (material assemblages of stone, brick, soil, and water), "social" properties (what people are afforded to do and how they might act within such assemblages), and "symbolic" properties (what meanings, lessons, and hopes they might derive from such assemblage) in order to enhance therapeutic efficacy. For instance, attention can be drawn to a whole array of eighteenth- and nineteenth-century "medico-moral" arguments about how specialist spaces, lunatic asylums in varying guises, could be manipulated to the end of upping cure rates for "acute" patients or at least bettering the lives of more "chronic" patients.

Elsewhere, we have charted and analysed such historical spatial interventions at length (e.g. Parr, 2008; Philo, 2004a), but here it will suffice to underline that all manner of efforts was made to create therapeutic asylum landscapes by selecting "fit localities" for them, laying out their grounds appropriately, and getting the architectures and internal spatial arrangements of the buildings right. The phrase "fit localities for an asylum" was coined by a writer in the *Asylum Journal* in the 1850s (Philo, 1987), and a wealth of locational debates, recommendations, and proscriptions graced the relevant journals, government enquiries, official inspectors' reports, lunacy legislation, newspaper articles, campaigning pamphlets, and more of nineteenth-century Britain (and elsewhere). The same was true with respect to both asylum grounds and asylum buildings, and all these elements spun tightly together in certain influential discourses of the time. Much was made of the place of nature – and hence a rural location – within these designs, there being a pronounced sense of tranquil nature being able to calm minds shattered by civilisation's cityward march. It is no exaggeration to state that the nineteenth-century asylums were subject to a pervasive "ruralisation" movement, with one historian nicely coining the phrase 'thoroughly rural-minded' (French, 1951, p. 73) when encapsulating views held by the English Lunacy Commissioners and others central to advising on asylum location.[3] The study discussed below is set in Scotland, and the centrality of the ruralisation agenda in the creation of Scotland's public (so-called "district") asylum system from the 1850s is made plain throughout Kim Ross's pioneering doctoral thesis (Ross, 2014).

Paying attention to this history furnishes critical lessons for more recent attempts to imprint a therapeutic mission into the design of mental healthcare facilities, including those inpatient facilities mentioned above as one part of a more broad-brush psychiatric transition. When addressing this transition, it is important to consider how treatment fashions have changed over time, often in ways recalling, sometimes reinventing or occasion simply forgetting the therapeutic landscapes created by the asylums of old. In what follows, we gesture to these longer-term shifts, attending chiefly to the external spaces (the situations, gardens, pathways) of the establishments involved. In so doing, we attend to the experiences, struggles, and voices of those people who experience mental healthcare as both receivers and givers, and whose reactions to the spaces planned "for" them to occupy and utilise must be heard when evaluating the success or failure of the therapeutic (or not-so-therapeutic) landscapes created. A critical geography of what we term "therapeutic carescapes" must foreground these voices, listening attentively when they either praise or criticise the locations, grounds, and buildings of mental healthcare provisions past and present, rural or otherwise. A key inspiration is a suite of papers by Sarah Curtis, Angela Wood, and co-workers (Curtis et al., 2013; Curtis, Gesler, Fabian, Francis, & Priebe, 2007; Curtis, Gesler, Priebe, & Francis, 2009; Wood et al., 2013, 2015) exploring the experiences of patients, staff, and carers relocated from older asylum settings to newer inpatient facilities in two different regions of England. Our own study engages equivalent experiences arising in the Scottish Highlands with the closure of an old asylum and opening of a new inpatient facility nearby, and – while we are returning to a project, and hence a 'story', from some time ago, the later 1990s into the early 2000s – our findings and their implications remain relevant for appraising current and future intersections of rurality and psychiatric transition.

"The Craig": "it's the grounds that made this place"

In 1864, the Inverness District Lunatic Asylum opened its doors for business. It was a public institution, part of a new breed of state-run lunatic asylums appearing across Scotland in response to the recommendations of an 1857 report and subsequent legislation. Intended to serve the whole Highlands and Islands region, a massive, if sparsely populated, rural region, it was sited a couple of miles or so outside the town of Inverness, the "capital" of this region but in reality a smallish provincial centre somewhat off the beaten track of power and influence. The asylum, its grounds and setting were purposefully chosen and, where possible, designed. It is instructive to hear the proposals from a group of memorialists of 1857 who:

> fixed upon Inverness as the site for a large public asylum on account of its central position, of its being a market town easily approached both by sea and land; of its commanding an unlimited supply of pure water, and its possession of a dry gravelly soil for buildings and airing grounds, and for the well-known amenity and salubrity of its climate.
>
> (A Copy of a Memorial, 1857, p. 2)

The authorities agreed with this diagnosis, and there is evidence that the resulting asylum on Dunain Hill very much squared with, and was almost certainly influenced by, the geographical preferences of the celebrated Scottish lunacy reformer, W.A.F. Browne, who urged a "moral treatment" of the insane requiring a location in the supposedly "moralising" context of an elevated natural (meaning rural) setting. Indeed, he commented favourably on the Inverness asylum in a paper of 1864, commending a site:

> where many acres of muir [moorland] have been reclaimed, where a group of houses and huts, situate on pleasant slopes and amid gardens, overlooking the Beaully Firth, accommodate some thirty or forty husbandmen who, with no other bonds, nor walls, nor restrictions other than the will of the governor, have made a large corner of desert to blossom like the rose.
>
> (Browne, 1864, p. 320)

The lack of an outer wall to the asylum was particularly novel, comprising a definite experiment in design with the goal of making the whole establishment seem as little like a prison as possible. Such practices extended into the building too, where "the window space and width of corridors were remarkable for the day and age" (Whittet, 1964, p. 16). These points could be elaborated, and are in Philo, Parr and Burns (2017), but the point is that the Inverness asylum was in many respects explicitly designed to create conditions thought, by a whole lineage of lunacy experts, to be therapeutic in cases of "madness".

The basic geography established in 1864 – the asylum on the hill, in substantial but unfenced grounds, with buildings full of windows and expansive corridors – remained little changed throughout the working life of the institution. Even when renamed Craig Dunain Hospital and brought under National Health Service control post–World War II, and despite the trajectory towards deinstitutionalisation from the 1960s onwards, these elements persisted. Even today, with the formal closure of the old institution in 2000–2001, the buildings and grounds still stand there on Dunain Hill, almost defiantly, as the policy-makers and developers scrabble to find a proper use for the site and structures. What this means, though, is that it is possible to talk to many people, ex-patients, relatives, staff, and neighbours, whose memories and judgements of the facility can be taken as verdicts on what was essentially a later nineteenth-century ruralised therapeutic carescape. This is exactly what we did, moreover, in the context of a larger Economic and Social Research Council (ESRC)–funded project from the early 2000s that explored the social geographies of mental health in the Scottish Highlands (Parr & Philo, 2003; Parr, Philo, & Burns, 2003; Parr, Philo, & Burns, 2004; Parr, Philo, & Burns, 2005; Philo, Parr, & Burns, 2017). In the course of interviewing over 100 users of psychiatric services, over 40 mental health workers, and a smattering of carers – for details of our field and interpretative methods, and also matters of ethics, see Parr and Philo references at close – we collected, as a supplement to our main dataset, a rich archive of personal experiences and feelings associated with "the Craig" on the Hill.

We cannot deny that the institution became somewhat feared in a wider regional context, with the sheer distance between it and many parts of the Scottish Highlands and Islands contributing to a stigmatising myth of this asylum in what might be termed a "regional imagination". People were terrified of being sent across the miles to the Craig, of being etched with the stigma of the place, and there was a clear reluctance on the part of families, friends, and parochial authorities to "release" their insane charges to the mercies of the distant asylum doctors. It is also true that for quite a few people who did end up as inmates of the Craig, the experience was frightening, disorientating, and almost wholly devoid of therapeutic merit. Several interviewees voiced these negative judgements:

> I was so desperate, as soon as I was there, I was desperate to be out. It was actually the old Craig Dunain, and it was this building, the whole thing. Although people grow affectionate to it if they're working here, … it was just … like a nightmare to me ….
>
> (Service user)

Unfavourable responses to the buildings, meaning the architecture – like "Colditz" or a "Frankenstein's Castle" were two descriptions from mental healthcare workers – and the cramped wards with little privacy, were forthcoming in many interviews. What this last quote also reveals is that some people could "grow affectionate" towards the Craig, however, and what genuinely surprised us – and what we must now emphasise – was the extent of really quite positive reactions. Tellingly, we believe, such judgements almost always attended to certain spatial dimensions of the asylum, particularly, if not exclusively, the grounds and countryside setting.

Let us hear some of these positive recollections, elaborating on one service user's simple statement that "[i]t's the grounds that made this place" and one carer's statement that "Craig Dunain was a wonderful place if you need it, there's no doubt about that and the grounds were lovely as well, it was … ideal for what it was there for". The grounds, woods, and, crucially, the duckpond were highly significant in the everyday lives of those who lived and worked in Craig Dunain:

> Oh aye, the duckpond, that was like, everybody would walk up there. Walk away up the road and feed the ducks, walk all the way round, go up through the trees, there was lots of places to sit on the ground.
>
> (Service user)

There is a suggestion that such tours of the grounds gave people a purpose and would be a key routine in the everyday lives of many patients:

> I used to love walking up to the duckpond and over stuff the ducks with bread, already been given five loaves that day! The grounds up there were brilliant, [I] used to wander round and … just a good hospital really.
>
> (Service user)

Interviewees drew upon images of tranquillity, calmness, and quietness to describe the external spaces of the asylum, perhaps contrasting with their own inner turmoil and the sometimes chaotic internal spaces of the buildings: "The Craig itself was quite helpful, quiet grounds to be in" (service user).

Interestingly, from the mid-1990s patients' groups utilised discourses about the "natural" environments of Craig Dunain being conducive to recovery from episodes of mental ill health as an input into debates about the closure of the hospital. A report by the Highland Users Group (HUG, 1996), considering what should be the qualities of any inpatient facility (or "new hospital") that might replace the Craig, listed the importance of features such as "peace, tranquillity and security" during periods of illness and recovery. On the basis of surveying users of Craig Dunain, moreover, the HUG report declared that:

> Almost all users considered the grounds within which the new hospital is situated to be of great importance. They wanted trees, grass, peace

> and quiet. Room to walk and feed the ducks all in an attractive, relatively private, environment. This environment was found to be soothing and relaxing in the more distressing stages of an illness and helpful as people recovered. People considered that this sort of environment helped their recovery tremendously.
>
> (HUG, 1996, p. 6)

This is an exceptionally clear statement about what service users in the region regarded as a therapeutic landscape, and there can be no doubting that the reference point for it was the physical environment of the old Craig set within its rustic, rambling, and secluded grounds. Staff too were aware of the therapeutic meaning held by the areas surrounding the hospital, recognising the value of patients being able to use the grounds, gaining some breathing space from others when experiencing acute phases of their condition.

Picking up on this last point, and as an important gloss on the original designing of the grounds as a therapeutic landscape, patients often used the grounds to *get away from* the formal – medical-psychiatric – therapeutic regime of the institution. In an unanticipated series of observations, Max (pseudonym), a service user, expressed this fact, as well as hinting at staff licence, what they would be prepared to allow, and the links between the grounds and his own inner worlds:

> Max mentioned that when in the hospital it was good to walk in the woods and at times the staff would allow you to camp in the grounds. This allowed him to "get away from the medication" – he couldn't explain this further. Max said that sometimes being alone with the voices helped to make you [him] stronger.
>
> (Interviewer notes)

A related quote from another service user, which first prompted us to conceive of the muddying of therapeutic geographies, ran as follows:

> I took the dirt track at the very back and walked right down past the graveyard. I came back covered in mud and I came back and they [nurses] gave me hell: "if anything happened to you, we wouldn't know where you were".

As well as escaping from the medical-psychiatric gaze, the external spaces of the Craig allowed for the pursuit of other activities such as illegal drug-taking and even sexual encounters:

> People used to do all sorts at the duckpond. When I was a member of the Patients' Council, people made it very clear to me that, when they got the new hospital, it was very important they had access to the duck pond 'cos they were very keen on it. I was arguing for this and it was much

> later I found out what that was all about. I wonder if the people I was telling how important the duck pond was, like the management, knew.
>
> (Service user)

This favourable response to the grounds evidently carried with it a sense of resistance to the establishment's norms, including the accessing of therapeutic alternatives such as space to "hear the voices", to take substances other than those approved by the institution, and to experiment with other ways of being a "real" person (not a disciplined inmate). They suggest a range of activities that may also alarm all of us now so fully inculcated into the "health and safety" – and new-moralised forms of – risk governance so prevalent throughout healthcare, social care, and indeed so many other establishments, all arguably central to a new species of neoliberal (capitalist) management.[4] These activities also undoubtedly muddied – but arguably enriched – what the nineteenth-century lunacy reformers supposed the outdoors therapeutic landscape of the asylum could offer to patients. Even so, it can still be speculated that some of the optimism possessed by the likes of Browne about the benefits of trying to mould a rusticated therapeutic landscape, notably one full of trees, walkways, and rural scenes, was not, after all, so wholly misguided.

New Craigs: the groundless "spaceship"

The old Craig closed its doors in 2000–2001, albeit there still being some continuing use of the out-buildings,[5] and it was replaced by a new purpose-built inpatient facility, New Craigs, located just down the hill from the old site, a little nearer to Inverness itself. Obviously, this new facility was designed with a whole range of therapeutic, administrative, and practical objectives in mind, and in the discourses of senior figures in the mental health services of the Highland Health Board there was no doubt that New Craigs entailed a great improvement over the old Craig. That said, it was transparently obvious in our interviews from the 2000s that responses to New Craigs as a therapeutic landscape – if not necessarily on the quality of the specific medical-psychiatric assistance there – were less than wholly laudatory, and indeed held certain less-than-complimentary claims in common. Indeed, a pronounced contrast emerged between positive responses to the old asylum, notably its grounds, and negative ones to the new facility, not least because the latter did not really have grounds at all and lacked the "rural" flavour of its predecessor.

Before elaborating this point about the grounds, let us add that the internal spaces of New Craigs also attracted criticism, most memorably for us when talking to two service users at a homeless shelter in Inverness who likened New Craigs to a "spaceship", all modern, sleek, and white inside, but strangely alienating as a place to spend any time. Another put it that "[w]hen you walk into New Craigs, it's like walking into a police station, a detention centre sort of place. There's no life, no fun, there's nothing" (also Högström & Philo, forthcoming b). In further comments the comparison with old Craigs also emerged:

> When you walk into New Craigs what do you see? Just bloody nurses … doors on either side. … When you walked into Craig Dunain you saw patients … [now] they are all in their wee single rooms which you can't see into, which baffles me, it's not good practice.
>
> (Ex-staff member)

> Newcraigs is like a modern office, it's busy, … while the old Craig Dunain, you walked in the main entrance and there was a big long carpeted hall-way and a reception desk, big old oak reception desk and a big old fire. It was just like going into a Victorian country house really. Certainly felt at ease. Whereas Newcraigs is very busy, fussy.
>
> (Service user)

That some interviewees disliked the internal spaces of the old asylum is nowhere more starkly represented than in the words of Jim Neville (no date), a one-time nurse at Craig Dunain, who hated the overpowering "geometry" of its corridors and wards (for a discussion, see Philo, 2017). Alternatively, another ex-staff member stressed how the old buildings could foster a sense of "home" (also Parr et al., 2003), something lost, perhaps, for service users transferred to New Craigs or into supported accommodation elsewhere:

> That awful place was home to hundreds of people and it was their community and they loved it …. I think some of the long-term residents really, really missed it and have lost their bearings because they have lost their home.

This closely parallels findings by Wood et al. (2015), relating to feelings of nostalgia – and what they term "solastalgia" (a sense of loss, with negative health implications, occasioned by how the place that people occupy has *changed*) – frequently expressed by patients and staff relocated from an old asylum to a new psychiatric inpatient facility (also Högström & Philo, forthcoming a, b).

Such feelings are often orientated to matters of *grounds*, with the most pronounced point of comparison between the old Craig and New Craigs being the lack of green space at the latter: the absence of that key ingredient of a nineteenth-century rural asylum landscape. "Well, that's what everyone misses, the grounds", laments one service user, while two other interviewees elaborated a little more:

> The grounds were comforting, [but] there are no grounds at New Craigs, beautiful view, but where's the pond? Where's the football pitch? Where's the golf course? They are all at Craig Dunain.
>
> (Ex-staff member)

> It had a sort of a feeling, it was a nice building, it had lovely walks, beautiful walks around there and it had an air of peace about it an air of tranquillity, which you don't get at New Craigs.
>
> (Service user)

The resonant connection between the old Craig and new Craigs, as one service user let slip, can be witnessed in the fact that "[p]atients go from New Craigs up to the old hospital for a joint, just for a walk". This remark hinted again at the transgressive possibilities afforded by the grounds of the old Craig, but more simply it paints a picture of patients based in New Craigs – this highly designed, state-of-the-art new site of inpatient care – feeling a need to return to the muddy pathways of a very old, seemingly outdated and outmoded, therapeutic landscape. Another example was shared by a carer:

> I know one lady who stayed in Craig Dunain for years and years and years and who now lives in a nursing home in town and still wanders, something she has always done, and wanders up here [to the grounds of Craig Dunain]. Just to look … because she identifies so strongly with it.

Similar evidence gathered from our study included claims about ex-residents and homeless people apparently choosing to sleep rough in the woods behind the old asylum buildings. Beyond these informal journeys of remembrance, the fate of the old Craigs site also became a topic of local debate, so that rather than being a stigmatised place (as has been the fate of some abandoned asylum sites elsewhere), the land and even maybe the buildings are now considered desirable for their aspect and location.[6] One service user's reflections about this redevelopment of the site highlighted tensions around the site, and also the problem of assuming that the site had become an empty one now bereft of inhabitants:

> Originally people were thrown up here so they would be away from the town, secluded, shut the nutters out. Now they've thrown us off the property here and put us in temporary accommodation down there [New Craigs] … To my mind all they've done is robbed us of something that should have been left … New Craigs isn't the same, the patients come up here for their walks, they're not going to be allowed to do that when there is a housing estate.

These words summarised the position taken by many when contrasting the old Craig and New Craigs, and nothing could be stronger in the politics of contemporary therapeutic landscapes than the insistence of having been "robbed … of something that should have been left". There is a profound insight here into an ongoing process of exclusion and even "dispossession", with patients initially shunted to the countryside away from the town – the "moral-medical" ideals of asylum location not being entirely untainted by an exclusionary logic (also Philo, 2004a, Chap. 2) – and then, a century or so on, being removed from what might have become, for some, a therapeutic refuge and resource, and instead metaphorically marched back to the city.[7]

Conclusion: the old and the new

The interventions made by interview respondents in a research project over 15 years ago sharply inflected our own thinking at the time about the intersections of rurality and mental healthcare, and we remain convinced of their relevance to debates about contemporary psychiatric facility design in the later 2010s. In 2019, for instance, the UK "Design in Mental Health Conference" will include a keynote speech about "green space" (for which read "rural-like space") and mental health in Scotland (https://www.designinmentalhealth.com/conference-programme-2019/). Questions of therapeutic relations with nature are clearly as relevant now as they were in the 2000s, perhaps even more so given the recent popularity of claims about rurality, the countryside, and what Richard Mabey (2005) has termed "nature cure" (see also Chapters 4, 5, and 7 in this collection). We hence find warrant for revisiting our older research, wherein we could indeed witness the views of patients – as well as of staff and carers – contrasting the merits and demerits of both an old asylum (the old Craig) and its new replacement (New Craigs). We must beware romanticising the old – placing on a pedestal some past "golden age" of asylum treatment and its landscapes – since there is no doubt that the asylums of old were often brutal, uncaring, and unforgiving places, too often serving as spaces of detention for those considered somehow "deviant" relevant to the cultural expectations of national, regional, and local societies (Foucault, 1967; Goffman, 1961; Rothman, 1971; Scull, 1979).

Neither must we simply suppose that the new is superior, though, slipping into progressivist notions of an ever-improving approach to psychiatric treatment and design that *automatically* takes the most recent schemes rolling off the architects' tables as an advance over what Browne or the founders of old Craig Dunain ever envisaged. In bald summary, from hearing the voices of experience in our study, it can be suggested that the presence of grounds, natural landscapes, and muddy pathways may be vitally important to both senses of self and possibilities for recovery, in a manner not wholly distant from what had once been envisaged by the lunacy reformers. Seen from this angle, moreover, a slither of "green space" in a new inpatient facility, a ribbon of grass bordering a busy road, a meagre rendering of the rural in the middle of the urban, is simply not going to suffice. Yet, there is more to the matter than *just* an evocation or even advocacy of mental healthcare through the lens of a Mabey-esque "nature cure", because – and this is a nuance, if potentially a significant one – what our interviewees also conveyed might be cast as a processual sensibility comforted by how an establishment has "aged", "weathered", and become in some register *part* of a local world, at one with its "nature", not an alien imposition. It is a sensibility dimly aware of how time and change have organically metamorphosed what might itself once have struck as a threatening new arrival on the healthcare landscape – the big, blocky asylum, solid, purposeful, amid freshly turned bare soil and clearly marked pathways – into something seemingly *in place*, mud, weeds, bugs, crumbling stone, stained wood, and all.

In this regard, it is instructive finally to return to what Osborne writes about becoming *part* of his valley, immersed in its natural contours and rhythms, while *also* remaining part of the modern human world clawing away at this rural scene and its resources:

> I'm still planted on a hill inside a valley bowl, ... a high place in a low area between two ridgelines; ... and I'm still part of that culture that wants to lay this land bare for profit and yet somehow leave the place looking untouched, so we won't have to face what we've done. Not an easy existence to make sense of ....
>
> (Osborne, 2001, p. 237)

Perhaps there are clues here about how the ex-patients of the old Craig, and maybe too some ex-staff members, were feeling in the early 2000s. On the one hand, the site of the old Craig, particularly its grounds, woods, and duckpond, provided them with that sense of immersion, almost of cradling, as described by Osborne, a sensation with enormous therapeutic value. Maybe too the fact that the old Craig was so old, its stark outlines on the rustic landscape softened, weather-beaten, and muddied through time, becoming an organic palimpsest of building and grounds, brickwork and earthwork (Figure 3.1), nature and culture, is what led some to feel safe here, at

Figure 3.1 "Organic" fusing ("muddying") of tree and wall at asylum.

home, relaxed, even mentally healthier. On the other hand, the structures of New Craigs, bereft of grounds or any deeper connectedness to the folds of the local topography, could not furnish them with the same attachments and emotions of wellbeing. Maybe too the fact that New Craigs was so new, this "spaceship" parachuted on to a pocket-handkerchief plot of land, an urban child of modern times obsessed with patient audits, waiting lists and business plans, was not incidental to some feeling less than happy when resident or attending there. "This is not an easy existence to make sense of", Osborne is right, and we know – as our interviewees knew – that there can be no simple turning back to the therapeutic asylum landscapes of the past. Even so, there is still much to be gained from at least acknowledging the tension between the old and the new, and acknowledging what some evidently find beneficial about the muddy terrains of former therapeutic landscapes, often set in their rural embrace, when designing the assemblages of inside and outside spaces (Tucker, Brown, Kanyeredzia, McGrath, & Reavey, 2019, p. 29) required by new, often urban, psychiatric geographies.

Acknowledgements

Thanks to the ex-patients and staff of Craig Dunain who gave their time and stories. Thanks to the UK ESRC for supporting the research through grant No. R000238453. We fulsomely acknowledge the work of Nicola Burns as research fellow in the original project (2001–2003). Thanks as well to the editors of the present volume.

Notes

1 In practice, of course, countless people with mental health problems continue to live *in* rural areas the world over (Philo, Parr, & Burns, 2003) or maybe even migrate *to* rural areas, sometimes precisely because those localities are reckoned to have qualities conducive to improved mental health (Philo & Parr, 2004). Acute questions are thereby raised about how the needs of these rural dwellers might best be met.

2 A staff interviewee in study of transitions at the Gartnavel Royal Hospital, one entailing a relocation from an old Victorian asylum "on the hill" to a new inpatient facility down below, remarked that "we managed to engage and work with each other far better in an old, dumpier building" (meaning the old institution) (in Högström & Philo, forthcoming a).

3 Extensive in-depth primary research led Philo (2004, esp. Chaps.6 & 7) to conclude that ruralisation really *was* the over-riding "geographical story" of the overall nineteenth-century asylum system. A pervasive ruralisation discourse dominated the siting of all but the earliest English public county asylums, even those provided after mid-century specifically for urban "boroughs", while the charitable lunatic hospitals and private madhouses inheriting an urban location from their eighteenth-century (or earlier) origins came under huge pressure to ruralise (albeit a few resisted). Alternative locational visions – urban-centred, community-based, anti-remoteness – did circulate during the century, increasingly so after the 1870s with declining moral-therapeutic optimism, but the rural

hegemony influenced asylum siting orthodoxies until well into the early twentieth century. Never entirely absent, though, was also a wish to rid the city of its troublesome people, those who might be disquieting to "sane" inhabitants. Some scholars have supposed this exclusionary impulse to be the *real* driver behind asylum ruralisation, mistrusting any voicing of the countryside's therapeutic advantages by contemporary experts, but the interpretative snares of this controversy can be sidestepped for present purposes (c.f. Philo, 2004a, Chaps.2 & 8).

4 The extent to which such risk governance can itself jar with ideal therapeutic regimes, particularly ones still prepared to allow a certain "geography of licence" (Goffman, 1961) to patients, is explored by Curtis et al. (2013); and it is also the fulcrum for a paper emerging from a more recent project recovering the "spatial stories" of Gartnavel Royal Hospital in Glasgow that considers what has happened to "fun at the asylum" (Högström & Philo, forthcoming b).

5 One external ward was being used by the Training and Guidance (TAG) unit, a scheme for helping people with mental health problems back into the labour market. Interestingly, as we recount at one point in Philo, Parr, & Burns (2005), users of the TAG unit also greatly appreciated the immediate environmental surroundings of the unit, meaning the grounds of the old Craig.

6 Various were suggested, including housing developments, a film studio, a campus for the University of the Highlands and Islands, or a new site for Scottish Natural Heritage.

7 We acknowledge that some patient voices, particularly from ex-patients who position themselves as "psychiatric survivors", would likely be less generous about the history (and geography) of closed mental healthcare institutions, seeing them as necessarily productive of abuses and hence ripe only for "abolition". In our own research – and also in the more recent Gartnavel project (Högström & Philo, forthcoming a, b) – we have rarely encountered such abolitionist views, but there is a complex, contentious debate to be had about the extent to which, in sum, "the asylum" can and should still have a place within worldly "post-asylum geographies".

References

A Copy of a Memorial from the inhabitants of inverness to the secretary of state for the home department; and of a minute of a general meeting of the commissioners of supply of the county of ross on the subject of a proposed Lunatic Asylum for the Northern Counties of Scotland (1857), Sess.2. Edinburgh: HMSO.

Browne, W. A. F. (1864). The moral treatment of the insane: A lecture. *Journal of Mental Science, 10,* 315–318.

Burns, T. (1998). Not just bricks and mortar: Report of the Royal College of Psychiatrists working party on the size, staffing, structure, siting, security of new acute adult psychiatry in-patients units. *Psychiatric Bulletin, 22,* 465–466. doi: 10.1192/pb.22.8.465

Curtis, S., Gesler, W., Fabian, K., Francis, S., & Priebe, S. (2007). Therapeutic landscapes in hospital design: A qualitative assessment by staff and service users of the design of a new mental health inpatient unit. *Environment & Planning C: Government & Policy, 25,* 591–610.

Curtis, S., Gesler, W., Priebe, S., & Francis, S. (2009). New spaces of inpatient care for people with mental illness: A complex 'rebirth' of the clinic? *Health & Place, 15,* 340–348.

Curtis, S. E., Gesler, W., Wood, V. J., Spenser, I., Mason, J., Close, H., & Reilly, J. (2013). Compassionate containment? Balancing technical safety and therapy in the design of psychiatric wards. *Social Science & Medicine, 97,* 201–209.

Foucault, M. (1967). *Madness and civilisation: The history of madness in the age of reason*. London: Tavistock.

French, C. N. (1951). *The story of St.Luke's Hospital*. London: Heinemann.

Gesler, W. M. (1992). Therapeutic landscapes: Medical issues in light of the new cultural geography. *Social Science and Medicine, 34*, 735–746.

Gesler, W. M. (1993). Therapeutic landscapes: Theory and a case study of Epidauros, Greece. *Environment and Planning D: Society and Space, 11*, 171–189.

Gesler, W., Bell, M., Curtis, S. E., Hubbard, P., & Francis, S. (2004). Therapy by design: Evaluating the UK hospital building program. *Health & Place, 10*, 117–128.

Högström, E., & Philo, C. (forthcoming a). 'The play of shadow and light': Illuminating worlds of a mental healthcare institution. *Transactions of the Institute of British Geographers*.

Högström, E., & Philo, C. (forthcoming b). Fun at the asylum: Devitalising mental healthcare. *Health & Place*.

Goffman, E. (1961). *Asylums: The social situation of mental patients*. London: Tavistock.

HUG. (1996). Closure of Craig Dunain. Report was available from HUG: Contact Graham Morgan, Highland Community Care Forum, 1 Ardross Street, Inverness IV3 5NN.

Mabey, R. (2005). *Nature cure*. London: Vintage.

Moon, G., Kearns, R., & Joseph, A. (2015). *The afterlives of the psychiatric asylum: The recycling of concepts, sites and memories*. Farnham: Ashgate.

Neville, J. (no date). The healing power of narrative, reflection and art: 'Minding your heart where extremes meet'. Unpublished ms. made available to researchers during project.

Osborne, T. (2001). *Sightlines: The view of the valley through the voice of depression*. Hanover and London: Middlebury College Press/University Press of New England.

Parr, H. (2008). *Mental health and social space: Inclusionary geographies?* Oxford: Blackwell.

Parr, H., & Philo, C. (2003). Rural mental health and social geographies of caring. *Journal of Social and Cultural Geography, 4*, 471–488.

Parr, H., Philo, C., & Burns, N. (2003). 'That awful place was home': Reflections on the contested meanings of Craig Dunain Asylum. *Scottish Geographical Journal, 119*, 341–360.

Parr, H., Philo, C., & Burns, N. (2004). Social geographies of rural mental health: Experiencing inclusions and exclusions. *Transactions of the Institute of British Geographers, 29*, 401–419.

Parr, H., Philo, C., & Burns, N. (2005). 'Not a display of emotions': Emotional geographies of the Scottish Highlands. In J. Davidson, L. Bondi, & M. Smith, M. (Eds.), *Emotional geographies* (pp. 87–102). London: Ashgate: London.

Philo, C. (1987). 'Fit localities for an asylum': The historical geography of England's nineteenth-century 'mad-business' as viewed through the pages of the Asylum Journal. *Journal of Historical Geography, 13*, 398–415.

Philo, C. (2000). Post-asylum geographies: An introduction. *Health & Place, 6*, 135–136.

Philo, C. (2004a). *A geographical history of institutional provision for the insane from Medieval Times to the 1860s in England and Wales: 'The space reserved for insanity'*. Lewiston, Queenston and Lampeter: Edwin Mellen Press.

Philo, C. (2004b). Scaling the asylum: Three different geographies of the Inverness District Lunatic Asylum (Craig Dunain). In L. Topp, J. E. Moran, & J. A. Andews (Eds.), *Madness, architecture and the built environment: Psychiatric spaces in historical context* (pp. 107–131). London: Routledge.

Philo, C., & Parr, H. (2004). 'They shut them out the road': Migration, mental health and the Scottish Highlands. *Scottish Geographical Journal, 120*, 47–70.

Philo, C., Parr, H., & Burns, N. (2003). Rural madness: A geographical reading and critique of the rural mental health literature. *Journal of Rural Studies, 19*, 259–281.

Philo, C, Parr, H., & Burns, N. (2005). 'An oasis for us': Some 'in-between' spaces of mental health in a rural region – TAG units in the Scottish Highlands. *Geoforum, 36*, 778–791.

Philo, C., Parr, H., & Burns, N. (2017). The rural panopticon. *Journal of Rural Studies, 51*, 230–239.

Ross, K. A. (2014). The locational history of Scotland's district lunatic asylums, 1857–1913. Unpublished PhD thesis, University of Glasgow, School of Geographical & Earth Sciences.

Rothman, D. J. (1971). *The discovery of the asylum: Social order and disorder in the New Republic*. Boston, MA: Little, Brown and Co.

Scull, A. T. (1979). Museums of madness: *The social organisation of insanity in nineteenth-century England*. London: Allen Lane.

Tucker, I. M., Brown, S. D., Kanyeredzia, A., McGrath, L., & Reavey, P. (2019). Living 'in-between' outside and inside: The forensic psychiatric unit as an impermanent assemblage. *Health & Place, 55*, 29–36.

Whittet, M. M. (1964). *Craig Dunain Hospital, Inverness: One hundred years, 1864–1964*. Inverness: Robt. Carruthers & Sons, Courier Office.

Wood, V. J., Curtis, S. E., Gesler, W., Spencer, I. H., Close, H. J., Mason, J., & Reilly, J. G. (2013). Creating 'therapeutic landscapes' for mental health carers in inpatient settings: A dynamic perspective on permeability and inclusivity. *Social Science & Medicine, 9*, 122–129.

Wood, V. J., Gesley, W., Curtis, S. E., Spencer, I. H., Close, H. J., Mason, J., & Reilly, J. G. (2015). 'Therapeutic landscapes' and the importance of nostalgia, solastalgia, salvage and abandonment for psychiatric hospital design. *Health & Place, 33*, 83–89.

4 Care farming, therapeutic landscapes, and rurality in the UK

Richard Gorman

Introduction

This chapter explores the ways in which "rurality" is entangled with ideas of the "therapeutic" and recruited (to varying extents and successes) into practices and performances associated with the facilitation of mental health and wellbeing. The conceptual framework of "therapeutic landscapes" has produced a rich literature that highlights how place matters for health (Kearns & Collins, 2009). However, despite lively historical, social, and cultural conflations and connections between ideas of rurality and health, the specific role and importance of rural identities and representations in producing therapeutic spaces, assemblages, and affects have not previously arisen to the fore.

To explore the interrelations between rurality, place, and the facilitation of positive mental health and wellbeing, I introduce care farming – an increasingly popular, place-based intervention which utilises agricultural settings to provide care for vulnerable groups. It operationalises rurality and agricultural spaces in order to promote and support mental and physical health. Drawing together different literatures, I discuss the specific connections that exist between care farming and notions of rurality. Mobilising empirical interview and ethnographic data, I move to consider the interrelationships between ideas of rurality and the production of therapeutic spaces, questioning how rurality is used to enact practices and performances of care farming, and the challenges and opportunities that these entanglements of rurality and care can produce.

Therapeutic landscapes and rurality

> A therapeutic landscape arises when physical and built environments, social conditions and human perceptions combine to produce an atmosphere which is conducive to healing. The term *healing* is used here in a broad manner to include cures in the biomedical sense (physical healing), a sense of psychological well-being (mental healing) and feelings of spiritual renewal (spiritual healing).
>
> (Gesler, 1996, p. 96, emphasis original)

The idea of a "therapeutic landscape" exists as a "geographic metaphor for aiding in the understanding of how the healing process works itself out in places" (Gesler, 1992, p. 743). The concept moves to recognise space and place as dynamic and evolving processes, moulded by the meshing and imbrication between physical, individual, and social factors (Gesler, 1992). The phrase has been used extensively as "a conceptual framework to organise ideas about how people experience landscape in ways that are important to their health" (Curtis, 2012, p. 7). As Kearns and Moon (2002, p. 611) describe, "for some, it is analogous to literally defined localities. For others it is a metaphor for the complex layerings of history, social structure and built environment that converge in particular places".

The tradition of exploring "therapeutic landscapes" arose alongside, and as part of, the development of a "new" geography of health (Kearns & Moon, 2002) which saw geographers develop an increased interest in the role and influence of an affective sense of place on health and wellbeing (Gesler, 1991); a concern for the significance of the relations between people and the environment in defining and enacting physical and mental health (Curtis, 2012). Rather than treating place as a defined location, place in this context is instead conceptualised as "a zone of experience and meaning", unique, specific, and constructed (Wilson, 2003, p. 84). Health is experienced and constructed within place, an embodied and situated experience. It is not possible to separate the experience of health from the place in which it is experienced (Andrews, 2002; Kearns, 1993). Ultimately, place matters for health (Kearns & Collins, 2009).

As Halfacree (2012) notes, "rural" landscapes have been an "especial" focus of geographic literature discussing ideas of "therapeutic landscapes". These have generally focussed on more "isolated" areas, rather than "everyday" rural areas, for example, rural retreats (Conradson, 2005b; Lea, 2008), camps in rural areas (Dunkley, 2009; Thurber & Malinowski, 1999), and rural wilderness areas (Palka, 1999). In his original conceptualisation of "therapeutic landscapes", Gesler (1992, p. 743) noted – and lamented – a tendency to associate a certain type of pastoral rural idyll with notions of "the therapeutic". Historically, Parr (2007, p. 540) notes how "rural nature in particular was understood as inherently healthy – with social, physical, and mental benefits". Rural spaces became associated with ideas of therapeutic value, with frequent historic preferences for "the establishment of asylums, lunatic hospitals and madhouses in tranquil, healthy and attractive rural environments" (Philo, 1987, p. 411).

Work within health geography has moved to consider and highlight "how the nature of rural space and place interacts with health and well-being" (Munoz, 2014, p. 2). Kearns and Collins (2000, p. 1049) noted that "rural places have frequently been constructed as therapeutic in opposition to urban places". Though, as Milligan (2007, p. 258) argues, whilst rural environments are regularly imagined as peaceful and "as places that individuals should visit in order to experience restoration or renewal", this idealised depiction of the rural can be starkly at odds with a more lived experience of rurality. Indeed, it is worth noting that the image of "the rural" that frequently emerges within discussions of therapeutic spaces is a very particular one. As MacKian (2008, p. 107) notes in her work on notions of health and therapeutic landscapes in Uganda, "rural landscapes are frequently associated with hardship and ill health".

The introduction of the therapeutic landscape concept encouraged a swathe of literature that "shed geometric and locational approaches to space and place" (Wilson, 2003, p. 84) to instead consider how affective atmospheres of place "have the potential to augment or diminish one's capacities" (Duff, 2011, p. 154). Drawing on this approach, I will not just consider the kind of therapeutic encounters that occur within rural settings (Conradson, 2005b), but also pay attention to the very role that "rurality" itself plays in actively affecting and shaping experiences of health and wellbeing. The logics of rurality can act as a "force" (Cloke, 2003, p. 2), with rurality itself having an ability to affect (Halfacree & Rivera, 2012). Rurality is a highly dynamic concept, produced through processes of imagination, representation, materialisation, and contestation (Woods, 2010). The rural exists as a "significant imaginative space" (Cloke, 2006a, p. 18). People's preconceived ideas about what rurality is, and should be like, can influence their attitudes and behaviours, with individuals developing relationships and practices that act to "protect or promote particular ideas about rurality" (Woods, 2004, p. 15).

This chapter seeks to explore how ideas of "the rural" come to be entangled with ideas of therapeutic spaces and the ways in which rurality is often "recruited" into the process of achieving wellbeing (Little, 2012). Though equally, the chapter seeks to explore how notions of the rural as a therapeutic space influence the "production, reproduction and contestation of discourses of rurality" (Woods, 2009, p. 851). In this sense, I mobilise rurality as "a set of both material spaces and symbolic imaginaries that converse with each other" (Gorman-Murray, Pini, & Bryant, 2013, p. 1); as a rurality that is processual and continuously in-the-making (Halfacree, 2006); a complex mix of representations, locality, and lived (material and embodied) experience (Halfacree, 2006). Through doing so, I move to take seriously the role of rurality within discussions of health and place, and consider the interrelations between "therapeutic affect" – "the encounters through which bodies acquire new capacities" (Andrews, Evans, & McAlister, 2013, p. 101) – and what Halfacree and Rivera (2012, p. 105) call "rural affect" – "the feelings, emotions and even actions brought about through engagement with rural materiality". I move now to briefly introduce care farming, paying attention to care farming's own entanglements and interrelationships with notions of rurality.

Care farming and rural–therapeutic landscapes

Care farming is a growing movement that seeks to connect agricultural spaces and enterprises with the provision of health, wellbeing, and care. Commonly defined as "the use of commercial farms and agricultural landscapes as a base for promoting mental and physical health through normal farming activity" (Hine, Peacock, & Pretty, 2008a, p. 247), care farms invite groups of (often vulnerable) individuals to become actively involved in the life, work, and rhythms of a farm as part of a structured programme of care, therapy, or rehabilitation. Care farming has been used as an intervention for a wide variety of different groups and conditions, including dementia (De Boer et al., 2015), people experiencing mental ill health (Iancu, Zweekhorst, Veltman, van Balkom, & Bunders, 2014), and people within the criminal justice system (Elsey et al., 2018). In the UK context, Hine, Peacock, and Pretty (2008b) suggest that the most common user group is people with learning difficulties (represented at 83% of all UK care farms), followed by disaffected youth (represented at 51% of all UK care farms), and people experiencing mental ill health (represented at 49% of all UK care farms).

Care farming is quickly becoming an important service and tool for the facilitation and promotion of mental health and wellbeing. The growth of the care farming sector has been provoked by efforts for agricultural diversification and multi-functionality (Hassink, Hulsink, & Grin, 2012), wider shifts from institutional to socialised and community forms of care provision (Kraftl, 2014), the effects of neoliberal forms of public service withdrawal (Elsey et al., 2018), interest in non-medicalised approaches to therapeutic care (Gorman & Cacciatore, 2017), locally specific cultures and histories (de Krom & Dessein, 2013), as well as the personal philosophies of individual farmers and landowners (Leck, Evans, & Upton, 2014).

An international portrait of care farming is not an easy one to paint. Definitions of what constitutes a "care farm" vary between countries (Haubenhofer, Elings, Hassink, & Hine, 2010), and the informality of the way in which many farms operate makes cataloguing the development of this novel approach difficult (Gorman & Cacciatore, 2017). Haubenhofer et al. (2010, p. 108) suggest that "The Netherlands is leading the way with approximately 1000 green care farms; in Belgium, Norway, Italy, and Austria a few hundred are already established, with numbers increasing". Greenleaf and Rosseger (2017, p. 87) suggest that "care farms remain rare in the United States", whilst in the UK, over 250 farms operate this way, providing therapeutic opportunities for an estimated 8,750 "vulnerable people" per week (Care Farming UK, 2017).

Care farming practices have been incorporated across the diverse spectrum of the food network; conventional and alternative forms of agriculture, horticultural and livestock, urban and rural. However, given their grounding within the sphere of agriculture, there is a tendency for them to be located in areas associated, identified, and imagined as "rural". Indeed, some scholars, such as Di Iacovo and O'Connor (2009, p. 11), explicitly embed "rural areas" into their working definitions of care farming, with care farming becoming a highly spatialised practice. Di Iacovo and O'Connor (2009, p. 12) argue that care farming "originates from the traditional rural self-help systems that were well-established in rural areas before the modernisation of agriculture and the rise of the public welfare system". Such a view perhaps appeals to the ideas of harmonious rural Gemeinschaft communities (Parr, Philo, & Burns, 2004), and highlights the ways in which certain imaginations of the rural, and rural idylls, become bound up in the practices and performances of contemporary care farming.

Hassink, Zwartbol, Agricola, Elings, and Thissen (2007, p. 31) describe how care farms can be considered as "examples of innovation in the rural area", and indeed, the tentatively growing body of scholarship on care farming has often evolved from discussions and funded projects around rural development (Di Iacovo & O'Connor, 2009; Hassink et al., 2012; RDPE Network, 2010). Indeed, care farming can play a significant role in the rural economy, leading to the creation of jobs and substantial investments in the agricultural sector (Hassink et al., 2007) – Leck et al. (2014, p. 316) discuss the frequent framing of care farming as a "revenue generating form of on-farm diversification" and cite press releases that claim "Care Farming is worth £149m to UK Rural Economy". A cursory search through ScienceDirect for "care farming" reveals that (at the time of writing) the majority of literature on care farming appears in the *Journal of Rural Studies*, more than double that found in any other publication. Care farming, it appears, is a rural issue. However, despite this strong grounding in "the rural", there has been little consideration of how discourses of rurality shape an engagement with care farming.

Attending to the ways in which rurality becomes enrolled and recruited (Little, 2012) into the production of care farming spaces and interventions becomes important when considering the ways in which stereotypes and imaginations of the rural influence "expectations of service delivery" (Best & Myers, 2017, p. 2). Assumptions made about rural life and rural places are actively involved, and subconsciously invoked, in the formation of care farming enterprises. As Conradson (2005b, p. 346) argues, "in order to understand a particular therapeutic landscape experience, it is useful to give attention to the broader relational configurations within which it occurs". The broader rural assemblage within which care farms are located moulds the ways in which the farms come to function, and preconfigures modalities of relating to, and being with, care farming spaces. I turn now to quickly discuss the methodologies that comprised and informed these investigations into the relationships between care farming, therapeutic landscapes, and rurality.

Methods for exploring rurality

> So, there'll be someone from the young homeless project, some of their clients, someone from the mental health with a few of their clients, and then they'll all just come, part of the idea is that they all mix and they all work with each other.
>
> (Dan, farmer involved in care farming)

As part of a larger project exploring the relationships between health, place, and animals (see also Gorman, 2017a, 2017b, 2017c), 55 semi-structured qualitative research interviews were conducted. These interviews took place with representatives from "rural" farms in the UK that were engaged in "alternative" agricultural paradigms, including care farming, as well as with representatives from groups who visited, and helped to facilitate visits to, these farms for health and wellbeing purposes. Sampling and recruitment drew on Curtis, Gesler, Smith, and Washburn's (2000) discussions of criteria for qualitative research in health geographies. Interviews were used to enable participants to tell stories about their experiences of agricultural and rural spaces; their "reflections on processes of becoming affected" (Dowling, Lloyd, & Suchet-Pearson, 2017, p. 826).

However, interview research tends to concentrate on talk, forgetting to pay attention to the material context of the talk, and how this influences what is said (Brinkmann & Kvale, 2014). A focus on the verbal can erase the more-than-human elements of the interview setting (Dowling et al., 2017). Recognising recent critiques of "neglecting the material dimensions of the rural condition that have a real impact on the experiences of people living, working and playing in rural space" (Woods, 2009, p. 851), ethnographic observation was also carried out in an attempt to attend to how rural materialities hold a potential to shape encounters, experiences, and feelings.

Ethnographic observation and participation creates a mode of being-in-the-world for researchers that enables research to question "what is important for people living and working in a particular setting, and to note and question when, where and why everyday time–space rhythms and routines get disrupted" (Crang & Cook, 2007, p. 56). Knowledge and understanding are produced via becoming similarly emplaced, experiencing co-presence, and sensorially and materially occupying the place that a researcher seeks to understand (Pink, 2009).

Writing accounts of the everyday life of these rural spaces existed as a form of representation. However, in writing these representations, I felt challenged as to how exactly to represent the many people who visited the farms for health and wellbeing purposes. The prevailing phrases for referring to human participants within care farming literature are "service user" (Leck et al., 2014) or "client" (Hassink et al., 2012). However, as McLaughlin (2009) notes, both of these phrases are somewhat problematic. They are indicative of hierarchical power relationships, privileging and homogenising one aspect of an individual's identity, creating binaries, and connotative of a level of passivity on the part of a "client" or consumption on the part of a "user". These phrases suggest a one-way relationship, whereas in a care farming context specifically, many of the individuals visiting the farms are actively involved in the upkeep and productivity of the farms. The participants are providing care for the animals, rather than simply receiving care themselves, for example. Thus, within my writing, I have chosen to use the word "visitors" to cover the diversity of human participants that visit the farms to benefit therapeutically. Additionally, by referring to the humans I observed within these spaces as visitors, I represent them as active co-constituents in these "therapeutic becomings" (Gorman, 2017b), rather than passive objects whom health is "done to".

The entanglements of therapeutic rurality

Thinking about the entanglements of rurality and ideas of therapeutic spaces involves recognising that "the rural" is a multifaceted space (Woods, 2009) full of "different countrysides" with "contrasting and sometimes contradictory understandings of rural processes" (Murdoch, 2003, p. 274). As Little (2013) describes, rural environments can have a nurturing effect, but they also produce atmospheres which act to control and regulate bodies. Recognising multiple (and contested) relational narratives of rural space is important in being able to successfully realise policies and practices aimed at improving wellbeing (Winterton, Hulme Chambers, Farmer, & Munoz, 2014). Rurality acts to produce and disrupt ideas of "the therapeutic", but so too do ideas of "the therapeutic" act to both produce and disrupt "the rural". Hence, in this chapter, I refer to the rural–therapeutic dyad to highlight the entangled co-constitution of rural–therapeutic spaces.

I move now to explore how being positioned within areas associated, identified, and imagined as "rural" influences practices of care farming. Here I draw on Woods' (2009. p. 851) concerns for the "production, reproduction and contestation of discourses of rurality". Firstly, I consider the opportunities that a specifically rural identity opens up, and how an entanglement of rurality and care can be generative. Secondly, I reflect how a state of rurality shapes certain challenges, and I question how the codifying of rural spaces as "therapeutic" may in fact be contested and disruptive – to both rural spaces and therapeutic practices.

Producing and recruiting the rural–therapeutic dyad

Views about the special qualities of rural spaces frequently became enrolled and bound up with the rationalisation and practice of care farming. Ideas and preconceptions about pastoral rural idylls were recruited to consolidate an identity, habitual relations, and particular routines, as Robin, a community farm manager involved in care farming, describes:

> Because where we are is quite rural, I think that adds to it you know, and it's quite important actually, that people come here and feel like they're somewhere special and different. So yeah, I guess we do play up to it, the rural-ness, because it helps people feel relaxed and feel good and special, and that's a large part of what we're here to do.
>
> (Robin, community farm manager, involved in care farming)

The stories told about the therapeutic qualities of rural landscapes end up having an effect on rural spaces themselves, as people attempt to fit the material world into their ideas of what rurality should be (DuPuis, 2006). Discourses of rurality also act to reproduce rurality. Thus, aligning the spaces and practices of care farming with notions of rurality also acts to influence how people behave when visiting the farms, and the type of activities that they want to get involved with. Visitors to the farms expected and wanted to meet animals, feel a connection to "nature", and experience quiet and tranquillity. Visitors felt aggrieved when cars drove past or planes flew overhead: a disruption to their idyllic, and therapeutic, rural space. The rural identity of these farms actively co-constitutes the ways that they are understood to be therapeutic. Rurality itself is attributed as having a crucial role within the care farming assemblage in co-producing and enacting therapeutic geographies. As William describes, a certain cultural imagination and conceptualisation of rurality (particularly one juxtaposed against urbanity) becomes positioned as an innovatory force for altering relations and knowledges, and opening up new (therapeutic) possibilities.

> I think that there's a sense of community, you know, with it being a rural area. There's a real chance to feel like you're part of contributing to the community, so yeah, it offers all that and there's something special about coming together, convalescing over a piece of land, doing something on a piece of land, doing something productive and actually feeding people. There's something about working together, getting your hands dirty, getting muddy, and then sitting down and having a cup of tea together. Immensely satisfying, there's an energy that comes from the land and the countryside that is quite magical you know, not quite the same as hanging out in a city centre or going to the cinema together!
>
> (William, community farm leader, involved in care farming)

People's individual ideas of rural idylls become invoked in the establishment and co-production of a "therapeutic landscape" (Conradson, 2005a). Playing up to, to draw on Robin's earlier language, these cultural tropes has a level of a generative potential for care farming as an intervention, positioning it within a broader landscape of associations, and accessing some of the cultural values and emotions commonly associated with rurality. To quote Bryant and Pini (2011, p. 6), "these include the centrality of nature, community cohesion, safety and physical gains associated with 'outdoor' lifestyles, harmony, permanence, security, inner strength, as well as family values". Framing care farming closely with these notions of the rural "opens doors" for acquiring support from various local funding bodies and institutions, as Ash, a representative from a scheme that aimed to match farms with groups seeking a therapeutic outlet, explains:

> It's very difficult to brand, and therefore the challenge is to get that information across, you know, the main challenge is being able to illustrate

> the benefits, but, people associate being in the countryside with all these benefits, right, so that opens doors when we try and sell it to people.
>
> (Ash)

In a similar way to how Gesler and Kearns (2002) highlight how naming an area causes people to relate in a certain way, fixing associations of health as an "understood truth", so too does the invocation of "the rural" with discourses of care farming. Focussing on "the rural", and invoking or recruiting it in this way appears as a strategic imperative for the growing care farming sector; embracing discourses of rurality acts to solidify and stabilise care farming as an intervention.

> The fact that we're in the heart of a very rural agricultural community is definitely part of our identity. It's what people want when they visit us, that sense of the countryside. Is it therapeutic? I think it helps for sure, just because of what people expect a place like this to be.
>
> (Owen, community farm owner, involved in care farming)

Situating practices of care within a "rural" space acts to simultaneously enact a vision of rurality, as well as recruiting rurality into the process of producing a therapeutic setting. As Owen describes above, particularly important here is the way in which expectation in itself becomes key in the emergence of therapeutic possibilities. The expectations that people have for their subjective experiences and encounters within place are important in affecting how places can become constituted as therapeutic (Watson, Murtagh, Lally, Thomson, & McPhail, 2007).

> Today we also moved the remainder of recent wood cuttings up to the top of the field, where Dan, the farmer, was building a firewood pile. There were a lot of heavier logs that had been left – most of the thinner material we'd already scavenged to build the wind shelter for the bees in previous sessions. Because of this, Dan got on his tractor and drove it down. This was hugely exciting to the visitors, especially as Dan let them ride on the back and in the trailer with them perched on top of a load of firewood. The visitors loved the tractor rides, one of them remarked "I felt good. On the tractor, I could forget about everything. I felt powerful. This is what the countryside is about, it's what I imagined".
>
> (Fieldnotes, 7 May 2015)

In this extract, the material and embodied experiences of the rural match up with imagined – and expected – representations and discourses to produce a level of "rural affect" (Halfacree & Rivera, 2012). The encounter with affective rurality here, in the space of the care farm, is also one which has a level of therapeutic affect, shaping opportunities for subjective experiences of, and capacities for, embodied wellbeing. A state of rurality opens up opportunities for different material and sensuous (therapeutic) encounters than might be found – or perhaps, noticed – in places without a "rural" identity. The specifically rural coding of place encourages people to seek out and take pleasure from certain experiences, whether paying attention to the sounds and smells of place or developing relationships with farm animals (Gorman, 2017a, 2017b). The rural aspect – in all its complexity – of care farms is an important part of the situated "therapeutic landscape experience" (Conradson, 2005b).

In this section, I have shown how a therapeutic sense of place emerges from, and is enacted through, a lens of rurality. The rural dimensions and logics of care farming spaces play a key role in their ability to act as "enabling spaces" (Duff, 2011) that transform body's potencies to "do different things" and "perform different actions" (Emmerson, 2017, p. 11). However, I move now to consider how notions of rurality might also act to produce certain challenges for care farming, and how the codifying of rural spaces as "therapeutic" can come to disrupt rural identities and therapeutic practices.

Contesting and disrupting the rural–therapeutic dyad

In the previous section, I discussed the way in which stereotypes and imaginations of the rural influenced therapeutic possibilities, with visitors' expectations of rurality acting to influence their subjective wellbeing experiences. However, the entanglement of these representations and discourses of the rural also at times acted to disrupt therapeutic practices, particularly when work at the farm did not live up to exciting or tranquil imaginaries of country life, or when their encounters with the farm animals proved unsuccessful, uneventful, or even negatively affective.

> One of the new members of the visiting group asked Dan why there were no cows, if it was supposed to be a farm. His interest in being part of the day's activities quickly dropped off once he found out that the animals he'd associated with the countryside wouldn't be present. The lack of cows produced a sense of disillusionment and disenchantment with the space of the farm, revoking its "therapeutic power". If anything, the lack of cows had a less-than-therapeutic impact, as the visitor withdrew, and refused to socialise with the rest of the group, excluding himself – a converse impact on what the farm was meant to produce.
>
> (Fieldnotes, 19 March 2015)

> There was disappointment that we still hadn't got to "meet" one of the lambs, people wanted to be able to touch it, and hold it.
>
> (Fieldnotes, 2 April 2015)

Visitors to care farms expect the full vibrancy of rurality – cuddly lambs, quietude, and tradition – and a failure by a care farm to deploy and realise this vision of rurality can fracture the potential for any form of therapeutic affect to emerge as feelings of resentment and missed opportunity colour how people perceive and experience the farms. Ideas and preconceptions about pastoral rural idylls are bound up with the formation of therapeutic geographies. As Woods (2010, p. 9) notes, the way in which the countryside is imagined in popular discourses may have little correspondence with the actual 'realities' of rural space and rural life:

> When it comes to actually being faced with the fact that actually the chickens have been got by a fox, they just don't like that, they like the nice side of things, that other side of things that aren't so great, but you know that is a normal part of farming isn't it, it's all part of rearing animals and life in the countryside.
>
> (Diana, manager of a care farming project)

This mismatch between popular ideas of "the rural" and the lived reality can shatter and disrupt the potential to realise a "therapeutic" space, as Diana's story above describes. As a result, care farms become implicated in a production and performance of rurality (Edensor, 2006) and have to create and deliver the affective, material, and sensual aspects that people expect of "the rural" as part of the therapeutic service they aim to provide in order to be successful. This can be quite a challenge, given that some of the idyllic imaginaries that people hold of "the rural" do not exist. Managing expectations of what these spaces are, and the experiences, encounters, and affects they might produce, becomes a key task for care farm staff.

Equally, this rural identity can be a barrier to the realisation of a therapeutic space. As Bryant and Pini (2011, p. 20) argue, "dominant socio-cultural constructions of rurality are intricately connected to circumscribing the discourses and practices that belong in the rural, and those that do not". Ideas of rurality are critical in defining and informing exclusionary (spatial) politics, and attempting to utilise rural spaces for providing care can bring actors into conflict, particularly about who belongs in rural spaces, and what a farm is for, as Diana describes:

> I think I was very cautious in the beginning as well, in a rural village, you have to be careful about what you do, because, that's the other thing, that the village got really upset, coz obviously all the gossip talk, it was going to be HM Prison, so we were going to have all rapists and you know! I was very careful, in a way, to manage that, so we had sort of, you know, people with low-behaviour issues or whatever on the farm, partly for the village. Well, now I think we could probably get away with a lot more. I think, in the village it's been really important that we started off very low key and I think, that's where, I hate to say it, but people with learning difficulties in a way have a great, a sort of, people are willing to help. Mental health, people are always quite dubious about, and then

> once you go and talk about addiction, any sort of crime or whatever, people are getting very wary to have them around their area.
>
> (Diana, manager of a care farming project)

As Parr et al. (2004) have shown, people affected by certain (mental) health conditions can be subject to carefully regulated socio-cultural boundaries, with certain illnesses being rendered as "out of place" in rural spaces. Cultural imaginations of "the rural", though beneficial as described earlier, can thus lead to significant challenges for care farming as an intervention, and one of the large tasks of those who wish to develop this type of work can be working to assuage concerns of their wider (rural) communities. It can also lead to, as Diana describes, a scaling down of ambitions and the loss of appetite and ability to provide a therapeutic space for certain groups. Cultural constructions of rurality move to position certain categories of people as being "out of place" in the rural (Woods, 2010). For care farming, this can lead to boundaries being built around who care farming can help – that is, who is capable of "benefitting" from being in these special rural places – and who care farming should help, drawing on discourses of "deserving" and "undeserving":

> One farm we worked with, they said we don't mind any group, but not substance misuse coz we're worried they'll come back and pinch things.
>
> (Ash, representative from a scheme that aimed to match farms with groups seeking a therapeutic outlet)

Both Diana's and Ash's stories here highlight that it is important to consider the way in which pre-existing cultural, social, and spatial structures act to (re)produce inequities within this emerging and innovative healthcare intervention and practice. As Gorman and Cacciatore (2017, p. 20) have noted, "there are few articles that are overtly critical or attend to the negative aspects of care farming". Work by Wydler and Gairing (2010) suggests that care farming practices are often highly bound up with rural and agricultural gender stereotypes and "traditional" distributions of gender roles. Similarly, Gorman (2017a) has discussed how activities on care farms that can result in therapeutic opportunities are frequently grounded in specific gender performances and identities. Producing "the rural" for its "therapeutic" benefits and associations may (re)produce inequalities and exclusions.

Indeed, the very "healthification" (Fusco, 2006) of rurality and rural spaces is not a neutral or uncontested process; it is one that can lead to a disruption of what is understood to be "rural" – by both local residents and people visiting care farms. It also produces a level of tension around the utilisation of "the rural" to benefit "the urban" (Kelly-Reif & Wing, 2016). Mason-Renton and Luginaah (2016, p. 47) suggest that processes of therapeutic place-making in rural landscapes are actively influenced by imaginaries of the urban, and contested and disrupted through "unwanted intrusions of urban by-products and processes". One person's gain from the establishment of "the rural as a therapeutic space" can be another's loss. Whilst it is perhaps easy to dismiss and critique those who feel that they lose out through the creation of therapeutic spaces for others, these tensions and contestations are worth recognising and paying attention to, perhaps in greater detail than literature presently has.

In their discussions, Di Iacovo and O'Connor (2009, p. 13) frame care farming as "the use of agriculture and farms for providing services to local inhabitants and rural communities". Again, there are tensions around who care farming should primarily look to benefit, and who care farms care for. This is a similar view to that suggested by Julia, below, when she describes the development of her farm's care work and how it became established through a boundedness linked to a specific invocation of locality:

> I think the fact that they were local people already probably had a massive impact on that, because people wanted to support them, and they knew who they were and they knew they were good people and part of the community, so rather than somebody coming in new, so I think, they did have that advantage.
>
> (Julia, community farm leader, involved in care farming)

There is a level of contestation around who should get to benefit from these rural spaces, in part developed through a desire to preserve a certain imagination of "the rural" for a certain group of people. Such a desire can disrupt and block opportunities for those outside of these specific identities and communities. Relatedly, there are also questions around how comfortable, confident, and interested different groups are in actually accessing rural idylls, in part shaped by the "complex interplay of belonging and alienation, inclusion and exclusion" (Gorman-Murray et al., 2013, p. 15) that both operates and operationalises "the rural". As William's quote in the previous section highlighted, care farms draw on discourses of rurality to open up ideas around a sense of community, sociality, and integration, yet representations of the rural can also produce a fear of not fitting in and of not belonging:

> One of the boys from the group visiting today refused to get take part in any of the activities. The leaders tried to encourage him to get involved, saying that it would make the time go quicker, but to no avail. He told me that "he wanted to be in a city" and felt that "he didn't belong here".
>
> (Fieldnotes, 19 March 2015)

Contemporary cultural constructions of rurality can be exclusionary from a number of different vantage points, more easily romanticised by certain groups than others (Bryant & Pini, 2011; Cloke, 2006b; Gorman-Murray et al., 2013). Likewise, thinking about care farming specifically involves recognising that the modern framing has complex associated histories and entanglements with practices such as "asylum farms" that produced a more exploitative framing of vulnerable groups as cheap agricultural labour (Parr, 2007; Philo, 2004). Representations and discourses of rurality can act to disrupt and discomfort an engagement with rural space as therapeutic. Rurality may be a crucial part of care farming's identity, and a resource in producing therapeutic spaces and encounters, but it is also one which brings challenges and requires careful navigation.

Conclusions

Within the context of British care farms, rurality acts to produce and disrupt ideas of "the therapeutic", but so too do ideas of "the therapeutic" shape the production, reproduction, and contestation of "the rural". Rurality becomes a key resource for producing a space beneficial to supporting and promoting mental health and wellbeing. Representations and discourses of "the rural" act to preconfigure perceptions, aligning rural spaces with specific values and emotional and affective responses. A rural identity positions, and fixes, these wellbeing interventions within a broader web of associations.

Yet, equally, a state of rurality can produce certain barriers and challenges towards establishing a therapeutic space. The codifying of rural spaces as "therapeutic" may be contested and disruptive – to both rural spaces and therapeutic practices. Actual encounters and experiences of rurality are often far removed from idyllic country visions; my time spent observing at a care farm involved dead sheep carcasses as much as (if not more) than cuddling cute lambs. When expectations are built so high through popular cultural imaginations of rurality, this failure to "perform the rural" can disrupt therapeutic processes. Equally, the notions of the rural as a space of community and cohesion, inclusion, and neighbourliness do not always emerge. The healthification of rural spaces can raise tensions, as imaginaries of who belongs, and what rural life should be, are invoked. For care farms, this can be a challenge, disrupting their ambitions, or producing conflict with their local communities.

Rurality – in all its complexity and diversity – plays an important role in the production of therapeutic geographies. Rurality shapes and defines the very potentialities of care farming as an innovative intervention, both opening up and closing down therapeutic possibilities.

References

Andrews, G. J. (2002). Towards a more place-sensitive nursing research: An invitation to medical and health geography. *Nursing Inquiry*, *9*(4), 221–238.

Andrews G. J., Evans J., & McAlister S. (2013). 'Creating the right therapy vibe': Relational performances in holistic medicine. *Social Science & Medicine*, *83*, 99–109.

Best, S., & Myers, J. (2017). Prudence or speed: Health and social care innovation in rural Wales. *Journal of Rural Studies*. doi:10.1016/j.jrurstud.2017.12.004.

Brinkmann, S., & Kvale, S. (2014). *InterViews*. London: SAGE Publications.
Bryant, L., & Pini, B. (2011). *Gender and rurality*. New York: Routledge.
Care Farming UK. (2017). *Care Farming in the UK and Ireland: Annual Survey 2016/17*. Bristol: Care Farming UK.
Cloke, P. (Ed.). (2003). *Country visions*. Harlow: Pearson.
Cloke, P. (2006a). Conceptualizing rurality. In: P. Cloke, T. Marsden, & P. Mooney (Eds.) *Handbook of rural studies* (pp. 18–28). London: SAGE Publications.
Cloke, P. (2006b). Rurality and racialized others: Out of place in the countryside? In: P. Cloke, T. Marsden, & P. Mooney (Eds.), *Handbook of rural studies* (pp. 18–28). London: SAGE Publications.
Conradson, D. (2005a). Freedom, space and perspective: Moving encounters with other ecologies. In: J. Davidson, L. Bondi, & M. Smith (Eds.) *Emotional geographies* (pp. 103–116). Hampshire: Ashgate.
Conradson, D. (2005b). Landscape, care and the relational self: Therapeutic encounters in rural England. *Health & Place, 11*(4), 337–348.
Crang, M., & Cook, I. (2007). *Doing ethnographies*. London: SAGE Publications.
Curtis, P. S. (2012). *Space, place and mental health*. Surrey: Ashgate.
Curtis, S., Gesler, W., Smith, G., & Washburn, S. (2000) Approaches to sampling and case selection in qualitative research: Examples in the geography of health. *Social Science & Medicine, 50*(7), 1001–1014.
De Boer, B., Hamers, J. P. H., Beerens, H. C., Zwakhalen, S. M. G., Tan, F. E. S., & Verbeek, H. (2015). Living at the farm, innovative nursing home care for people with dementia–study protocol of an observational longitudinal study. *BMC Geriatrics, 15*(1), 144.
de Krom, M. P., & Dessein, J. (2013). Multifunctionality and care farming: Contested discourses and practices in Flanders. *NJAS-Wageningen Journal of Life Sciences, 64*, 17–24.
Di Iacovo, F. P., & O'Connor, D. (2009). *Supporting policies for social farming in Europe: Progressing multifunctionality in Responsive rural areas*. Firenze: ARSIA.
Dowling, R., Lloyd, K., & Suchet-Pearson, S. (2017). Qualitative methods II: 'More-than-human" methodologies and/in praxis'. *Progress in Human Geography, 41*(6), 823–831.
Duff, C. (2011). Networks, resources and agencies: On the character and production of enabling places. *Health & Place, 17*(1), 149–156.
Dunkley, C. M. (2009). A therapeutic taskscape: Theorizing place-making, discipline and care at a camp for troubled youth. *Health & Place, 15*(1), 88–96.
DuPuis, E. M. (2006). Landscapes of desires? In: P. Cloke, T. Marsden, & P. Mooney (Eds.), *Handbook of rural studies* (pp. 18–28). London: SAGE Publications.
Edensor, T. (2006). Performing rurality. In: P. Cloke, T. Marsden, & P. Mooney (Eds.), *Handbook of rural studies* (pp. 18–28). London: SAGE Publications.
Elsey, H., Farragher, T., Tubeuf, S., Bragg, R., Elings, M., Brennan, C., … Cade, J. (2018). Assessing the impact of care farms on quality of life and offending: A pilot study among probation service users in England. *BMJ Open, 8*(3), e019296.
Emmerson, P. (2017). Thinking laughter beyond humour: Atmospheric refrains and ethical indeterminacies in spaces of care. *Environment and Planning A, 49*(9), 2082–2098.
Fusco, C. (2006). Inscribing healthification: Governance, risk, surveillance and the subjects and spaces of fitness and health. *Health & Place, 12*(1), 65–78.

Gesler, W. M. (1991). *The cultural geography of health care*. Pittsburgh, PA: University of Pittsburgh Press.

Gesler, W. M. (1992). Therapeutic landscapes: Medical issues in light of the new cultural geography. *Social Science & Medicine*, *34*(7), 735–746.

Gesler, W. M. (1996). Lourdes: Healing in a place of pilgrimage. *Health & Place*, *2*(2), 95–105.

Gesler, W. M., & Kearns, R. (2002). *Culture/place/health*. London: Routledge.

Gorman, R. (2017a). Smelling therapeutic landscapes: Embodied encounters within spaces of care farming. *Health & Place*, *47*, 22–28.

Gorman, R. (2017b). Therapeutic landscapes and non-human animals: The roles and contested positions of animals within care farming assemblages. *Social & Cultural Geography*, *18*(3), 315–335.

Gorman, R. (2017c). Thinking critically about health and human-animal relations: Therapeutic affect within spaces of care farming. *Social Science & Medicine*. doi:10.1016/j.socscimed.2017.11.047.

Gorman, R., & Cacciatore, J. (2017). Cultivating our humanity: A systematic review of care farming & traumatic grief. *Health & Place*, *47*, 12–21.

Gorman-Murray, A., Pini, B., & Bryant, L. (Eds.). (2013). *Sexuality, rurality, and geography*. Lanham, MD: Lexington Books.

Greenleaf, A. T., & Roessger, K. M. (2017). Effectiveness of care farming on veterans' life satisfaction, optimism, and perceived loneliness. *The Journal of Humanistic Counseling*, *56*(2), 86–110.

Halfacree, K. H. (2006). Rural space: Constructing a three-fold architecture. In: P. Cloke, T. Marsden, & P. Mooney (Eds.), *Handbook of rural studies* (pp. 18–28). London: SAGE Publications.

Halfacree, K. H. (2012). Diverse ruralities in the 21st century: From effacement to (re-)invention. In: L. J. Kulcsar & K. J. C. White (Eds.), *International handbook of rural demography. International handbooks of population v. 3*. Dordrecht, New York: Springer. pp. 387–400.

Halfacree, K. H., & Rivera, M. J. (2012). Moving to the countryside… and staying: Lives beyond representations. *Sociologia Ruralis*, *52*(1), 92–114.

Hassink, J., Hulsink, W., & Grin, J. (2012). Care farms in the Netherlands: An underexplored example of multifunctional agriculture—Toward an empirically grounded, organization-theory-based typology. *Rural Sociology*, *77*(4), 569–600.

Hassink, J., Zwartbol, C., Agricola, H. J., Elings, M., & Thissen, J. T. (2007). Current status and potential of care farms in the Netherlands. *NJAS – Wageningen Journal of Life Sciences*, *55*(1), 21–36.

Haubenhofer, D. K., Elings, M., Hassink, J., & Hine, R. E. (2010). The development of green care in western European countries. *Explore: The Journal of Science and Healing*, *6*(2), 106–111.

Hine, R., Peacock, J., & Pretty, J. N. (2008a). Care farming in the UK: Contexts, benefits and links with therapeutic communities. *Therapeutic Communities*, *29*(3), 245–260.

Hine, R., Peacock, J., & Pretty, J. N. (2008b). *Care farming in the UK: Evidence and opportunities*. Colchester, Essex: University of Essex Report for the National Care Farming Initiative (UK).

Iancu, S. C., Zweekhorst, M. B., Veltman, D. J., van Balkom, A. J., & Bunders, J. F. (2014). Mental health recovery on care farms and day centres: A qualitative comparative study of users' perspectives. *Disability and Rehabilitation*, *36*(7), 573–583.

Kearns, R. (1993). Place and health: Towards a reformed medical geography. *The Professional Geographer, 45*(2), 139–147.

Kearns, R., & Collins, D. (2000). New Zealand children's health camps: Therapeutic landscapes meet the contract state. *Social Science & Medicine, 51*(7), 1047–1059.

Kearns, R., & Collins, D. (2009). Health geography. In: T. Brown, S. McLafferty, & G. Moon (Eds.), *A companion to health and medical geography* (pp. 15–32). Oxford: Wiley.

Kearns, R., & Moon, G. (2002). From medical to health geography: Novelty, place and theory after a decade of change. *Progress in Human Geography, 26*(5), 605–625.

Kelly-Reif, K., & Wing, S. (2016). Urban-rural exploitation: An underappreciated dimension of environmental injustice. *Journal of Rural Studies, 47*, 350–358.

Lea, J. (2008). Retreating to nature: Rethinking 'therapeutic landscapes'. *Area, 40*(1), 90–98.

Leck, C., Evans, N., & Upton, D. (2014). Agriculture–who cares? An investigation of 'care farming' in the UK. *Journal of Rural Studies, 34*, 313–325.

Little, J. (2012). Transformational tourism, nature and wellbeing: New perspectives on fitness and the body*. *Sociologia Ruralis, 52*(3), 257–271.

Little, J. (2013). Pampering, well-being and women's bodies in the therapeutic spaces of the spa. *Social & Cultural Geography, 14(*1), 41–58.

MacKian, S. C. (2008). What the papers say: Reading therapeutic landscapes of women's health and empowerment in Uganda. *Health & Place, 14*(1), 106–115.

Mason-Renton, S., & Luginaah, I. (2016). Interfering with therapeutic tranquility: Debates surrounding biosolid waste processing in rural Ontario. *Health & Place, 41*, 42–49.

McLaughlin, H. (2009). What's in a name: 'Client', 'patient', 'customer', 'consumer', 'expert by experience', 'service user'—what's next? *British Journal of Social Work, 39*(6), 1101–1117.

Milligan, C. (2007). Restoration or risk? Exploring the place of the common place. In: A. Williams (Ed.), *Therapeutic landscapes* (pp. 255–272). Hampshire: Ashgate.

Mills, S, Kraftl, P (Eds.). 'Alternative' education spaces and local community connections: A case study of care farming in the United Kingdom. In: *Informal education, childhood and youth* (pp. 48–64). London: Palgrave Macmillan.

Munoz, S. A. (2014). Rural health geography. In: W. Cockerham, R. Dingwall, & S. Quah (Eds.), *The Wiley-Blackwell encyclopedia of health, illness, behavior, and society.* Chichester: Wiley-Blackwell.

Murdoch, J. (2003). Co-constructing the countryside: Hybrid networks and the extensive self. In: P, Cloke. (ed.), *Country visions*. Harlow: Pearson. pp. 236–281.

Palka, E. (1999). Accessible wilderness as a therapeutic landscape. In: A. Williams (Ed.), *Therapeutic landscapes: The dynamic between place and wellness* (pp. 29–52). Lanham, MD: University Press of America.

Parr, H. (2007). Mental health, nature work, and social inclusion. *Environment and Planning D: Society and Space, 25*(3), 537–561.

Parr, H., Philo, C., & Burns, N. (2004). Social geographies of rural mental health: Experiencing inclusions and exclusions. *Transactions of the Institute of British Geographers, 29*(4), 401–419.

Philo, C. (1987). "Fit localities for an asylum": The historical geography of the nineteenth-century "mad-business" in England as viewed through the pages of the Asylum Journal. *Journal of Historical Geography, 13*(4), 398–415.

Philo, C. (2004). A *geographical history of institutional provision for the insane from medieval times to the 1860's in England and Wales: The space reserved for insanity*. Lewiston: Edwin Mellen Press.

Pink, S. (2009). *Doing sensory ethnography*. London: SAGE Publications.

RDPE Network. (2010). Support for care farming through the rural development programme for England. Cheltenham: RDPE Network.

Thurber, C., & Malinowski, J. (1999). Summer camp as a therapeutic landscape. In: A. Williams (Ed.), *Therapeutic landscapes: The dynamic between place and wellness* (pp. 53–70). Lanham, MD: University Press of America.

Watson, D. B., Murtagh, M. J., Lally, J. E., Thomson, R. G., & McPhail, S. (2007). Flexible therapeutic landscapes of labour and the place of pain relief. *Health & Place, 13*(4), 865–876.

Wilson, K. (2003). Therapeutic landscapes and first nations peoples: An exploration of culture, health and place. *Health & Place, 9*(2), 83–93.

Winterton, R., Hulme Chambers, A., Farmer, J., & Munoz, S. A. (2014). Considering the implications of place-based approaches for improving rural community wellbeing: The value of a relational lens. *Rural Society, 23*(3), 283–295.

Woods, M. (2004). *Rural geography: Processes, responses and experiences in rural restructuring*. London: Sage.

Woods, M. (2009). Rural geography: Blurring boundaries and making connections. *Progress in Human Geography, 33*(6), 849–858.

Woods, M. (2010). *Rural*. New York: Routledge.

Wydler, H., & Gairing, M. (2010). *Care farming in Swiss farm households–Gender aspects in pluriactivity*. Paper presented at 9th European IFS Symposium, 16/09/2010.

5 Non-clinical wellbeing interventions in rural regions

Sarah Morton and Sara Bradley

Introduction

In Scotland, approximately one in six adults reported experiencing symptoms of a mental health condition between 2012 and 2015 (Mental Health Foundation, 2016). This figure appears to be increasing year on year. The Scottish Government Report (2015a) *What Research Matters for Mental Health Policy in Scotland* found that 75% of people with common mental health problems are not in receipt of any form of treatment; the remaining 25% are provided with medication or psychological therapies, such as counselling, via a primary care healthcare practitioner (Mental Health Foundation, 2016).

Non-clinical-based treatments, such as peer support groups, are also offered for mental health problems. A review by Repper and Carter in (2011) highlighted the wider, positive effects of peer support such as reducing mental health stigma (Mental Health Foundation, 2016). Social prescribing, which aims to provide non-clinical interventions such as those that involve the arts, physical exercise, volunteering, and peer support (and can run in conjunction with other treatments), is also increasingly being utilised for those with mental health conditions (Mental Health Foundation, 2016).

The availability of services and treatments, particularly non-clinical interventions, is variable across Scotland, and this is especially so in more remote and rural locations. This chapter explores existing evidence about different non-clinical approaches, and considers how these fit within rural settings, including adaptations that may be necessary in order for the services to be sustainable and other logistical factors. Three case studies are offered: Branching Out (nature on prescription service; in two locations), Velocity Cycle to Health (Inverness), and Nature Walks for Well-being (Inverness). The chapter concludes by suggesting mechanisms that could facilitate a more joined-up way of working across services, health boards, and local decision makers (including councils), and highlighting the need to be aware of the impact that may be caused as a result of changes to service offering or local service provision (e.g. transport availability).

Background

It is reported that a third of all GP consultations in the UK involve some element of concern for mental health. However, it is estimated that just one in three people who would benefit from some form of intervention to address or treat their condition actually receive it (Scottish Government, 2017, p. 7). In the longer term, people with life-long mental illness are likely to die 15–20 years prematurely because of physical ill health (Scottish Government, 2017, p. 7). Of those who do receive treatment in the form of medication, there can be various side effects including notable weight gain. Keeping physically active can address this side effect and can also have a positive effect on mood (Scottish Government, 2017, p. 32), motivation, and general wellbeing. Evidence suggests that increasing the amount of physical activity that a person engages in could enable them to live longer and healthier lives. Evidence also indicates that by providing people with appropriate tools to manage their own health – including being supported to do so, such as through social prescribing – their wellbeing may be improved (Scottish Government, 2017, p. 35).

When implemented correctly, the hugely positive effects of being active on a regular basis are well evidenced. Generally, the risk of "visible" diseases such as diabetes, stroke, cardiovascular disease, and obesity are significantly reduced. More subtle mood-related benefits are also associated with being active, and those who are active on a regular basis indicate feeling more energetic, confident, happier, having increased motivation, and less likely to suffer from depressive or clinical mood-related issues. Specifically relating to mental health, many studies have explored the relationship between improved mental health and being physically active. Almost all report a positive effect, including on cognitive function (Mental Health Foundation, 2016, p. 81). When coupled a group activity in the outdoors, these effects can be enhanced, and can help support engagement with regular activity on a more independent, self-managed basis.

Greenspace and health

Evidence on the relationship between greenspace and health indicates that access to greenspace (Mitchell & Popham, 2008) is important to improving health and wellbeing among the general population (Bowler, Buyung-Ali, Knight, & Pullin, 2010; Mitchell & Popham, 2008). Access to greenspace also improves outcomes for people suffering from dementia, diabetes (Astell-Burt, Feng, & Kolt, 2014), mental health problems (Maas, Van Dillen, Verheij, & Groenewegen, 2009), and cardiovascular issues (Arnold, Smolderen, Buchanan, Li, & Spertus, 2012; Pereira et al., 2012). Being exposed to greenspaces has been associated with, among other things, improvement of perceived general health, pregnancy outcomes (e.g. birth weight), brain development in children, cognitive function in adults, mental health, risk of a number of chronic diseases (e.g. diabetes and cardiovascular conditions), and likelihood of mortality (Dadvand, 2019).

A study of 38 healthy participants exploring the effects of exposure to walking in nature on neural activity in the subgenual prefrontal cortex found a reduction in activity in this part of the brain – or more simply, a reduction in negative thinking for those participants [n=19] exposed to the nature walk, compared to those participants [n=19] who walked in an urban location (Bratman, Hamilton, Hahn, Daily, & Gross, 2015). Since many people with mental health issues experience low mood, anxiety, and negative thoughts, activation of the subgenual prefrontal cortex through exposure to nature could be hugely beneficial for this patient population.

Existing availability of greenspace interventions in Scotland

In Scotland, there is a relatively abundant offering of established and emerging non-clinical interventions for those experiencing mental health issues. The following list gives examples of some of the different types:

The Scottish Association for Mental Health (SAMH) – offer therapeutic horticulture at sites across Scotland and believe their horticulture services can help mental health recovery (Scottish Association for Mental Health, n.d.).

Earth for Life – a social enterprise specialising in environmental education and eco-therapy, working with adults with mental health issues, young people with developmental difficulty, community groups, and corporations. Delivering "educational and therapeutic woodland based activities such as bushcraft, foraging and wild cookery, games, story-telling, guided walks, bug-hunting and pond-dipping, drumming and percussion, willow craft and trapeze sessions in the woodlands" (Earth for life, n.d.).

Open Aye – a social enterprise offering participatory photography workshops. In autumn 2013, they ran a participatory photography project with people in recovery, through COMAS's Serenity Café project in Edinburgh and Glasgow Association of Mental health (GAMH). The project aimed to demonstrate the effect of outdoor health-based activities on wellbeing and quality of life (Open Aye, n.d.).

Mind Ecotherapy – aims to improve mental and physical health and wellbeing by supporting people to be active outdoors, e.g. gardening, farming, exercise, art and craft, conservation work, forestry, growing food, tending animals, conservation work, building ponds, and reclaiming land. Mind believe participants are doing an activity they enjoy which enables them to meet people and get outdoors in the fresh air (Mind, n.d.). Evidence from Mind's lottery-funded Ecominds scheme found that seven out of ten people experienced significant increases in mental wellbeing by the time they left an ecotherapy project (Mind, 2013).

In 2016, Bragg and Atkins (2016) produced a comprehensive review of "nature-based interventions" for mental health on behalf of Natural England with the aim of raising awareness and increasing the number of projects commissioned (Scottish Government, 2017, p. 7). Their literature review encompassed what they deemed to be the most typical types of intervention, namely therapeutic horticulture, environmental conservation, and "care farming". Bragg and Atkins (2016) identify the following types of nature-based interventions in the UK: Social and therapeutic horticulture (STH), environmental conservation, care farming, animal-assisted interventions (AAI), green exercise, ecotherapy, and wilderness therapy. They find that the interventions share common aims and similar characteristics such as engaging with the natural environment and participating in "meaningful activities" (Scottish Government, 2017, p. 32). Benefits include enhanced mental wellbeing; decreases in depression, anxiety and stress; improved self-confidence and mood; improved cognition; increased sense of satisfaction and quality of life; feelings of safety and security; greater social contact and sense of belonging; and increase in skills and sense of achievement (Scottish Government, 2017, p. 32).

Bragg and Atkins (2016) outline substantial evidence that demonstrates the positive effect of nature on mental health and wellbeing. They cite Ward-Thompson et al. (2012), who describe the ways in which mental health is influenced by the natural environment: firstly, directly via the "restorative effect" of nature; and then, secondly, indirectly by enabling social contact and encouraging physical activity. Bragg and Atkins outline three important theories about human interaction with nature and its restorative effect: (i) the biophilia hypothesis (Wilson, 1984); (ii) the attention restoration theory (ART) (Kaplan & Kaplan, 1989); and (iii) the psycho-evolutionary stress reduction theory (PET) (Ulrich, 1981). They conclude:

> Throughout this published evidence base, there is therefore consensus that nature contributes to enhanced wellbeing, mental development and personal fulfilment. Natural, green environments are places to relax, escape and unwind from the daily stresses of modern life; places to socialise and be physically active, thus having a positive effect on our wellbeing.
>
> (Bragg & Atkins, 2016, pp. 11–12)

In recognition of the evidence on the benefits of the natural environment on mental and physical health, Scottish Natural Heritage (the lead public body advising Scottish Government on nature conservation, landscape, and outdoor recreation) is one of the main partners in the "Our Natural Health Service" (Scottish Natural Heritage, n.d.) which "aims to show how greater use of the outdoors can help to tackle physical inactivity, mental health issues and health inequalities". The focus is on increasing awareness of the advantages of "green exercise" and incorporating nature-based interventions alongside mainstream healthcare.

Case studies of greenspace interventions for mental health

This section of the chapter outlines three case studies of outdoor, non-pharmaceutical programmes that are available to mental health service users in Scotland. The programmes provide users with an intervention that is non-clinical in nature, is conducted outdoors, and affords opportunity for social contact:

1 Branching Out for Mental Health (in two NHS health board locations – Highland, and Argyll and Bute)
2 Velocity – Cycling to Health
3 Nature Walks for Wellbeing

Case study sites were selected in order to include a mixture of established and newer services, activity types, and geographical location (including in and/or near a regional city and remote rural – including one island). From the range of non-clinical interventions available for mental health service users, these case studies were specifically selected because they allow us to focus on physical activities taking place in the outdoors. In gathering the data for these case studies, we took an ethnographic and interview-based approach. We spent time with service providers and users at each organisation, conducted structured and unstructured interviews, and spent time with the groups – participating in activities alongside them. Discussions with service providers were also conducted on an informal basis.

We interpreted the information collected during our field visits using the Individual, Social, Material (ISM) model (Figure 5.1), which looks to understand the influence of habit, skills, emotions, values, networks and relationship, meanings, roles and identity, infrastructure, rules and regulations, norms, attitudes, and infrastructure, on an individual's decision-making process, and what influences that person to choose to do something. Table 5.1 elaborates on how these components were explored.

Branching Out

Branching Out is an award-winning greenspace on referral programme for adults (aged 18+) in Scotland with formally diagnosed mental health issues – some serious and long term. The service was set up in 2007 by Forestry Commission Scotland and consists of three hours per week of woodland-based activity over a 12-week period. Examples of activities include health walks, vegetation management, bush craft, photography, and willow sculpture. On completion of the course, participants are awarded certificates to recognise individual achievements. The programme is currently available in nine NHS board areas: Greater Glasgow and Clyde, Lothian, Forth Valley, Lanarkshire,

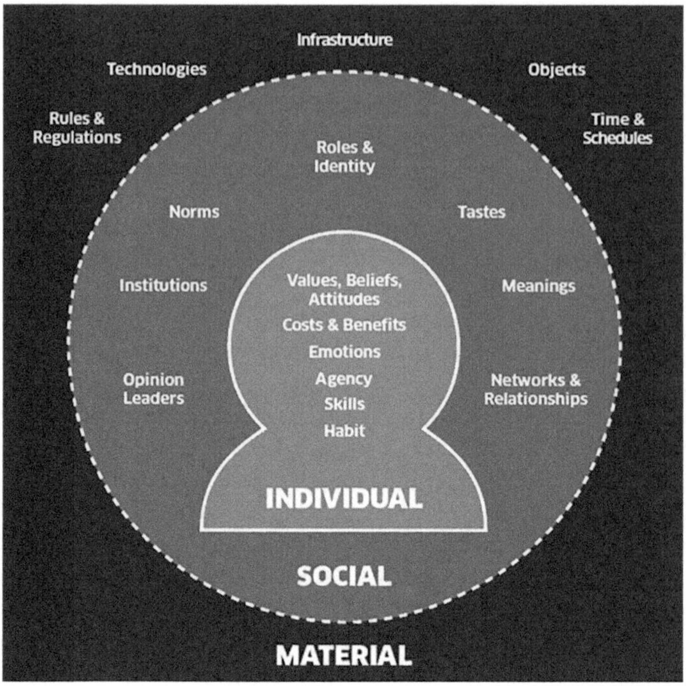

Figure 5.1 Individual, social and material model.

Table 5.1 ISM model used to interpret information collected from case study sites

What	*How*
Individual	1 What they do and how often they do it (habit). 2 How they know what to do, where to go, and how to get there (skills). 3 What they think and feel about what they do (emotions). 4 What they have to do to be able to do what they do, and what they get out of doing it (costs and benefits). 5 What is important to them and the perceived benefit that can be achieved from doing it (values, beliefs, attitudes).
Social	1 Who they do it with (networks and relationships). 2 What it means to do these things (meanings). 3 How they fit in with others who are doing the same thing (roles and identity). 4 What sort of things everyone does (norms). 5 Where they look to for guidance, awareness raising, and sources of information (institutions/opinion leaders).
Material	1 When they do these things (times and schedules). 2 What they need to do these things (objects/infrastructure/technology). 3 What needs to be in place for these things to work smoothly and how they are/were intended (rules and regulations).

Ayrshire and Arran, Borders, Tayside, Fife, and Highland. All leaders complete an accredited training course, and this ensures consistent delivery across Scotland (Scottish Forestry, n.d.).

Branching Out in Highland

The Highland service has been operating under the Branching Out umbrella since 2013. The site that is used is a working forest, owned and managed by the local community, who successfully negotiated buyout of the land in 1998. It is a well-established site with a forest school used by a number of local school primary school groups, a play park for children, a curling pond, woodland walks (which link to one of Scotland's long-distance way walks), mountain bike trails, and sites of historic interest. Located on the outskirts of the Highland capital of Inverness, the site is accessible easily by private transport, but less so by public transport – which is irregular and requires a significant walk from the nearest bus stopping point. Participants who use the Branching Out service at this site get there by private taxi, the cost of which is covered by the service.

Staff at the site are employed on a full-time basis and facilitate several woodland-based activities in addition to the Branching Out programme. This site hosts the training programme for all new Branching Out leaders and plays an integral role in the success of the programme Scotland-wide. Staff play a key role in delivery of this training and can be considered as pioneers of the programme. Since becoming a Branching Out provider in 2013, approximately 30 new Branching Out leaders for Highland and Argyll and Bute have been trained here. We attended one session of the training and recorded in our field notes that a dedication to sustaining the service whilst evolving to meet user need and local context is clearly understood and communicated by the staff. One key focus when inviting participants to join the course was indicated to be balancing healthcare provision with access to greenspace. To do this, staff invite NHS employees to attend the training as part of ongoing continuing professional development (CPD) development and have found this to be a very useful bridge to encouraging referrals of patients to the Branching Out programme. However, not all NHS employees will be in a position to attend the training, so invites are also extended to "try it out", and this has also been a useful approach to increase referrals.

Staff at the Highland site run three Branching Out programmes per year and work closely with participants to understand what they want to achieve over the course of the 12 weeks. Staff are excellent at helping participants to identify these goals and objectives, as well as helping to monitor and to encourage on occasions when motivation can be low. One of the key assets at this site is that the Branching Out participants have access to a weekly volunteering programme, meaning that they can continue to come to the site on a regular basis after their completion of the 12-week programme. Another asset is the excellent network of signposting (to other activities and services) that staff here have built up over the many years that the programme has been running. Staff are intricately involved with the local community and, through their networks, opportunities are identified and tapped into. Analysis of our case study materials suggests this to be a critical component of the programme that makes it successful from the perspective of the participants.

Participants who use the Branching Out service in Highland reported experiencing hugely positive benefits, including reduced anxiety and increased confidence. These can be considered two very important factors of any person's day-to-day living but are even more significant for those with mental health issues, who experience difficulty with both on a regular basis. Many participants reported feeling better about themselves physically; feeling, for example, that being part of Branching Out helps to get them off the sofa and out of the house – leading to increased movement, even if it is just for one day per week. This was discussed as being of importance because of the dampening effect of certain medications. Participants also explained that they felt they have gained weight since taking medication but found that Branching Out helped them to dwell less on that and rather to enjoy feeling generally better. Some participants reported that they slept better following a Branching Out day. However, in contrast, many discussed feeling anxious the evening before a Branching Out day – usually in relation to fears that they may not make it to the site in time for the programme start; with some saying that they often experienced a sleeplessness night. The social benefit of attending the programme, however, was very clear. Participants indicated the importance of shared experiences and being around people who understood what they had been through, and what they continued to go through. Participants highlighted being able to discuss healthcare appointments and medications, as well as any other therapies that they are currently engaged in, with other people who are non-judgemental and can provide feedback based on their own experiences. This helped participants to develop strong relationships with each other, and this transition into friendship was particularly observed by those who went on to participate in the weekly volunteering sessions.

Staff reported observing similar health and wellbeing benefits to those that the participants told us about. It was clear that having staff with a wealth of experience and knowledge was a key driver of these benefits. Staff clearly had an intuition that recognised when, and when not, to provide input, support, guidance, advice, or simply a listening ear. The staff clearly had the ability to provide this in a manner that made participants feel safe and trusting of their facilitators.

This success of this service represents a strong and dedicated team who have a great desire to utilise greenspace and the outdoors as a mechanism for improving the lives of those living with mental health issues in Highland. In order to sustain this success "buy in" is required. Firstly, from a healthcare perspective, more staff should consider referring patients to this service, and for those who are already active in doing this, follow-up is required, including documenting and producing case studies that could be useful in encouraging other healthcare staff to appreciate the benefit of participating in the Branching Out programme. Secondly, funders should consider providing longer-term support for programmes such as this, including large-scale funding that supports the service to evolve and develop over a, for example, ten-year period, rather than drip-feeding small sums of money for specific, individual projects. Thirdly, much effort is required on the part of local services, including local councils, to develop and maintain triangular working structures that support each other, and this could take the form of provision of transport, sharing tools and materials, or food donations.

Branching Out in Argyll and Bute

The Argyll and Bute Branching Out service has been running since 2015 and is available to access at six different sites – on mainland and island communities. Each of the sites is unique in terms of geography and local community but are all similarly difficult to access (since they are remotely located with limited access to transport links) and have limited healthcare provision. Since 2015, the service in Argyll and Bute has received 226 referrals, with 120 of these individuals completing the 12-week programme. Two of the Argyll and Bute delivery sites are considered in this case study: a remote village on the west coast and an island accessible by commercial ferry services. Both locations are classified by the Scottish Government as remote and rural and the area of Argyll and Bute in which they are situated is ranked sixth on the Scottish Index of Multiple Deprivation (2016), meaning that they are among the 15% most deprived areas in Scotland (Argyll and Bute Council, 2016). Generally, access to services in these areas is exceptionally limited, with many settlements having only one bus service in and out per day or no bus service at all, and most do not have a resident medical service.

Branching Out service users in these areas have transport to the programme sites provided by a local taxi company. The cost of this is covered by the service. The driver responsible for transportation of participants was highlighted as a key person in "getting people out of the house". Through conversation with the driver, it was possible to understand why this individual played such a critical role, including their ability to gently encourage participants to attend the Branching Out session when it was clear they just didn't feel like doing so on a particular day, and their ability to bring participants out of their shell by identifying their interests and engaging them in conversation about these. The driver also had a clear skill for assessing participants on an informal basis and being able to aptly handle situations; for example, he knew when empathy was required, when some motivational chat was required, and when it was appropriate to just let participants have some quiet time to themselves.

One concern was acceptance of the service by residents. Some people worried that local residents may not have experience of encountering mental health service users and be wary of them due to cultural stigma around mental illness. However, in contrast, it was appreciated that the service, being visible (from the roadside in one of the locations), could act as a step towards helping locals to change their mind-set towards mental health.

Staff facilitating the Branching Out service are employed by each of the sites they work at and are not solely employed for the purposes of facilitating the Branching Out programme. Therefore, staff undertake several roles at the sites in addition to facilitating the Branching Out groups. Staff have a range of experience, but all have a genuine connection to the area and a love of the outdoors – all discussed a strong appreciation of the health benefits of participating in activity in outdoor and woodland spaces. Some staff are more experienced than others, and those staff aid the professional development of the less experienced members of staff – a mix of job shadowing, transfer of knowledge and skills, and demonstration was observed to take place. Staff undertake training specific to Branching Out at the Highland site, discussed in the first case study section. One of the main challenges for staff is securing funding to sustain their posts, and this was highlighted as a constant concern that requires a lot of effort, and staff time, to keep abreast of.

Although a relatively new site, development has been efficient and there are several permanent buildings, including poly tunnels with plant and vegetable growing beds, a classroom/workshop, a sawmill, and a storefront. The site is open to the local community (including the primary school) and general public (e.g. for walking). Plans for future development include building affordable housing on the site (using timber felled and processed at the woodland), a camping site, a play park, and an extended path network. Branching Out service users access the site once per week and participate in activities such as woodworking, growing, crafting, and general site maintenance. Following competition of the 12-week programme, it is possible for some service users to access a service exclusively available at this site called Moving On. The Moving On service is effectively a step up from Branching Out, and users participate in more project-based activities and have, for example, recently completed the building of a wooden round house. Moving On is exclusive to the Argyll and Bute site, and was developed in response to the need for continuation activities.

The second site that we visited within Argyll and Bute was just completing its first Branching Out programme. The site is on an island and the community woodland where activities take place has just recently been purchased. It is a much smaller site; however, it is perhaps more accessible for locals. There is limited signage or indication of the work that is going on at the site, but as it is close to the road the local population are becoming more and more aware of activity going on here – particularly as it is on the main route to one of the ferry ports. Currently, there is a small area of the woodland allocated as a "hub" for the Branching Out group – it has been roofed with tarpaulin, and there is a fire pit surrounded with rustic, raw wood plank benches. The benches are covered with cosy sheepskin pads – handwoven by the users. Dotted around the woodland are artefacts crafted by the users – dream catchers, wooden plaques, and sculptures made from "found" wood, moss, leaves, etc. The current group are pioneering the shape of this site for the future, and it was very special to spend some time there.

Our fieldwork clearly demonstrated that service users in Argyll and Bute perceive the programme to have significant benefits for them, potentially life-saving for some. It also showed us that Branching Out plays a critical role in developing their social networks, which for the majority would not exist if they did not have access to this service. Most of the service users that we spoke to indicated that they enjoyed accessing the service and felt that it was an asset to have the routine that comes from having something to do on a set day each week. The discussions that we had with service users about benefits centred around acceptance, feeling free to speak openly, share ideas, and work as a group, as well as the generation of feelings of being valued and enjoying social interactions in a non-judgemental environment. Of concern to both facilitators and users was the limited time available to access the service. Twelve weeks was not considered a sufficient amount of time to offer a long-term solution – something desperately needed by service users. Some spoke of feeling "dropped" and discussed with fearful anticipation how they might feel on the last day of the programme. Some participants even indicated a reluctance to see the programme through to the end, already concerned about the feelings they anticipated experiencing when the 12 weeks was up. Facilitators highlighted a follow-on option as the obvious and necessary solution to address this major issue, but in the absence of much needed funding and financial input, this was indicated as something of an ongoing effort. However, the enthusiasm and dedication of facilitators was very apparent, and it was obvious that they would take whatever action they could to ensure sustained provision of the service, as well as exploring options for providing more long-term input for service users.

Velocity – Cycle to Health

Operating from its café and workshop in the centre of the Highland capital, Inverness, since 2015, Velocity's Cycle to Health project is targeted at people experiencing mild mental health difficulties, social isolation, low mood, or anxiety. The project is funded by the Smarter Choices, Smarter Places (SCSP) Open Fund, supported by Transport Scotland. Focussing on behaviour change, the fund aims to encourage everyday walking or cycling, and sustainable travel methods for longer journeys. The Velocity project looks at ways of using cycling to help people adopt healthier lifestyles, to encourage sustainable travel, and to improve emotional wellbeing. Velocity believes the combination of physical activity and the social element of the project has a positive effect on mental health.

Most participants self-refer, although they can be referred by a healthcare professional, e.g. GP and community mental health team. However, the person is required to make the initial contact with Velocity themselves. Velocity advertises the project in, for example, the Inverness City Advertiser (ICA – what'sonhighlands.com), GP surgeries, and New Craigs psychiatric hospital, which is a secure in- and outpatient facility, located on the outskirts of Inverness.

Following an initial one-to-one assessment of cycling skills and needs, participants join a small weekly group comprising three or four people of similar ability and confidence, which runs over four weeks. The initial 2.5-hour sessions are open to all abilities and aim to increase cycling skills and confidence, enabling people to progress to Velocity's regular social rides if they wish. As part of the initial assessment and project evaluation, each participant completes the Warwick-Edinburgh Mental Well-Being Scale (WEMWBS), a scale of 14 positively worded items for assessing mental wellbeing. At the end of the four-weekly sessions, this form is completed again. After three months, it is mailed out to participants to complete at home. The evaluation includes a questionnaire on transport and behaviour change, as well as giving participants an opportunity to reflect on their progress. The team has three project workers and a project co-ordinator, who are qualified cycle trainers and cycle leaders. They do not have dedicated mental health training but do have professional backgrounds in areas like healthcare and/or counselling. The team aims to create a nurturing environment and to support people to challenge themselves. The high staff/participant ratio (2:4) helps people to feel safe. People are usually contacted within a couple of days to arrange the one-to-one meeting, but it can take longer to match them with the most appropriate group. All necessary equipment, such as bikes, helmets, waterproofs, and lights, is provided, so that there are no costs for the participant. On Tuesday evenings, participants meet at the café for soup and then go out on a cycle ride as a group. Social rides also take place on alternate Saturday mornings. The rides usually start from the Velocity café, encompassing locations and routes in and around the outskirts of Inverness, offering traffic free rides, e.g. along the Caledonian Canal towpath, as well as riding in traffic. Velocity also offer workshops on bike maintenance, for which they have recently started to charge on a donation basis according to the user's income. Since introducing this payment system, workshop attendance has dropped.

Although there is no formal mechanism or checklist for assessing participants in order to signpost follow-on services, project workers will give out cards with contact numbers for mental health organisations. Signposting is dependent on individual interests, and how willing they are to share personal information. By building relationships and having conversations with participants, project workers can signpost to other services such as counselling, wellbeing walks, or Branching Out (Scottish Forestry, n.d.), as well as other cycling initiatives like WheelNess (led by Cycling UK, it offers free access to a bike) (Cycling UK, n.d.).

Benefits reported following participation in the Cycle to Health programme included improvements in mental health and wellbeing; for example, one interviewee found the group cycling reduced his anxiety and he found cycling fast particularly beneficial, saying, "I can think clear moving fast". Two others had found "me time" through cycling as well as increased self-confidence. Goal-setting and a sense of achievement are key factors, enabling participants to both feel and measure progress, growth, and development. They are pushing and challenging themselves in order to achieve a goal they have set themselves within the group. When outside their comfort zone, they benefit from the supportive environment engendered by reassuring and knowledgeable leaders. One participant drew an analogy between cycling challenges and mastering difficult things in one's head, finding that the determination and fighting spirit needed in cycling were similar to that required to overcome mental health issues. Welcoming, friendly, and open, the group helps to reduce social isolation by providing an opportunity for social contact and to make friends with other participants. One key benefit of taking part was discussed as a shared understanding of mental health issues and spending time with people in a similar situation with an interest in maintaining and improving their mental health. Participants encourage one another – the social contact is actively nurturing rather than just getting together for a chat. The open-minded and non-judgemental atmosphere is appreciated particularly by those whose friends and family may not be able to fully understand their situation.

Being outside is a key aspect of the project's success by giving people the opportunity to enjoy fresh air and exercise as well as engage with the natural environment and thereby "enjoy somewhere calm where you can hear the birds, be by water, in amongst nature". According to one participant, cycling is multi-sensory and "spiritually cleansing", allowing one to connect to the environment, see wildlife, enjoy the scenery, and notice things they would not see if they were travelling by car. Another participant said she would choose the cycling over the café "social bit" because of the sense of release and freedom: "the air's rushing past you when you're on the bike and you just feel great". Even poor weather, which is common in Inverness and the Highlands of Scotland generally, was not perceived to be a deterrent for participants. Extreme weather can cause groups to be cancelled, but the project encourages participants to go out even when it is "miserable" outside, if it is possible and safe to do so. Not limited to sunny days, participants should, therefore, be prepared for all weathers. This is considered liberating – since you can get out even in the rain, this enables cycling to become a part of regular everyday routine. Remembering an "epic monsoon day" one interviewee recounted the sense of achievement and "being in it together" engendered in the group. Sometimes they are "buzzing" when the weather is bad and the sense of achievement can be greater. Cycling in the dark can have a similar impact. People would not necessarily go out on their own in the dark or bad weather. When it is particularly cold or windy, a greater sense of camaraderie is generated because everyone is helping each other along.

Even though the service is in a relatively central part of the city, a range of different barriers to participation were reported. Initial contact has to be made by the (potential) participant; therefore, they need to have the motivation to take this first step. According to one project worker, people are drawn to the project for the same reason that they may find it difficult, i.e. lack of self-confidence and mental ill health. If a person cancels a session, then they can feel bad about themselves and it can exacerbate their lack of confidence. The project workers try to reach out to people without making assumptions about why they do and do not come on any particular occasion. In following up non-attendance, project workers have to balance being concerned for the individual and not being intrusive. Caring responsibilities and lack of childcare can also act as a barrier to participation. The timing of sessions can be inconvenient depending on employment and other commitments. Some employers have been supportive and given people time off to participate. People do not need any equipment to take part in the sessions, but participants are not allowed to borrow bikes if they want to cycle outside the project. According to one participant, living in the countryside can make taking part more difficult because of busy country roads, lack of cycle paths, and the necessity of driving to locations as starting points.

In terms of improvement, it was difficult for service providers and users to generate suggestions since the project experienced a high level of satisfaction. Suggestions included increasing the number of rides, accommodating those who wanted more challenging rides, and not charging for bike workshops.

Nature Walks for Wellbeing

Nature Walks for Wellbeing are organised by the Inverness Heritage Officer at the Scottish Waterways Trust (Scotland's national waterways charity), which devises canal-based projects to bring people and the natural environment together in order to enhance health and mental wellbeing, improve employment opportunities, and help local communities. Offering nature-based group walks for people with mental illness, the scheme has been running regularly for the last five years.

Walks take place every Thursday at pre-determined locations around Inverness, and the schedule is emailed monthly to individuals and healthcare professionals. Participants do not have to book, no one is required to introduce themselves, and leaders aim to create an inclusive atmosphere where everyone feels welcome, accepted, and safe. The sessions can also include a range of art-based activities, storytelling, poetry, nature tracking, wildlife watching, and mindfulness exercises. The walks last 1.5 hours and include a break for refreshments. Using a Kelly kettle, the leader, helped by participants, makes tea and coffee outdoors. There are eight different leaders with a range of outdoor, nature, arts, or physical exercise experience and skills. Sometimes there are specific nature-based activities and the leaders talk to the group about the natural environment as they walk along, e.g. seasonal changes. The leaders go on a once-a-year getaway together where they can share experiences and have training sessions on nature and the outdoors as well as on mental health and wellbeing.

Participants accompanied by healthcare staff (usually occupational therapy assistants) come from acute wards in the New Craigs psychiatric hospital, Aonach Mor (a community unit for people with long-term enduring mental health problems), and Birchwood Recovery Centre (run by a Registered Charity, the unit provides accommodation and support for people recovering from mental ill health). The group can also include unaccompanied individuals living in the community, who may or may not have stayed in the psychiatric hospital or other mental health facility in the past. The number ranges from 10 to 30 participants. The majority of participants are male and it is recognised as a good way of engaging men in activities. The scheme costs about £8,000 per year to run, and funding comes from a variety of sources such as charitable funding from national lottery schemes and private trusts.

The project leader, healthcare staff, and participants reported a range of benefits of participating in the Nature Walks for Wellbeing programme. Increased motivation is one of these benefits. People may intend to increase physical activity but if experiencing a low mood, the day can pass and they do not do it according to one participant. If something has been arranged with others, then they are more likely to turn up. The atmosphere engenders a sense of mutual understanding and acceptance because it is non-clinical, informal, and friendly without any forms to fill in. This helps participants to feel comfortable and not feel embarrassed if they do not want to take part in activities. Self-reported improvements in mental health and wellbeing included feeling calmer, more relaxed, and sleeping better. Self-confidence can also grow over the weeks, eventually enabling participants to take part in activities or to try other groups. Some may leave the group early or stay back from others at first but join in gradually over time. Participants can experience a strong sense of achievement by, for example, managing to walk a mile or keeping up with the group. Participation can improve physical health and fitness. The exercise is beneficial, but it is not too intense like being on a gym treadmill and therefore is not beyond most participants' ability, meaning they are prepared to give it a go. Increasing activity can often be difficult because of a lack of motivation as well as medication side effects like weight gain. Being outdoors is an extremely important factor and an attraction for the participants. For those staying in the psychiatric hospital, the Nature Walks offers a welcome contrast to the acute wards which can be very noisy and in which one cannot open windows. It is completely different being outdoors in the fresh air without walls or central heating. Often patients cannot leave the hospital alone due to a lack of confidence or because they need to be accompanied, which can be difficult because of staff availability. Staff and facilitators said they could see the difference in participants after their walk in the outdoors. One reported that participants chatter in the car on way back to hospital and, when they are used to going on the Nature Walks, they chatter on way down to the meeting point too. Staff also find it beneficial. Although one participant does not always feel like going out, she knows she will feel great afterwards. During the walk, leaders talk about the environment and identify plants and birds, point outing how different species can be reliant on each other. One participant explained how she can feel cut off in the hospital ward, but when she goes outdoors, she can see, hear, smell, and touch which makes her feel much more connected and uplifted. She finds other participants from the hospital or other facilities tend to visibly relax and become more talkative.

Conclusions

The evidence demonstrating the benefits of nature-based interventions and "green exercise" for those with mental health issues is substantial. Not only can direct health-related benefits such as weight loss, reduced anxiety, and lower risk of cardiovascular issues be gained, there are also great social benefits that can be as helpful for participants as the immediate intended outcomes. Our case studies have illustrated the capacity of non-clinical outdoor interventions to help different groups of people with a range of mental health conditions. We surveyed a range of services and identified four to act as case studies by spending time within them and speaking to their staff and users. Overall, we found there to be a largely positive response to these services but not without challenges. Our key conclusions are summarised below:

Key benefits

Evidence from the case studies indicates that participation in these projects increases physical activity, improves mental health, reduces anxiety, builds self-confidence, and increases social contact. These activities enable participants to set goals and experience a sense of achievement. Being outdoors is a key aspect of the projects' success by giving people the opportunity to enjoy fresh air and exercise whilst engaging with the natural environment. In addition to the intended health benefits, these programmes also benefit participants in a more social way, engendering a sense of belonging, encouraging them to engage with others, and to develop a social network with peers in a safe, inviting, and encouraging environment.

Factors for success

Skilful facilitation by supportive, experienced, and knowledgeable leaders is one of the main factors in the success of these projects, particularly in the long term. This important element helps to create the informal, welcoming, and non-judgemental atmosphere, which allows participants to share experiences, feel accepted, and offer peer support. Service users also need access to support to enable them to attend the services, including information about what it entails, how to sign up, and how to get there, including transportation. A "taster day" may be beneficial for some participants, as might information about appropriate clothing and equipment that is required to take part. Local businesses, charities, and government organisations should look to support these types of interventions by ensuring they play an active role promoting them within local communities and working alongside service providers to consider what is needed to support the long-term running of these programmes.

Barriers

In her evaluation of the Green Exercise Programme, Hynds (2010) outlines some widespread barriers experienced by people trying to access local greenspace, including lack of transport, lack of knowledge about sites, lack of self-confidence, and poor weather and individual health. Similar barriers are found in our case studies. Key examples include personal factors such as feeling motivated to make initial contact with the service, lack of self-confidence, and caring responsibilities. Timing with work was also identified as a potential barrier for some since most services are available on weekdays and during normal working hours. In addition, there are overarching problems with funding and access. This is considered an issue in the first instance for providers, who appear to be continuously sourcing financial support and making applications to funders. Replication of these programmes in more remote and rural areas is considered to be significantly challenging, and costs of provision in these areas are anticipated to be greater than those sites with access to public transport links. The potential for extending these projects in more remote and rural areas needs further examination. However, the relationship between physical activity and mental wellbeing is recognised and supported by policy as shown in the Scottish Government Mental Health Strategy: 2017–2027 (Scottish Government, 2017), which includes "Action 31. Support the physical activity programme developed by SAMH". According to SAMH (2017), physical activity is beneficial for mental health:

> Being active isn't just good for our physical health; it's also proven to have a positive effect on our mental health and wellbeing. Yet we know that people experiencing a mental health problem can find it difficult to participate in physical activity and sport. And research suggests that the less physical activity a person does, the more likely they are to experience low mood, depression, tension and worry.

The need to address the apparent lack of parity between mental and physical health in service planning, resourcing, and delivery has been highlighted. A 2018 Royal College of Nursing (RCN) report states:

> Across the UK there have been commitments to achieve parity of esteem for those with the most serious mental health problems. This is

> based on the knowledge that those with mental health problems like schizophrenia and bipolar disorder die between 15–20 years before the general population.
>
> (Royal College of Nursing, 2018)

In order to increase the sustainability of this type of non-clinical intervention and thereby build on the successes illustrated in these case studies, there are issues to be addressed in health and social care practice: firstly, the lack of funding for interventions and trained staff; and secondly, the lack of transport and problems accessing meeting-points and "greenspace".

References

Argyll and Bute Council. (2016). Retrieved from https://www.argyll-bute.gov.uk/info/scottish-index-multiple-deprivation-2009-argyll-and-bute.

Arnold, S. V., Smolderen, K. G., Buchanan, D. M., Li, Y., & Spertus, J. A. (2012). Perceived stress in myocardial infarction: Long-term mortality and health status outcomes. *Journal of the American College of Cardiology, 60*(18), 1756–1763.

Astell-Burt, T., Feng, X., & Kolt, G. S. (2014). Is neighborhood green space associated with a lower risk of type 2 diabetes? Evidence from 267,072 Australians. *Diabetes Care, 37*(1), 197–201.

Bowler, D. E., Buyung-Ali, L. M., Knight, T. M., & Pullin, A. S. (2010). A systematic review of evidence for the added benefits to health of exposure to natural environments. *BMC Public Health, 10*(1), 456.

Bragg, R., & Atkins, G. (2016). A review of nature-based interventions for mental health care. *Natural England Commissioned Reports, 2014*, 18.

Bratman, G. N., Hamilton, J. P., Hahn, K. S., Daily, G. C., & Gross, J. J. (2015). Nature experience reduces rumination and subgenual prefrontal cortex activation. *Proceedings of the National Academy of Sciences, 112*(28), 8567–8572.

Cycling UK. (n.d.). Retrieved from https://www.cyclinguk.org/wheelness

Dadvand, P. N. M., (2019). Green space and health. In: K. H. Nieuwenhuijsen (Eds.), *Integrating human health into urban and transport planning* (pp. 409–423). Cham: Springer.

Earth for life. (n.d.). Retrieved from https://www.earthforlife.org/

Hynds, H. (2010). *Green exercise programme evaluation, natural England research reports, Number 039.* Published on 29 March 2011. Natural England: Peterbourgh copyright 2011. ISSN 1754–1956

Kaplan, R., & Kaplan, S. (1989). *The experience of nature: A psychological perspective.* Cambridge: Cambridge University Press.

Maas, J., Van Dillen, S. M., Verheij, R. A., & Groenewegen, P. P. (2009). Social contacts as a possible mechanism behind the relation between green space and health. *Health & Place, 15*(2), 586–595.

Mental Health Foundation. (2016). *Mental health in Scotland: Fundamental facts.* Retrieved from https://www.mentalhealth.org.uk/publications/mental-health-scotland-fundamental-facts. [Accessed on: 19/12/2020].

Mind. (n.d.). Retrieved from https://www.mind.org.uk/ecotherapyworks

Mind. (2013). *Feel better outside, feel better inside: Ecotherapy for mental wellbeing, resilience and recovery: A briefing for Health and Wellbeing Board Chairs.* Retrieved from https://www.mind.org.uk/media/399857/Ecotherapy-briefing-health-wellbeing-boards.pdf

Mitchell, R., & Popham, F. (2008). Effect of exposure to natural environment on health inequalities: An observational population study. *The Lancet, 372*(9650), 1655–1660.

Open Aye. (n.d.). Retrieved from https://www.openaye.co.uk/

Pereira, G., Foster, S., Martin, K., Christian, H., Boruff, B. J., Knuiman, M., & Giles-Corti, B. (2012). The association between neighborhood greenness and cardiovascular disease: An observational study. *BMC Public Health, 12*(1), 466.

Repper, J., & Carter, T. (2011). A review of the literature on peer support in mental health services. *Journal of Mental Health, 20*(4), 392–411.

Royal College of Nursing. (2018). *Parity of esteem: Report of the spring 2018 RCN survey of mental health professionals, 2018, RCN: London.* Retrieved from https://www.rcn.org.uk/professional-development/publications/pub-007109

Scottish Association for Mental Health. (n.d.). Retrieved from https://www.samh.org.uk/about-us/our-work

Scottish Forestry. (n.d.). Retrieved from https://scotland.forestry.gov.uk/supporting/strategy-policy-guidance/health-strategy/branching-out

Scottish Government. (2015a). The Scottish health survey: 2015 edition, volume 1, main report. Retrieved from http://www.gov.scot/Publications/2016/09/2764/downloads

Scottish Government. (2015b). What research matters for mental health policy in Scotland. Retrieved from http://www.gov.scot/Resource/0049/00494776.pdf [Accessed on: 26/07/2016].

Scottish Government. (2017). *Scottish Government Mental Health Strategy: 2017–2027.* Retrieved from http://www.wellscotland.info/priorities/Social-Prescribing-and-Self-Help

Scottish Index of Multiple Deprivation. (2016). Argyll and Bute. Retrieved from https://www.argyll-bute.gov.uk/info/scottish-index-multiple-deprivation-2009-argyll-and-bute

Scottish Natural Heritage. (n.d.). Retrieved from https://www.nature.scot/professional-advice/contributing-healthier-scotland/our-natural-health-service

Ulrich, R. S., (1981). Natural versus urban scenes: Some psychophysiological effects. *Journal of Environment and Behaviour, 13*, 523–556.

Ward-Thompson, C., Rose, J., Aspinall, P., Mitchell, R., Clowd, A., Miller, D. (2012). More green space is linked to less stress in deprived communities: Evidence from salivary cortisol patterns. *Landscape and Urban Planning, 105*, 221–229.

Wilson, E. O. (1984). *Biophilia: The human bond with other species.* Cambridge, MA: Harvard University Press.

6 Delivering effective treatment in rural regions

James Ikonomopoulos, Ya-Wen Melissa Liang, Karen Furgerson, and Kristopher Garza

Introduction

In this chapter, we consider the delivery of effective mental health treatments in rural areas. By using a global perspective, we review existing literature and provide case study examples to illustrate a conceptualisation of mental health needs that includes depressive disorders and suicidality, as well as exploring the impact of natural disasters, and effects of domestic violence in a number of rural regions around the world. The authors discuss the implementation of various treatment programs, theories, and therapeutic techniques used to effectively deliver treatment for these issues. To efficiently implement treatment to individuals living in rural communities, a counsellor, a therapist, or a helper in mental health must understand the needs of these communities. Due to the lack of mental health resources and referral opportunities in rural areas, working with individuals and groups is going to require more in-depth understanding of treatment feasibility. This chapter explores these issues by reviewing a variety of treatments and strategic approaches identified as effective for a number of rural populations. Attention is given to the implementation of such treatments and the multicultural considerations for treatment in rural areas.

Depression and suicide in rural areas

Depression is a major mental health disorder, affecting over 300 million people globally (World Health Organization [WHO], 2018). Depressive disorders differ from common mood changes and brief emotional reactions to daily living. Because depressive symptoms can be ongoing with varying degrees of severity, depressive disorders are a serious health condition warranting special attention. Individuals struggling from depressive symptoms may experience poor functioning at work, school, and in relationships with others (American Psychiatric Association [APA], 2013). A great number of people who struggle with depressive disorders are also at an increased risk for attempting suicide. An estimated 800,000 people die from suicide each year worldwide (WHO, 2018). For individuals aged 15–29, suicide continues to be the second leading cause of death globally (WHO, 2018).

Despite there being effective and well-established treatment interventions for depressive disorders, fewer than half of all people affected globally receive such treatments (WHO, 2018). There are a number of challenges to delivering effective treatments such as a disparity in community resources, a lack of well-trained treatment providers, cultural stigmas connected to depression, and other disorders, as well as the perceived stigma of receiving treatment (WHO, 2018). When comparing occurrences of health-related disorders, a disparity exists between rural and urban areas with some relatively consistent differences seemingly apparent. Residents living in rural areas are shown to have greater levels of depression, increased rates of domestic violence, as well as increased risk of having experienced physical, emotional, and sexual abuse as children (Peek-Asa et al., 2011). Rural residents are also more likely to experience suicidality, behavioral problems, and risk-taking behaviors (Peek-Asa et al., 2011).

Challenges to effective treatment

A challenge to effective treatment is the need for thorough and valid assessment of mental health conditions. Depression is a disorder that is commonly misdiagnosed around the world, regardless of socio-economic status (WHO, 2018). A descriptive study from India (Chavan, Sahni, Das, & Sidana, 2017) reported that a large number of people in rural communities have poor knowledge regarding mental illness, and only a few have average levels of knowledge. In rural areas, depression may go unrecognized in up to 70% of the cases, and even when it is recognized and treated, fewer than 50% of these cases receive an adequate dose or duration of treatment (Chavan et al., 2017; WHO, 2018). Continual assessment and establishment of normative data for various populations is necessary and warrants the need for valid assessment development, training on administration, and interpretation leading to appropriate treatment recommendations tailoring the needs of underserved populations. Despite the challenges to assessment, we are seeing a global rise in mental health disorders. In May of 2013, the World Health Assembly resolution passed and called on every nation to recognize and respond to the rise of mental health needs prevalent in their countries (WHO, 2018).

Types of depression

Several mental health disorders are associated with depression, including major depressive disorder, persistent depressive disorder, bipolar disorder, seasonal affective disorder, and postpartum depression (APA, 2013). A depressive episode can be categorised as mild, moderate, or severe (APA, 2013) based on the number of symptoms and degree of severity. Depressive symptoms can occur over a prolonged period of time, and relapse may happen if depression is left untreated (APA, 2013). The symptoms of a depressive disorder can include ongoing feelings of severe sadness, feelings of hopelessness or helplessness, anger and irritability, feelings of worthlessness, loss of interest in activities that were once enjoyable, changes in sleep and appetite, tiredness and fatigue, trouble focusing, difficulties with decision-making, problems with memory, and recurring thoughts about death or suicidality (APA, 2013).

Suicide in rural areas

Rural areas have generally higher rates of suicide (Hirsch, 2006). Suicide is death caused by self-directed injurious behavior with intent to die as a result of that behavior (Jackson-Cherry & Erford, 2018). Suicidal ideation and history of attempts are common symptoms of depressive disorders. Handley et al. (2012) conducted a study aiming to explore the relationship between depression and suicidality as similar but separate constructs. Their sample consisted of New South Wales residents aged 18 and up, who were randomly selected from the Australian Electoral Roll and resided in one of 60 Local Government Areas from the Greater Western, Hunter New England, or North Coast rural health service regions of New South Wales (Handley et al., 2012). These regions cover approximately 70% of the geographic area of non-metropolitan New South Wales. Handley et al. (2012) discovered that over one-third of individuals with lifetime suicidal ideation and approximately one-third of individuals with lifetime suicide attempts had no history of a depressive disorder, suggesting that depression and suicidality may be separate constructs. These results correspond with research previously done in an urban Australian population (Fairweather-Schmidt, Anstey, & Mackinnon, 2009), which also found supporting evidence for depression and suicidality as separate conditions. The results of these studies reveal similarities in mental health states despite different geographical regions. On the other hand, lifetime depressive disorders have a high relationship with suicidal ideation and suicide attempts, creating an increase in the likelihood of an individual struggling with either depression or depression and suicide (Handley et al., 2012).

Treatment for depression

Several interventions have shown effectiveness for treating moderate and severe depressive disorders. Mental health practitioners may offer psychological interventions, including cognitive behavioral therapy, behavioral activation, and interpersonal psychotherapy (IPT) as well as antidepressant medication such as selective serotonin reuptake inhibitors (SSRIs) and tricyclic antidepressants (TCAs) (Cuijpers et al., 2013). Healthcare and other service providers need to be aware of the common side effects associated with medication treatment, and the barriers to treating underserved populations, such as those living in rural regions.

Treatment for depressive disorders is one of the major priorities covered by WHO's mental health Gap Action Programme (mh GAP) (WHO, 2018).

The Program works toward helping countries to increase the services available for groups with mental, neurological, and substance use disorders, by training non-specialist helpers to provide care (WHO, 2018). WHO, along with other organisations, has created brief treatment manuals that can be delivered by trained non-specialist helpers for treating depressive disorders (WHO, 2018). One intervention manual is *Problem Management Plus* (PM+) that utilizes strategies such as behavioral activation, strengthening social support, problem-solving treatment, and relaxation training (WHO, 2010).

Problem Management Plus (PM+)

WHO developed a five-session client-paced curriculum called Problem Management Plus (PM+) which may be delivered by trained lay workers or non-specialist helpers (Dawson et al., 2015). The WHO PM+ program involves a series of brief psychological tools that aim to alleviate symptoms of common mental health conditions, including depression. A consultant of the University of New South Wales, Australia, wrote the intervention protocol for the WHO (Dawson et al., 2015). PM+ works to reduce depressive symptoms, as well as symptoms of anxiety, PTSD, trauma, and stress to improve mood and activity level. PM+ is made up of evidence-based strategies, including: (a) problem solving, (b) stress management, (c) behavioral activation, and (d) accessing social support (Dawson et al., 2015).

The motivation for creating the PM+ curriculum came from a request to the Department of Mental Health and Substance Abuse at the WHO in Geneva to develop interventions that may be delivered in such a way that they are applicable in remote and rural areas where resources are scarce and adherence to fidelity of established psychological interventions are difficult (e.g. exposure therapy, cognitive processing therapy, eye movement desensitization and reprocessing). Moreover, other promising approaches that can be integrated in rural areas include the manual *group interpersonal therapy* (IPT) which is a group program for treating depression.

Group interpersonal therapy (group IPT)

Dr Gerald L. Klerman and Dr Myrna M. Weissman developed interpersonal psychotherapy (IPT) in the 1970s for use by mental health specialists to treat depressive disorders (WHO, 2019). IPT has been modified for diverse populations, age groups, and mental health conditions in community and medical settings worldwide. Positive treatment outcomes have been demonstrated in a number of research studies in countries with all income levels using both individual approaches and group approaches. The group interpersonal therapy (group IPT) manual modifies IPT for treating depressive disorders for group treatment involving eight sessions in a simplified format for non-specialized helpers who may have not received training in psychotherapy or mental health. The WHO offers a group IPT curriculum on their website to further spread awareness that IPT can be utilized by supervised non-specialists, including regions that regulate the term "psychotherapy" around the world (WHO, 2019).

Concept of depression in rural India

People from different cultures and geographical areas may have different perceptions of depression and its causes. Local residents in a rural area of Chandigarh, India, were interviewed regarding their concept of depression (Chavan et al., 2017). The participants explained that in addition to feeling sad, the most common descriptions of depressive symptoms were having disturbed sleep, suicidal thoughts, remaining withdrawn, talking less, being irritable, and using the word "tension" to describe depressive symptoms. Many of these patients with depression might have generalised weakness, aches, and pains without any diagnosable medical illness, and negative thoughts (Chavan et al., 2017). Many participants also mentioned that similar responses were common with family or relatives.

The participants discussed how a depressed person does not have to be socially withdrawn or stuck in bed the whole day, and it was further stressed that self-expression of depressive thinking is there in most of the cases. It was also mentioned that despite having depression, some of the patients still continue to work with reduced efficiency (Chavan et al., 2017). When one asks such a person "How are you feeling inside?", the person will most likely say that they are not feeling well. The participants realized that in their village, if somebody says that they aren't feeling well, they are generally not listened to and family feel that either they are experiencing a physical illness, or they are presumed to have some sort of evil curse or black magic. A person in this situation may at times be accused of giving lame excuses to avoid working.

When the community leaders were asked about their overall concept of depression, they mostly mentioned that a depressed person would get tense very easily, would remain withdrawn and alone, and would interact less (Chavan et al., 2017). However, none of the participants mentioned somatic symptoms (including bodily and anxiety symptoms), appetite disturbances, low confidence or self-esteem, hopelessness, death wishes, or suicidal ideas. The closest word for depression for them was "tension". The general perception among the participants was that it is not a common illness and does not affect everyone equally (Chavan et al., 2017).

Alleviating symptoms in rural India

Chavan et al. (2017) then attempted to investigate the methods used by rural residents when someone in their community needed relief from depressive symptoms and mental health problems. The participants shared their preference for "local faith healers" despite some not having established credentials. Many of the local residents didn't feel they received answers about their depression and mental health problems from local medical practitioners (Chavan et al., 2017). In contrast, these "local faith healers" attempted to give them an explanation and listen to their problems. The participants also shared how the local practitioner would resort to injections for most ailments, and complained how the injections only gave temporary relief and worried that in the future, they would be dependent on injection medications without ever having a cure. The participants suggested that there should be more awareness about such mental health illness in the community, adequate facilities addressing these concerns where they can be heard, and standards against wrongful practices should be established (Chavan et al., 2017).

Remote collaborative care programs

There is a scarcity of specialized mental health care resources available within rural areas, which may diminish treatment management for patients struggling with depressive disorders. In the treatment of depressive disorders, primary care teams are becoming more prevalent, as researchers have found them helpful when integrated into a collaborative care model for management of health disorders. Researchers are finding evidence that some of the main components of collaborative care programs for depressive disorders can be delivered remotely, allowing better accessibility to treatment for vulnerable or underserved populations, especially true for people living in rural areas (Fortney, 2017). Researchers conducting studies in the United States and the United Kingdom have discovered that remote collaborative care programs for depressive disorders (i.e., interventions in which elements of treatment are delivered by the use of information and communications technology (ICT)) are at minimum just as efficacious as those collaborative care programs delivered in person (Fortney, 2017).

Remotely delivered collaborative care programs are interventions well designed to remotely support rural primary care teams to treat patients, adhering to established clinical practice guidelines for those areas (Ministerio de Salud, 2013; Rojas et al., 2018), retaining treatment decisions within local health authorities (Rojas et al., 2018). Various models of collaborative care programs involving primary care teams working together with case managers and mental health specialists (Vanderlip et al., 2016) have shown to be cost effective and promising with treatment outcomes for depressive disorders (Woltmann, 2013), which has led to efforts promoting their use in regular practice (Solberg et al., 2013).

Program of treatment for depression in primary healthcare (PTDPHC)

An example of such a collaborative care program is the Program of Treatment for Depression in Primary Health Care (PTDPHC), a program in Chile that started in the early 2000s, that was later supplemented with universal health insurance coverage and the implementation of quality standards for clinical practice. Despite the uneven distribution of collaborative care models in rural areas, the use of ICT advances the opportunity for mental health practitioners to remotely assist primary care teams in rural and underserved locations (Hoeft, Fortney, Patel, & Unutzer, 2018). These collaborative care programs aided by ICT have shown their effectiveness for treating depressive disorders (Fortney et al., 2007).

Rojas et al. (2018) aimed to test the effectiveness of remotely delivered collaborative care programs in rural areas of Chile for patients with depression. Rural primary care teams who provided care to depressed patients were made up of physicians, psychologists, social workers, midwives, and nurses (Rojas et al., 2018). These rural primary care teams were directly contacted through ICT with a specialized mental health team at the University of Chile Clinical Hospital in Santiago, Chile's capital city (Rojas et al., 2018).

Patients had a completion rate of 84% (221/250) for six-month follow-up assessments. The remote collaborative care program attained greater user satisfaction scores and better treatment adherence rates at six months in comparison to treatment as usual (Rojas et al., 2018). Significant differences were found for mental health–related quality of life between the remote collaborative care program and usual care for three months after baseline assessment but not for three and six months after baseline for depressive symptoms. Rojas et al. (2018) reported a high occurrence for treatment fidelity in the remote collaborative care program suggesting that technology-assisted interventions may support rural primary care teams in the treatment for patients with depression. Rural primary care teams that do not have the possibility to collaborate with an on-site psychiatrist may be supported by remote collaborative care programs by providing timely advice to primary care teams working with depressed patients in distant parts of a Lower-Middle Income (LMI) country.

Responding to rural suicidality

Reviews of rural suicide literature reveal the importance of individual characteristics, cultural factors, and social determinants for reducing the risk of suicide (Hirsch, 2006). Protective factors are characteristics that prevent the likelihood for individuals to consider, attempt, or die by suicide (Jackson-Cherry & Erford, 2018). Protective factors comprise a number of levels, including (a) individual (e.g. genetic predispositions, personality traits), (b) family (e.g. cohesion,), and (c) community (e.g. availability of mental health services) (Jackson-Cherry & Erford, 2018). Taking action to introduce a number of protective factors into rural communities may assist in reducing factors that contribute to suicide (Jackson-Cherry & Erford, 2018). These protective factors include integrating effective clinical care for mental, physical, and substance abuse disorders in rural areas through primary care teams and through remote collaborative care programs using ICT, which can assist with delivery of effective treatment and improve the access to clinical interventions. By implementing ICT, primary care teams in rural areas can establish protocols for crisis interventions services, including the use of crisis hotlines, mobile crisis outreach teams, and remotely supervised care and safety planning to reduce risk of harm.

Another protective factor is promoting family and community support (connectedness) which reduces perceptions of loneliness and isolation. This can include using strategies to build relationships with teachers, coaches, mentors, and creating peer programs and community engagement activities through sports, clubs, and spiritual or religious groups in those regions (Jackson-Cherry & Erford, 2018). People living in rural communities can also benefit from support from ongoing medical and mental health care relationships. Individual characteristics serving as protective factors include learning skills in problem solving, conflict resolution, and nonviolent ways of handling disputes using curriculums recommended by WHO such as Group IPT and PM+ that can be easier to implement compared to specialized care in rural areas with limited resources, which can be facilitated by non-specialized trained helpers (WHO, 2019).

A case of natural disasters in rural areas in Taiwan

Natural disasters endanger people all over the world and can suddenly result in severe crises among numerous individuals, especially toward vulnerable populations and rural areas. The research of Xiong et al. (2016) revealed significant differences in intrusion between rural and urban disaster survivors. Residents in rural areas responded to higher level of intrusion after natural disasters compared to residents in urban areas (Xiong et al., 2016). It is possible that residents in rural areas have limited resources to rebuild communities and have fewer opportunities to receive professional mental wellness services after experiencing a natural disaster.

Disasters refer to situations or events that meet one of the following criteria: (a) resulting in ten or more deaths of individuals, (b) affecting a minimum of 100 individuals, (c) an alert for an international incident, or (d) an announcement of a state-level emergency (Xiong et al., 2016). The impacts of natural disasters would also result in environmental threats, public health issues, psychological disorders, and adjustment issues. Residents in rural areas are exposed to high risks of re-experiencing natural disasters (Xiong et al., 2016). It is recommended that the local government in rural areas receive more funding and resources to establish disaster recovery and provide mental wellness services to residents.

Flooding is considered as a significant natural disaster that threatens every country (Xiong et al., 2016). Taiwan is ranked as a top vulnerable country that faces a combination of hazard natural disasters, including typhoons, floods, and earthquakes (Jha, Barenstein, Phelps, Pittet, & Sena, 2010). A research study of global risks by World Bank Hazard Management indicated that 73% of the island and populations in Taiwan are at risks of more than three hazards per year (Dilley et al., 2005). Here, we consider the following case study to introduce ways of delivering effective therapy after a natural disaster in rural areas in Taiwan.

Background of natural disasters and rural areas in Taiwan

Taiwan is an island of 36,000km^2, which is in the path of western North Pacific typhoons. Several typhoons landfall Taiwan each year, especially from summer through to early autumn. The tropical cyclone that is also known as a typhoon brings heavy rains, results in severe flooding, and triggers muddy floods and landslips in mountain areas of Taiwan. Over 55 diverse Indigenous tribes reside in rural mountain areas in Taiwan, with most in the East and West rural mountain areas 9,800 feet above sea level, in the area in which most typhoons landfall. Indigenous tribes remain minorities, and each tribe has its unique language, cultures, and traditions.

The case of Typhoon Morakot

According to the report of Chao (2016), Chen et al. (2015), Lin and Lin (2016) and Wu (2014), Typhoon Morakot struck mountain areas in Taiwan on 8 August 2009. The heavy 2,500 inches of rain was followed by Typhoon Morakot from August 7th through to August 9th and severe flooding in rural areas in Central, Eastern, and Southern Taiwan. It resulted in deadly landslides in mountain areas. As reported, the muddy flood swept the mountains, buried 40 rural villages, swept away 13 rural schools with 85 students found dead, and destroyed 80% of Indigenous communities. Based on the reports, 140,000 houses were flooded, 25,000 households were forced for evacuation, 619 people found dead, and 408 individuals were missing. Approximately 25,000 residents in rural areas were temporarily relocated, 9,000 individuals were permanently relocated, and 924 individuals were injured. The majority of affected individuals were from Indigenous populations residing in rural villages locating in the high mountains in Southern and Eastern Taiwan.

Fourteen out of 55 Indigenous tribes resided in high mountain ranges where the only main road for transportation was swept away after the muddy flood following Typhoon Morakot. Many villages became completely unreachable. The surviving individuals had to climb on unstable cliffs and hike in the mountains for hours to reach out for assistance.

Effects on rural mental health after natural disasters

Experiencing natural disasters can traumatise individuals. Natural disasters can not only be life threatening but also trigger mental disorders. Survivors can experience helplessness, anxiety, and depression.

Post-traumatic stress disorder (PTSD)

Experiencing severe rain, flooding, landslides, property destruction, life-threatening incidents, injuries, and death caused by natural disasters can trigger individuals' post-traumatic stress disorder (PTSD). PTSD can be defined as unpleasant and intrusive memories, thoughts, emotions, reactions, or psychological symptoms after a traumatic incident. PTSD is the top psychological problem that most individuals would experience after flooding (Xiong et al., 2016).

A study on rural and urban residents with PTSD symptoms indicated that 53% of rural residents reported PTSD symptoms compared to 40% of urban residents PTSD (Xiong et al., 2016). It is not uncommon for rural residents to have fewer opportunities to access mental health services and limited recourses to cope with psychological distress when compared to urban residents. Research on 120 Indigenous individuals aged over 55 revealed that 30% had developed PTSD syndrome three to six months after the natural disaster of Typhoon Morakot (Chen et al., 2015). The triggers were identified as depression, relocation, poor health, death of family members, and stress related to loss of careers and income (Chen et al., 2015). A prolonged trauma of losing housing, surviving in a flooded village, and the inability to rebuild the community can exaggerate Indigenous individuals' anxiety, depression, and PTSD symptoms. The possibilities of being removed from remote communities in the mountains to other safer housing areas can also traumatise Indigenous populations because they are used to their own farming and hunting living styles. Untreated anxiety or depression can trigger PTSD, panic attacks, or other severe psychological disorders.

Depression

A study on 120 Indigenous people aged over 55, residing in mountains after Typhoon Morakot, indicated that they experience significant and persistent depression symptoms (Chen et al., 2015). Approximately 73% of the participants reported experiencing depression symptoms alone without PTSD syndrome (Chen et al., 2015). It is possible that depression symptoms affect individuals' daily energy levels and mood; thus, participants tend to easily observe their depression symptoms compared to PTSD syndromes.

Another study on 292 Indigenous refugees over 65 years old revealed that participating in outdoor activities related to community cohesion significantly reduce these refugees' depression symptoms (Chao, 2016). According to Chao (2016), when these elderly individuals perceive safety, support, and kindness from the community, they are more likely to enhance interpersonal contacts and participating in outdoor activities. The results correspond to Maslow's hierarchy of needs theory. When individuals' physiological and safety needs are met, they are able to move forward to pursue the need of social belonging.

Delivering effective therapy after natural disasters

Maslow's hierarchy of needs

The theory of Maslow's hierarchy of needs is an effect theory for treating individuals experiencing natural disasters and dealing with the aftermath. Maslow theorised five levels of basic human needs, including physiological needs, safety needs, love and belonging needs, esteem needs, and self-actualisation.

Physiological needs

Physiological needs are fundamental prior to attaining any other needs in Maslow's theory. Clients will not be interested in receiving counselling services if they are starving or in need of basic medical services. Individuals' basic physiological needs ought to be met before they can move toward achieving other needs. In the case of Typhoon Morakot, survivors of Indigenous tribes were facing damaged housing with limited clean water, insufficient food, a shortage of electricity, loss of families or relatives, medical issues, and threats of potential landslide on the top of psychological trauma. It is crucial that counsellors work with health professionals, rescue teams, and relief teams to stabilize victims' emotions, guide them to a temporary shelter, lead them to receive free medical services, and ensure they have food, clean water, and clothes to maintain healthy conditions. A counselling strategy for this level of needs includes directional counselling with empathy. Counsellors also need to use observations to detect whether survivors are injured or in need of clothing, water, food, or medical services. This could help survivors perceive empathy from counsellors, which is crucial for establishing a therapeutic relationship.

Safety needs

Many Indigenous survivors experienced the loss of families, tribe members, and housing. Using directional counselling to stabilize survivors' emotions and ensure their safety is essential. Many residents might be unwilling to be relocated to a safe shelter because they were anxious to search for members from families and tribes. They may also be unwilling to leave their tribes even though the community was buried by muddy flood. Counsellors need to work with the rescue team and maintain a firm attitude with empathy to re-direct survivors to a safe shelter to help survivors meet their safety needs.

Love and belonging needs

Many Indigenous children were forced to separate from their parents when the educational agencies tried to relocate these children for continued education while parents needed to rebuild the communities (Wu, 2014). It is not uncommon for survivors (especially children who experience the death of a family member) to feel abandoned. Counsellors need to help survivors establish connections and social structures to the new community and enhance their social support to satisfy survivors' needs of love and belonging. Facilitating group counselling, community activities, and psychoeducational workshops would be effective strategies to help survivors share their grieving process, adjust to the new social environment, and receive support and love from the community and group members who have experienced similar grieving and trauma after a natural disaster.

Esteem needs

Survivors who lost their houses, jobs, income, and family support would experience low self-esteem. Survivors with insufficient income due to natural disasters would experience difficulties re-building a home or resettling to a new community, which would also negatively impact their esteem. Counsellors can normalize survivors' disappointments and encourage survivors to enhance esteem. Using encouragements is an effective technique to rebuild clients' esteem.

Self-actualisation

The need of self-actualisation would arise after survivors achieve other four needs. Counsellors are recommended to use a holistic approach to effectively help survivors achieve self-actualisation. Unfolding the recovery process requires a holistic, relational, and historical approach (Hsu, Howitt, & Miller, 2015). Counsellors are required to understand the historical backgrounds of Indigenous communities before exploring with survivors their goals of self-actualisation. Understanding the holistic and relational components of Indigenous tribes helps counsellors to facilitate treatments helping survivors reach their unique self-actualisation.

Understand cultures and norms

Understanding Indigenous cultures and norms are crucial for counsellors to work with survivors. Without comprehending Indigenous cultures and norms, counsellors might unintentionally impose personal values and beliefs on clients, which would harm the clients. The worldviews and values of Indigenous tribes are different from the mainstream culture in Taiwan (Lin & Lin, 2016). Under the influence of non-acquisitiveness culture, Indigenous tribes shy away from material gain and only cultivate what they need; they refrain from taking advantages of Mother Nature and large-scale agriculture (Lin & Lin, 2016). As a result, their personal income is between US$500 and 1,000 per month and most elderly Indigenous individuals live on a government pension of US$100–200 per month with an unstable income from bamboo harvesting (Jha et al., 2010). The non-acquisitiveness culture makes it difficult for Indigenous tribes to accept relocation or receive counselling services for enhancing mental wellness. "I've given you homes, free homes, and you *still* won't come down from the mountain?" (Hsu et al., 2015, p. 315). When counsellors understand the cultures and norms of Indigenous tribes, they can better facilitate psychoeducational groups through local churches to help Indigenous individuals feel more comfortable with participating in the relocation plans and receiving mental wellness services. Approximately 90% of Indigenous populations in Taiwan reside in mountain villages ministered by Christian missionaries and churches (Wu, 2014). Most Indigenous tribes in Taiwan also worship an eternal soul and believe in both evil and good spirits (Lin & Lin, 2016). Christian missionaries and churches can strength Indigenous individuals' mental wellness, spirit, and resilience. Counsellors can utilize religion as a media to help Indigenous individuals receive tangible recourses and social support through psychoeducational groups.

Counsellors need to pay attention when facilitating addiction counselling among Indigenous tribes. "We keep being admonished to stop smoking, drinking, eating [raw] meat … We've already had to suffer relocation from our homeland because of Typhoon Morakot, and must still comply with lifestyle tips?" (Hsu et al., 2015, p. 315). Eating the raw meat of boars, smoking, and chewing bing lang and then spitting out bloody juice are practical methods that Indigenous tribes use to attain nutrition and energy. The cultural norms negatively impact Indigenous individuals' willingness to receive relocation or adjustment counselling because Indigenous individuals perceive their lifestyles and norms are devalued by the mainstream culture. When counsellors facilitate addiction counselling, they need to explore with Indigenous individuals their cultures and norms to avoid offending clients.

Connecting professional volunteers

In the event of disaster counselling, it is crucial that counsellors work with professionals or skilled volunteers. Counsellors need to seek verbal consent from clients in the first place because most clients will not feel ready to sign a consent form. From our experience of helping survivors, they are guarded from talking to a counsellor because they do not want to be identified as having a mental disorder. Utilizing professionals or skilled volunteers from a rescue team to reach out to survivors may be an effective strategy to bring survivors to meet with counsellors for professional help.

Domestic violence and families in rural areas

We have seen that culture influences how individuals perceive stress, distress, and their emotional reactions to events as well as the ways in which they seek help or even if they seek help at all (Sue, Sue, Neville, & Smith, 2019). Further, culture is not narrowly defined as just one's ethnicity or religion.

The views and values of individuals from rural communities can differ from those living in urban environments within the same country or region. For example, violence against women in rural areas of Brazil has been cited as accepted as "normal" (Bervian, da Costa, da Silva, Arboit, & Honnef, 2019). The women saw their mothers beaten, they expect to be beaten, and assume that their daughters will be as well. They rationalise that it is just the way things are. Although violence against women occurs in both rural and urban settings, it is less "acceptable" in urban areas. The violence may occur, but it is not accepted as the norm (Bervian et al., 2019).

The WHO has defined domestic or intimate partner violence as "behaviour by an intimate partner or ex-partner that causes physical, sexual or psychological harm, including physical aggression, sexual coercion, psychological abuse and controlling behaviours" (WHO, 2017). While the language of this definition is purposefully gender-neutral, women are most likely to be abused, and this is most likely to be by a male partner. (Asay, DeFrain, Metzger, & Moyer, 2016; Wriggins, 2018) As Tonsing (2016) noted, "Domestic violence is a global issue that cuts across ethnic, class, and culture. Its manifestations are also shaped by the values and circumstances of particular cultures" (p. 442). While domestic or intimate partner violence occurs globally and is ubiquitous throughout most countries and cultures (Zorn, Wuerch, Faller, & Hampton, 2017), there can be no single definition. What domestic or intimate partner violence is, and how it is addressed, depends greatly upon the environment in which it occurs. The values and perception of the community will impact whether domestic violence is condoned, tolerated, or accepted.

Perceptions of domestic violence and violence against women

The prevailing attitude of the community toward domestic violence will in turn drive not only the response of the community to such occurrences but also impact how victims view their experience and whether they accept their situation as inevitable (Tonsing, 2016). Oyefara, Jegede, and Ojo (2018) reported that in some cultures, the community not only condoned violence against women but also viewed it as justified. They recounted one study of Indian women where violence toward women who were bad cooks, were disrespectful to their in-laws, or produced too many girl children was considered justified by men and women alike. Zorn et al. (2017) encountered significant concerns about how their participants defined intimate partner violence and the terminology used by the researchers based on regional differences. They found that asking questions using terminology that is "standard" hindered their interviews with participants who were from rural areas. They found that each small, isolated area had its own unique view and way of communicating exactly what domestic or intimate partner violence actually meant and how they perceived its impact in their particular area. Neither researchers nor those hoping to provide help or services to victims of domestic or intimate partner violence can afford to become encumbered by our own biases concerning violence within families.

Cultural values and personal identity

The cultural values and expectations, particularly in rural areas, influence how an individual perceives her role within the family, her place within the community, and her behaviors and beliefs about herself. Further, these factors can influence her willingness to share her experiences with others or seek out support or help, especially from perceived outsiders. Tonsing's (2016) research found that the majority of the women who participated in her study were under pressure not to speak about what happened inside the family because it would bring shame to the family and lead to them being ostracised by the community. Further, the personal identity and status of the women were wholly tied to their marriage and place within the family. Should the family be dishonoured in any way, the result for their status and identity could be devastating. Such concerns make it even more difficult for victims to seek help or even share experiences with anyone, even mental health providers. This can further exacerbate the feeling of isolation.

Asay et al. (2016) noted that the cultural attitudes condoning domestic or intimate partner violence leave victims with few options. If the occurrence of domestic or intimate partner violence is considered a private matter and condoned or at least ignored by the community, violence is perpetuated and victims have little choice but to accept it. Tonsing's (2016) research also noted that even when a victim of domestic or intimate partner violence may wish to remove herself from the violent situation, the cultural values of the community, particularly in rural areas, can be a significant barrier for her. Many of the respondents in her study spoke specifically about needing to maintain the marriage in spite of the abuse due to the stigma of divorce in the community. They feared being ostracised from the community and the loss of respect of family and friends, leaving few options for self-support and support of her children. Several of the women studied recounted experiences where family members, even parents, viewed the victim as a "bad woman" or shameful. They were advised by their mothers to keep silent and endure the violence and were threatened with disowning or shunning by their fathers. In essence, the cultural norms of the community make it more difficult to remove herself from the violent situation than to stay and accept the violence.

Effects of domestic and intimate partner violence

As reported by Asay et al. (2016), there are significant difficulties in addressing problems that are denied or ignored and even further barriers exist in rural areas where even if help is sought, few services are available. Particularly in rural or isolated areas, addressing domestic or intimate partner violence is further hindered because the victims simply have nowhere to seek help. Lack of communication with other communities, economic problems, fear of retaliation, few social policies, extremely limited resources in isolated areas or at least lack of knowledge of any resources which may be available, limited availability of transportation, and few, if any, culturally sensitive intervention programs can leave victims with few ways to get help even if they want it (Asay et al., 2016; Ragusa, 2017; Tonsing, 2016; Zorn, et al., 2017). Victims of domestic or intimate partner violence also encounter barriers such as lower education levels which impact employability, inadequate medical facilities, limited childcare, and a lack of social support from both friends and family as well as social or governmental agencies (Ragusa, 2017). It is therefore understandable that victims may feel stuck between two equally difficult situations. They can remain in a violent situation where they have their other basic needs met (shelter, food, security for the children, and the regard of their family and community), or they can remove themselves from the dangers at home only to face the loss of financial and social support and uncertainty that they can provide for themselves or their children.

It is not surprising that experiencing domestic or intimate partner violence in such situations can result in significant mental health concerns. Anxiety, depression, post-traumatic stress, and substance misuse are common diagnoses for survivors of domestic or intimate partner violence. In a study conducted with women from the Democratic Republic of the Congo, significantly greater incidence of major depressive disorder, post-traumatic stress, suicidal ideation, and suicide attempts were reported in women who had suffered domestic or intimate partner violence than in those who had not (Tol et al., 2017).

Given the serious mental health consequences of domestic or intimate partner violence, and the restrictive cultural views and dearth of resources in rural communities, mental health professionals who do attempt to work with victims from rigid, rural cultures must be mindful in developing multicultural competence and selective in the methods they use with such clients. The very conditions which contribute to feelings of isolation, acceptance of domestic or intimate partner violence, and lack of trust in outsiders (social and cultural views and values and the lack of adequate resources for victims) also contribute to barriers counsellors face in working effectively with survivors within the structure of their environments (Crumb, Haskins, & Brown, 2019). Traditional counselling may not be possible within the confines of the environments and cultural restrictions of clients in rural areas. To be effective, delivery formats and practices need to be altered to consider the clients' specific experiences and cultural views. As stated by Crumb et al. (2019), "Counselors practicing in rural, impoverished areas must be prepared to address systems of oppression, discrimination, marginalized statuses, and the impact these factors have on counseling services and clients' well-being" (p. 20). Effective counsellors, regardless of the cultural identification or specific diagnosis, should "meet the clients where they are" and approach each therapeutic relationship with attention to each client's specific needs, limitations, and strengths which are specific to the client's cultural views and values (Ivey, Ivey, & Zalaquett, 2014, p. 72). Counsellors should not only be mindful of the clients' cultural background and its impact upon the experiences of the clients but our own as well. Such mindfulness of our own cultural background, values, and views and how they may inform, and shape personal biases will allow greater immediacy and acceptance of the clients' experiences and promote a non-judgmental therapeutic relationship (Ivers, Johnson, Clarke, Newsome, & Berry, 2016).

Approaching survivors

Mainstream counselling and therapy have moved toward a medical model with the publication of the fifth edition of the *Diagnostic and Statistical Manual of Mental Disorders* (DSM-5). However, this approach may not sufficiently account for the specific cultural barriers faced by counsellors who attempt to provide services to victims of domestic or intimate partner violence whose cultural background may inhibit the development of trust in an outsider and condones the acts of violence which contribute to the clients' mental health challenges. When the counsellor focuses on the development of a therapeutic relationship that is built upon sensitivity to the specific cultural environment, values, and attitudes specifically pertaining to the individual client, a more effective working relationship between counsellor and client can be developed. Such a relationship can also allow for the counsellor to observe and better understand the specific challenges a client may face when domestic or intimate partner violence is an accepted part of the culture of reference for the client. Tomlinson-Clarke and Georges (2014) cited the multipath model of Sue et al. (2019) which considers a more holistic approach using biological, psychological, social, and sociocultural dimensions to better understand the aetiology of the mental health consequences of domestic or intimate violence in clients in rigid and rural cultures. Such an approach focuses upon the intrapersonal strengths of the client and the therapeutic relationship between the counsellor and the client in developing coping mechanisms for dealing with the effects of the violence and the clients' limited options. Rather than focusing on "mental illness" and symptoms of dysfunction, which can seem judgmental and inhibit the development of a trusting relationship, a collaborative and wellness-focused model allows the counsellor to engage with the client and obtain the information needed to fully understand the challenges facing the client. Using a wellness forward method rather than an illness and deficiency approach can help counsellors better assess the client's strengths and options in minimizing the consequences of the violent circumstances and learn more effective functioning within the particular environment.

Conclusion

A number of interventions have shown their effectiveness for treating moderate and severe depressive disorders. Treatment for depressive disorders is one of the major priorities covered by the WHO's mental health Gap Action Programme (WHO, 2018). The Program works toward helping countries by increasing the services available for groups with mental, neurological, and substance use disorders, by training non-specialist helpers to provide care (WHO, 2018). WHO, along with other organisations, has created brief treatment manuals that can be delivered by trained non-specialist helpers for treating depressive disorders (WHO, 2018). Individual characteristics serving as protective factors include learning skills in problem solving, conflict resolution, and nonviolent ways of handling disputes using curriculums recommended by WHO such as Group IPT and PM+ that can be easier to implement compared to specialized care in rural areas with limited resources, which can be facilitated by non-specialized trained helpers (WHO, 2019).

Protective factors are characteristics that prevent the likelihood for individuals to consider, attempt, or die by suicide (Jackson-Cherry & Erford, 2018). Protective factors comprise a number of levels, including (a) individual (e.g. genetic predispositions, personality traits), (b) family (e.g. cohesion,), and (c) community (e.g. availability of mental health services) (Jackson-Cherry & Erford, 2018). Taking action to introduce a number of protective factors into rural communities may assist in reducing factors that contribute to suicide (Jackson-Cherry & Erford, 2018). Integrating effective clinical care for mental, physical, and substance abuse disorders in rural areas through primary care teams and through remote collaborative care programs using ICT can assist with delivery of effective treatment and improve the access to clinical interventions.

Primary care teams in rural areas can establish protocols for crisis interventions services, including the use of crisis hotlines, mobile crisis outreach teams, and remotely supervised care and safety planning to reduce risk of harm. Promoting family and community support reduces perceptions of loneliness and isolation in people living in rural areas. People living in rural communities can also benefit from support from ongoing medical and mental health care relationships.

The theory of Maslow's hierarchy of needs is an effective theory for treating individuals experiencing natural disasters and dealing with the aftermath. Maslow theorised five levels of basic human needs, including physiological needs, safety needs, love and belonging needs, esteem needs, and self-actualisation. Physiological needs are fundamental prior to other needs in Maslow's theory. Individuals' basic physiological needs ought to be met before they can move forward to achieving other needs. Using directional counselling to stabilize survivors' emotions and ensure their safety is essential. Counsellors need to help survivors establish connections and social structures to the new community and enhance their social support to satisfy survivors' needs of love and belonging. Counsellors can normalize survivors' disappointments using encouragement to rebuild clients' esteem. The need of self-actualisation would arise after survivors achieve the other four needs. Counsellors are recommended to use a holistic approach to effectively help survivors. Understanding Indigenous cultures and norms are crucial for counsellors to work with survivors. Without comprehending Indigenous cultures and norms, counsellors might unintentionally impose personal values and beliefs on clients, which could potentially harm them. In the event of disaster counselling, it is crucial that counsellors work with professionals or skilled volunteers.

Domestic and intimate partner violence continues to be a problem in rural communities and around the world. Building a therapeutic relationship, along with focusing on the intrapersonal strengths of a person, can help them overcome many of the psychological and socio-cultural effects of domestic violence. Integrating a biological, psychological, social, and sociocultural lens can help us better understand the aetiology of domestic and intimate partner violence and the mental health needs for people living in rigid and rural cultures. Traditional counselling just may not be possible within the confines of the environments and cultural restrictions of clients in rural areas. To be effective, delivery formats and practices need to be altered to consider the clients' specific experiences and cultural views. Counsellors ought to be prepared to address systems of oppression, discrimination, marginalised statuses, and impoverished areas counselling services and clients' wellbeing. Effective counsellors, regardless of the cultural identification or specific diagnosis, should "meet the clients where they are" and approach each therapeutic relationship with attention to each client's specific needs, limitations, and strengths which are specific to the client's cultural views and values (Ivey et al., 2014, p. 72).

References

American Psychiatric Association. (2013). *Diagnostic and statistical manual of mental disorders* (5th ed.). Washington, DC: American Psychiatric Association.

Asay, S. M., DeFrain, J., Metzger, M., & Moyer, B. (2016). Implementing a strengths-based approach to intimate partner violence worldwide. *Journal of Family Violence, 31*, 349–360.

Bervian, G., da Costa, M. C., da Silva, E. B., Arboit, J., & Honnef, F. (2019). Violence against rural women: Conceptions of professionals in the intersectoral network of care. *Enfermería Global, 18*(2), 168–179.

Chao, S. F. (2016). Outdoor activities and depressive symptoms in displaced older adults following natural disaster: Community cohesion as mediator and moderator. *Aging & Mental Health, 20*(9), 940–947. doi: 10.1080/13607863.2015.1044940

Chavan, B., Sahni, S., Das, S., & Sidana, A. (2017). Concept of depression in rural community of Chandigarh. *Indian Journal of Social Psychiatry*, (3). Retrieved from http://search.ebscohost.com/login.aspx?direct=true&db=edsgao&AN=edsgcl.578164035&site=eds-live

Chen, Y. L., Hsu, W. Y., Lai, C. S., Tang, T. C., Wang, P. W., Yeh, Y. C., … Chen, C. S. (2015). One-year follow up of PTSD and depression in elderly aboriginal people in Taiwan after Typhoon Morakot. *Psychiatry and Clinical Neurosciences, 69*(1), 12–21. doi: 10.1111/pcn.12227

Crumb, L., Haskins, N., & Brown, S. (2019). Integrating social justice advocacy into mental health counseling in rural, impoverished American communities. *The Professional Counselor, 9*(1), 20–34.

Cuijpers, P., Sijbrandij, M., Koole, S. L., Andersson, G., Beekman, A. T., & Reynolds III, C. F. (2013). The efficacy of psychotherapy and pharmacotherapy in treating depressive and anxiety disorders: A meta-analysis of direct comparisons. *World Psychiatry, 12*(2), 137–148.

Dawson, K. S., Bryant, R. A., Harper, M., Kuowei Tay, A., Rahman, A., Schafer, A., & van Ommeren, M. (2015). Problem Management Plus (PM+): A WHO transdiagnostic psychological intervention for common mental health problems. *World Psychiatry, 14*(3), 354–357.

Dilley, M., Chen, R. S., Deichmann, U., Lerner-Lam, A. L., Arnold, M., Agwe, J., Buys, P., … Yetman, G. (2005). *The world bank hazard management Unit.* Retrieved from http://documents.worldbank.org/curated/en/621711468175150317/pdf/344230PAPER0Na101official0use0only1.pdf

Fairweather-Schmidt, A. K., Anstey, K. J., & Mackinnon, A. J. (2009). Is suicidality distinguishable from depression? Evidence from a community-based sample. *Australian & New Zealand Journal of Psychiatry, 43*(3), 208–215. doi: 10.1080/00048670802653331

Fortney, J. C. (2017). Practice-based versus telemedicine-based collaborative care for depression in rural federally qualified health centers: A pragmatic randomized comparative effectiveness trial. *Focus*, (3), 361. Retrieved from http://search.ebscohost.com/login.aspx?direct=true&db=edsbl&AN=RN612733841&site=eds-live

Fortney, J. C., Pyne, J. M., Edlund, M. J., Williams, D. K., Robinson, D. F., Mittal, D., & Henderson, K. L. (2007). A randomized trial of telemedicine-based collaborative care for depression. *JGIM: Journal of General Internal Medicine, 22*(8), 1086–1093. doi: 10.1007/s11606-007-0201-9

Handley, T. E., Inder, K. J., Kay-Lambkin, F. J., Stain, H. J., Fitzgerald, M., Lewin, T. J., … Kelly, B. J. (2012). Contributors to suicidality in rural communities: Beyond the effects of depression. *BMC Psychiatry, 12*(1), 105–114. doi: 10.1186/1471-244X-12-105

Hirsch, J. K. (2006). A review of the literature on rural suicide: Risk and protective factors, incidence, and prevention. *CRISIS -TORONTO-*, (4), 189. Retrieved from http://search.ebscohost.com/login.aspx?direct=true&db=edsbl&AN=RN200871891&site=eds-live

Hoeft, T. J., Fortney, J. C., Patel, V., & Unutzer, J. (2018). Task-sharing approaches to improve mental health care in rural and other low-resource settings: A systematic review. *Journal of Rural Health, 34*(1), 48. doi: 10.1111/jrh.12229

Hsu, M., Howitt, R., & Miller, F. (2015). Procedural vulnerability and institutional capacity deficits in post-disaster recovery and reconstruction: Insights from Wutai Rukai experiences of Typhoon Morakot. *Human Organization, 74*(4), 308–318. doi: 10.17730/0018–7259–74.4.308

Ivers, N., Johnson, D. A., Clarke, P, B., Newsome, D. W., & Berry, R. A. (2016). The relationship between mindfulness and multicultural counseling competence. *The Journal of Counseling and Development, 94*(1), 72–82.

Ivey, A. E., Ivey, M. B., & Zalaquett, C. P. (2014). *Intentional interviewing and counseling: Facilitating client development in a multicultural society*. Belmont, CA: Brooks/Cole.

Jackson-Cherry, L. R., & Erford, B. T. (2018). *Crisis assessment, intervention and prevention* (3rd ed.). Upper Saddle River, NJ: Pearson Education.

Jha, A. K., Barenstein, J., Phelps, P. Pittet, D., & Sena, S. (2010). *Safer homes, stronger communities: A handbook for reconstructing after natural disasters*. World Bank Group. doi: 10.1596/978-0-8213-8045-1

Lin, J., & Lin, W. (2016). Cultural issues in post-disaster reconstruction: The case of Typhoon Morakot in Taiwan. *Disasters*, *40*(4), 668–692. doi: org/10.1111/disa.12172

Ministerio de Salud, Gobierno de Chile. (2013). Guía clínica AUGE. Depresión en personas de 15 años o más. *Serie Guías Clínicas MINSAL*, 26–28. Disponible en: http://www.minsal.cl/portal/url/item/7222754637c08646e04001011f014e64.pdf

Oyefara, O. O., Jegede, S., & Ojo, R. C. (2018). Rural-urban differentials in the prevalence and perception about determinants of domestic violence among couples in Lagos state, Nigeria. *IFE PsychologIA: An International Journal*, *26*(2), 114–128.

Peek-Asa, C., Wallis, A., Harland, K., Beyer, K., Dickey, P., & Saftlas, A. (2011). Rural disparity in domestic violence prevalence and access to resources. *Journal of Women's Health (15409996)*, *20*(11), 1743–1749. doi: 10.1089/jwh.2011.2891

Ragusa, A. T. (2017). Rurality's influence on women's intimate partner violence experiences and support needed for escape and healing in Australia. *Journal of Social Service Research*, *48*(2), 270–295.

Rojas, G., Guajardo, V., Martínez, P., Castro, A., Fritsch, R., Moessner, M., & Bauer, S. (2018). A remote collaborative care program for patients with depression living in rural areas: Open-label trial. *Journal of Medical Internet Research*, *20*(4), 1. doi: 10.2196/jmir.8803

Solberg, L. I., Lauren Crain, A., Jaeckels, N., Ohnsorg, K. A., Margolis, K. L., Beck, A., … Van de Ven, A. H. (2013). The DIAMOND initiative: Implementing collaborative care for depression in 75 primary care clinics. *Implementation Science*, *8*(1), 1–23. doi: 10.1186/1748-5908-8-135

Sue, D. W., Sue, D., Neville, H., & Smith, L. (2019). *Counseling the culturally diverse: Theory and practice*. Hoboken, NJ: John Wiley & Sons.

Tol, W. A., Greene, M. C., Likindikoki, S., Misinzo, L., Ventevogel, P., Bonz, A. G., … Mbwambo, J. K. (2017). An integrated intervention to reduce intimate partner violence and psychological distress with refugees in low-resource settings: Study protocol for the Nguvu cluster randomized trial. *BMC Psychiatry*, *17*(1), 186. doi: 10.86/s12888-007-1338-7.

Tomlinson-Clarke, S. M., & Georges, C. M. (2014). DSM-5: A commentary on integrating multicultural and strength-based considerations into counseling training and practice. *The Professional Counselor*, *4*(3), 272–281.

Tonsing, J. C. (2016). Domestic violence: Intersection of culture, gender and context. *Journal of Immigrant Minority Health*, 18, 442–446. doi: 10.1007/s10903-015-0193-1.

Vanderlip, E. R., Rundell, J., Avery, M., Alter, C., Engel, C., Fortney, J., & Williams, M. (2016). *Dissemination of integrated care within adult primary care settings: The collaborative care model*. Washington, DC: American Psychiatric Association and Academy of Psychosomatic Medicine.

Woltmann, E. (2013). Comparative effectiveness of collaborative chronic care models for mental health conditions across primary, specialty, and behavioral health care settings: Systematic review and meta-analysis. *Focus-American Psychiatric Publishing Inc*, *4*, 552. Retrieved from http://search.ebscohost.com/login.aspx?direct=true&db=edsbl&AN=RN343318971&site=eds-live

World Health Organization (WHO). (2017, November 29). *Violence against women*. Retrieved from https://www.who.int/en/news-room/fact-sheets/detail/violence-against-women

World Health Organization (WHO). (2018, March 22). *Depression*. Retrieved from https://www.who.int/en/news-room/fact-sheets/detail/depression

World Health Organization (WHO). (2019, April 30). *Mental health gap action programme (mhGAP)*. Retrieved from https://www.who.int/mental_health/mhgap/en/

Wriggins, J. (2018). Domestic violence and gender equality: Recognition, remedy, and (possible) retrenchment. *University of Toledo Law Review*, *49*(3), 617–629.

Wu, H. C. (2014). Protectors of Indigenous adolescents' post-disaster adaptation in Taiwan. *Clinical Social Work Journal*, *42*(4), 357–365. doi: 10.1007/s10615-013-0448-z

Xiong, C. Z., Hao, H. J., Liong, C. W., Loon, C. W., Chenn, K. S., Kai, S., … bin Yaacob, M. J. (2016). Prevalence of post traumatic stress disorder (PTSD) among flood victims in Malaysia: Difference between Kuala Lumpur and Kelantan. *International Medical Journal*, *23*(2), 114–117.

Zorn, K., Wuerch, M. A., Faller, N., & Hampton, M. R. (2017). Perspectives on regional differences and intimate partner violence in Canada: A qualitative examination. *Journal of Family Violence*, *32*, 633–644.

7 Wildlife

Exploring the potential of an innovative digital narrative approach to improve mental health interventions for adolescents in indigenous rural populations of low- to middle-income countries

Mark Grindle and Johannes H. De Kock

Introduction

In Chapter 6, Ikonomopoulos, Liang, Furgerson, and Garza argued that the lack of mental health resources and referral opportunities in rural areas necessitates more in-depth counselling and therapy. They illustrated how mental health professionals working with rural communities and populations must become aware of the best treatments available. These can be costly to deliver and new approaches to mental health interventions for rural areas are needed. Online therapies are available increasingly and evidence is emerging about the potential of mixed reality (MR) as a clinical and therapeutic tool for mental health treatment. In this chapter, we consider *Wildlife: South Africa* – a case study in the deployment of an innovative digital narrative approach (DNA) to online and blended behaviour change interventions and therapies. Comparative work took place under the auspices of the same project at related sites *Wildlife*: *Myanmar* and *Wildlife: India.*

This chapter first considers rural mental health from an international comparative perspective by contrasting South Africa's (SA) mental health workforce to the other low- and middle-income countries (LMICs) included in the study and then to the high-income countries (HICs) discussed in this book. This illuminates how rurality and mental health interact to create risk but also opportunity for innovative mental health care in rural LMICs. We argue that there is a need for more innovative approaches and cite the use of DNA as one such approach to address the global implications of rural mental health.

Background

The global burden of mental illness

As discussed elsewhere in this volume, neuropsychiatric conditions, including mental illness, constitute approximately 13% of the global burden of disease, making them the official third largest cause of disability in the world (World Health Organization, 2013a). With life expectancy rising, populations aging, and mortality rates waning, it is argued that non-lethal outcomes of diseases are becoming a larger component of the global burden of disease and that current appraisals vastly underestimate the burden of mental illness (Vigo, Thornicroft, & Atun, 2016, Whiteford et al., 2013).

Mental illness is responsible for 30% of disability-adjusted life-years (DALYs), the disability component of the burden of disease calculation (World Health Organization, 2012a). New estimates place mental illness first in burden of disease when considered in terms of years lived with disabilities (YLDs), and on a par with circulatory and cardiovascular diseases in terms of DALYs (Vigo et al., 2016). The global need for the treatment of mental illness and associated YLDs and DALYs outweighs the current capacity to provide appropriate services dramatically. According to the World Health Organization (WHO), the global shortage of mental health care professionals is dire (Shah & Beinecke, 2009, World Health Organization, 2012b). Worldwide, the treatment gap for mental illness is undisputable, with 85% of people in LMICs and between 35% and 50% of people in HICs living with severe mental disorders receiving no medical intervention (WHO, 2012a). While these figures suggest that mental illness is affecting a vast proportion of the global population, it is clear that LMICs carry the heaviest burden of mental illness (Bruckner et al., 2011; World Health Organization, 2013c, 2017b).

Mental illness in LMICs and HICs: a comparative perspective

The most recent WHO's ATLAS report for mental health (WHO, 2017b) indicates immense disparities between LMICs and HICs in mental health system governance and financial and human resources for health and mental health service availability (Bruckner et al., 2011): By 2014, over 75% of HICs had stand-alone laws for treating and preventing mental illness, contrasted to the less than 10% of LMICs in Africa who had these laws in place (World Health Organization, 2015). Government mental health expenditure per capita in the European region and other HICs are more than 20 times higher than that in the LMICs in the African and South East Asian Regions. This translates to people with less disposable income having to pay more for mental health services (WHO, 2017b). While the global median of mental health workers per 100,000 population remained at 9 between 2014 to 2017, the discrepancy between LMICs and HICs is widening. HICs have 71.7 mental health workers per 100,000 population compared to 1.6 in low-income countries. The same trend is observed in regional classifications where the median number of mental health workers per 100,000 population in Europe is 50 compared to that of countries in Africa and South East Asia at 0.9 and 2.5 per 100,000 population respectively (WHO, 2017b). This brief examination of comparative access to mental health services exposes the mental health resource crisis faced by LMICs, especially those in the WHO Africa and South East Asia

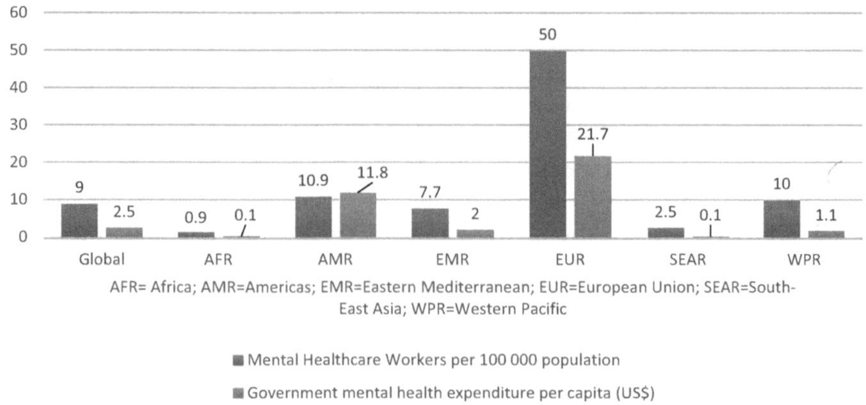

Figure 7.1 Comparison of mental health care workers per 100,000 population and government mental health expenditure per capita by region.

regions. The three LMICs included in our study – Myanmar, India, and SA – fall within these sparsely resourced regions. Figure 7.1 provides an overview of the mental health workforce per population, and government expenditure per capita by WHO region.

South-East Asia and Africa: regions with a dearth of mental health resources

South-East Asia

With over a quarter of the world's population, South-East Asia has a disproportionately large share of the global disease burden for mental disorders (World Health Organization, 2013b). This area is made up of 11 countries, all belonging to the LMIC World Bank classification and with substantial challenges to mental health care delivery. The vast majority of mental health care professionals in the South-East Asia region are confined to a limited number of urban tertiary-care mental hospitals (Anwar & Thamarangsi, 2017). The limited reach is evidenced by a treatment gap in this region of between 76% and 90% for patients with neurological and mental disorders (Demyttenaere et al., 2001; World Health Organization, 2013d). Despite WHO (2013a) endorsed programmes to integrate mental health into already existing primary care health facilities, major challenges with regard to mental health legislation, widespread prejudice, and stigma persist, hindering progress. The high morbidity and low mortality associated with mental health disorders furthermore detract from donor support and government expenditure prioritisation (Anwar & Thamarangsi, 2017).

Despite overwhelming supportive evidence of the efficacy of integrating mental health services into primary care in this region (WHO, 2013d), this amalgamation remains only an ambition for most of the area. The most notable lack of mental health human resource is that of mental health specialists with numbers of psychiatrists and psychologists falling well below that of the global norm (WHO, 2017b). The ambition of integrating mental health with primary care necessitated a paradigm shift in the training of health professionals. The focus has been on training non-specialists to deliver care in primary care settings that specialists would have delivered in tertiary healthcare settings (World Health Organization, 2008). Even though governments have partially subscribed to this WHO-endorsed task-shifting approach to mental health care, significant shortfalls remain within mental health human resources in these settings (Anwar & Thamarangsi, 2017). India and Myanmar have, for example, respectively only 0.8 and 0.32 mental health nurses per 100,000 population compared to the 90 and 122 that Australia and Scotland have, correspondingly. Table 7.1 indicates the comparative dearth of relevant, efficacious, and accessible mental health human resources in India and Myanmar, two countries in this South-East Asia region, compared to other selected countries discussed in this book.

Africa

The African region, with its high concentration of LMICs, endures arguably the highest disease burden of mental illness in the world, accounting for a fifth of all disability in this continent (WHO, 2013b). In this region, as in the South-East Asia region between 85% and 90% of people suffering from mental illness do not receive medical treatment for their conditions (World Health Organization, 2013c). This, together with the WHO expectation that the disease burden of mental disorders is likely to increase on this continent, is disconcerting for public health policy makers in this region (WHO, 2012a).

South Africa (SA), like other African countries, faces mental health workforce shortages and socio-economical risk factors likely to increase rates of mental illness. SA furthermore faces higher rates of tuberculosis, maternal and child mortality, and communicable and non-communicable diseases in comparison to countries with similar World Bank income group classification (Bradshaw, 2008). Non-communicable diseases, including mental illness, have been linked to poverty and deprivation, and in SA its impact is immense (Ataguba, Day, & Mcintyre, 2015), accounting for around 35% of years of life lost (Massyn et al., 2014). In this region, poverty, unemployment, and the impact of the HIV/AIDS pandemic increase the risk and burden of neuropsychiatric disease markedly (Hanass-Hancock, 2009; Vlassova, Angelino, & Treisman, 2009).

Out of SA's population of 53 million people, 11% are living with HIV/AIDS and more than half the population live below the poverty line. The damaging social impact due to the mortality and morbidity caused by HIV/AIDS is enormous with the occurrence of child-headed households increasing. This, together with underdeveloped social care systems, increases the risk of intergenerational mental illness (Karim & Karim, 2010; Patel & Kleinman, 2003). In SA, it is estimated that approximately half of the population live in rural areas (Kok & Collinson, 2006; Lehohla, 2013a; Reid, Couper, & Nobel, 2002), and that 75% of poor South Africans live in these settings (Reid, 2006). The psychosocial difficulties associated with poverty have been evidenced as having a direct positive correlation with vulnerability to mental illness (Patel & Kleinman, 2003; Skeen, Lund, Kleintjes, Flisher, & Consortium, 2010). Compounding these risk factors, SA and the wider African region face an unequal distribution of mental health workers, with the majority centred in urban areas (De Kock & Pillay, 2018; Vergunst, 2018).

SA is, however, one of the only LMICs in the African region with reliable estimates of the rural mental health workforce. The findings of a recent audit in the country (De Kock & Pillay, 2018) suggest severe discrepancies between the national mental health workforce and the rural mental health workforce.

The drive towards primary healthcare and task-shifting

As in the South-East Asian region, the South African Government has adopted the WHO-endorsed approach (WHO, 2013d) of integrating mental health services into the primary healthcare (PHC) system – the system that is accessible to rural populations (Vergunst, 2018). Since 1994, SA's governmental health policy drive towards inclusivity has motivated the move towards PHC. The adoption of the *White Paper for the Transformation of the Health System* (1997b), followed by the *National Health Policy Guidelines* for improved Mental Health in South Africa (1997a), underlined the government's commitment towards shifting mental health treatment to the PHC level.

With regard to ensuring mental health human resources, SA has been struggling, with lower workforce numbers than that of many LMICs (Burns, 2011). Table 7.1 shows SA's mental health human resources compared to those of the other countries discussed in this book. The consequence of the lack of human resources for mental health is that the country's highly acclaimed human rights–based Mental Health Care Act serves merely as an unattainable ambition in rural settings: it is seen as a prime example of a health policy, aiming to improve access to care at PHC level, that through being too complicated and human resource heavy becomes undeliverable in rural settings (Versteeg & Couper, 2011). The problematical implementation of the primary mental health care model in a rural SA has been assessed to be "fraught with complications" leading to overburdened rural healthcare professionals (De Kock & Pillay, 2018) falling back on or adopting an overly medicalised approach to mental health care (Burgess, 2016) in these settings.

It is in SA's rural primary care areas where mental health shortages are the greatest (Lund, Petersen, Kleintjes, & Bhana, 2012; Petersen, Lund, Bhana, & Flisher, 2012). The implementation of SA's innovative, person-centred PHC service has unfortunately been sporadic: in the 40+ years, that have now passed since the famous PHC-centred Alma Ata conference (Kautzky &

Tollman, 2008; World Health Organization, 1978), accessible mental health for all has not been achieved in rural settings. Across all cadres, SA's rural areas are falling short of the global mental health workforce benchmarks (WHO, 2017b), having in total only 1.55 mental health professionals per 100,000 population (De Kock & Pillay, 2018). Table 7.2 depicts SA's national mental health workforce compared to its rural workforce and to that of other World Bank income group classifications.

In an effort to alleviate workforce shortages in rural settings, SA, just like countries in the South-East Asia region, has started to implement the WHO-endorsed strategy of task-shifting (WHO, 2008). As we will see in the next section, implementing task-shifting approaches are complex in SA's rural settings – largely due to the dearth of available healthcare providers to whom the tasks of the specialists can be shifted. The next section of this chapter provides historical context and then moves on to evidence the lack of mental health specialists in SA's rural settings in terms of psychiatrists (De Kock & Pillay, 2017) and clinical psychologists (De Kock & Pillay, 2016b). It then focuses on WHO-endorsed solutions to mental health specialist shortages by illustrating the case of mental health nurses (De Kock & Pillay, 2016a) – earmarked as the cadre to whom many of the specialists' tasks are to be shifted.

Psychiatrists

As SA was becoming a democracy in 1994, its psychiatric services were restricted to a hospital-centric approach and limited to metropolitan areas (Emsley, 2001). While SA's psychiatry training programmes are held in high international regard, the services offered by psychiatrists are only accessible by an exclusive portion of its population – those able to afford it. It is estimated that by 1994, more than 30 million South Africans were dependent on the public health system (Council for Medical Schemes, 2014). Less than 170 psychiatrists were practicing there at the time (CFMS, 2014) and fewer than 5% worked in rural settings, which, at that point, comprised the majority of SA's population (Allwood, 1997; Kok & Collinson, 2006; Reid et al., 2002). At the advent of SA's democracy, the drive to integrate mental health into the country's PHC system was initiated (Allwood, 1997; Emsley, 2001; Freeman, 1998). Today there are 762 psychiatrists registered in SA (Health Professions Council South Africa, 2013), but only a total of seven psychiatrists are employed in rural public health facilities – a system that serves a population of over 17 million people (Kok and Collinson, 2006; Lehohla, 2013a, 2013b). Psychiatrists are therefore represented at a rate of 0.03 per 100,000 population in SA's public rural settings (De Kock & Pillay, 2017). Furthermore, over 60% of rural public health facilities receive no monthly psychiatric outreach by a psychiatrist (De Kock & Pillay, 2017). As a stop-gap, 63 medical doctors dedicated to mental health are employed in rural public health facilities at a rate of 0.37 per 100,000 population.

Clinical psychologists

Psychology in SA has transformed since the dawn of the country's democracy in 1994. SA's apartheid political system left social inequality and a disproportionate distribution of resources with the majority of psychologists practicing in the private sector in urban settings (Pillay & Petersen, 1996). At this time, the profession of psychology faced a crisis of applicability – utilising Western-based psychological theory and practice in a country where most of the population is African. This profession therefore faced not only a human resource dilemma but also a practical one: how was the profession of psychology to serve a population with a demographically diverse society if they are utilising Eurocentric approaches to care and treatment (Rock & Hamber, 1994)? With the shift towards integrating psychology into the PHC system in 1994, it was clear that these challenges of relevance and accessibility needed to be addressed. By 1994, SA had practically no psychologists working in rural PHC settings. The establishment of human resources for psychology within PHC system was, therefore, seen as a priority, and clinical psychologists were regarded as the appropriate professionals to provide this resource as they already assess, diagnose, and treat relatively serious forms of psychopathology in medical settings (Forum, 1993). Over the last 25 years SA has made some effort to provide this human resource in its rural settings: SA currently employs 81 clinical psychologists, at a rate of 0.47 per 100,000 rural population. This figure remains well below the international criteria set for quality of care (World Health Organization, 2011). This figure, albeit indicative of some improvements, suggests that the relevance and accessibility dilemma of psychology services in SA, especially for people living in rural settings, have not yet adequately been addressed. The issue of cultural relevance has even far-reaching implications and should be seen as on par with accessibility of services (De Kock & Pillay, 2016b). The critical importance of cultural sensitivity and relevance in the provision of mental health services and policies are discussed below.

Mental health nurses

In SA, nurses are regarded as the backbone of the health sector, making up the majority of the human resources for health (South African Nursing Council, 2013). WHO (2011) estimates suggest that SA has a ratio of 9.7 nurses trained in mental health per 100,000 population. The discrepancy between this figure and the fact that this cadre is practicing at a rate of only 0.68 per 100,000 population in SA's public rural facilities (De Kock & Pillay, 2016a) indicates the severe shortage of mental health care professionals in rural SA. Table 7.3 summarises SA's mental health workforce in rural settings per province.

Due to the lack of psychiatrists and clinical psychologists in SA (WHO, 2017b), especially in its rural areas (De Kock & Pillay, 2018), the treatment of mental illness at rural PHC-level falls onto the shoulders of understaffed medical doctors and mental health nurses (Petersen et al., 2012). The previous section elucidated the shortage of these professionals.

Attempts to de-centralise mental health care to speciality-trained PHC nurses have been falling short of the set benchmarks (Petersen & Lund, 2011). While worthwhile arguments are made for the adoption of widespread task-shifting in SA's rural settings (De Kock, 2016; Vergunst, 2018), the training of cadres of healthcare professionals (De Kock & Pillay, 2018) to whom such tasks can be shifted is much slower than the proportional population growth rate in SA (Lehohla, 2013a, 2013b). Other than this practical critique of the task-shifting approach, one has to consider the cultural relevance of addressing rural African health inequalities from a Western biomedical (Vergunst, 2018) and Eurocentric psychological (De Kock & Pillay, 2016b) perspective. Further, culturally sensitive innovation is proposed to alleviate the rural mental health workforce crisis.

Applicable and relevant innovation through necessity

Despite its rural mental health workforce crisis, SA has, over the last quarter of a century, been on the cutting edge of developing novel healthcare policies. Necessity has long been regarded as a motivator for healthcare innovation (Miller & French, 2016), and it can be argued that this has fuelled SA's innovative strategies. The implementation problems associated with these strategies in rural areas may not only be due to workforce shortages but also to the narrow, biomedical, and Western-based psychological approaches to populations that largely subscribe to more traditional, African worldviews (Kirmayer & Swartz, 2013; Vergunst, 2018). The shifting of tasks from psychiatrist to mental health nurse would mainly be prescribing psychotropic medication (WHO, 2008). In the same vain, the shifting of tasks from clinical psychologists to mental health nurses, social workers, or clinical associates runs the risk of being boxed into the managed care formula of cognitive therapies associated with, and developed in conjunction with, the Western biomedical approaches to mental health care (Meichenbaum, 2014). African scholars argue for the inclusion of culture (Kirmayer & Swartz, 2013) when it comes to treating mental illness in rural settings (Musyimi, Mutiso, Nandoya, & Ndetei, 2016), in keeping with the dominant narrative, ideology, or worldview of that culture (Burns & Tomita, 2015).

In Chapter 6, Ikonomopoulos, Liang, Furgerson, and Garza advocated the delivery of cognitive behavioural treatment (CBT) and dialectical behaviour therapy (DBT) in rural areas in America. They argued for the rural healthcare worker's sensitivity to the most relevant of efficacious treatment modalities which, in their case study, was in-depth counselling and individual therapy. However, where approaches like CBT and DBT may be appropriate in America's rural settings, it may not be as relevant in SA's rural settings. With the majority of rural South Africans describing themselves as being African (Lehohla, 2013a, 2013b), the focus of their internal and external life will more likely be centred on local geographical community (Nwoye, 2006) than that of their Western counterparts. African psychology is centred around the community narrative (Mkhize, 2004), and approaches that take this into account will be likely to be more culturally relevant and, therefore, more applicable and accessible.

The inclusion of the wider community in mental health interventions is emphasised as crucial in rural health contexts (Musyimi et al., 2016). Thus, culturally sensitive interventions may be more likely to lead to healing and social integration, associated with positive outcomes and recovery of mental health disorders in African contexts (Kirmayer & Swartz, 2013). The risks of emphasising professional, Western-based mental health interventions may undervalue indigenous forms of helping and healing in SA's rural settings, and could be seen as an impediment of integrating mental health care successfully into the PHC system (Kirmayer & Swartz, 2013).

Blending realities to improve adolescent mental health

While it is argued that the scale-up of biomedical services could marginalise more traditional, community-engaged healing (Cooper, 2016), several successful cultural adaptions of psychosocial interventions across settings and mental disorders have been made (Degnan et al., 2018). When done successfully, participants were included in intervention design – allowing a blend of empirical knowledge with community preference. A prime example of a case in which this method is being advocated is the WHO's recent guidance on the global accelerated action for health of adolescents (WHO, 2017a).

The WHO suggests that the principle of positive development be used in the treatment and prevention of adolescent mental health disorders. It is centred on the premise that adolescents should not be seen only as a problematic group to treat but rather as a population group capable of transforming the societies in which they live (World Health Organization, 2001). This requires a paradigm shift away from the conventional top-down public health approach of risk and protective factors, towards seeing adolescents as societal assets whose contributions can be nurtured through engagement and participation. It is suggested that adolescent participation in intervention design would promote their sense of competence, confidence, and community connection, while developing their capacity for caring by increasing their sense of belonging (WHO, 2017a).

With self-harm ranking as the second highest global cause of death for older adolescents, depressive disorders the third largest cause of adolescent DALYs lost globally, and anxiety disorders the fifth largest cause of DALYs lost among adolescent girls, adolescent mental health interventions have never before had such a high priority on the WHO's Global Strategy for Women's, Children's and Adolescents' Health (Kuruvilla et al., 2016). Furthermore, the WHO rates adolescents who are living in remote areas as "particularly vulnerable" and suggests the roll-out of adolescent-friendly, participatory e-health and m-health services in these settings.

In the previous sections we highlighted that scaling-up strategies and even novel task-shifting approaches alone would prove to be inadequate to meet the mental health needs of SA's rural population, if they remain based on current orthodoxies. We highlighted not only how SA's health policy makers, but also SA's mental health services, were struggling with issues of accessibility and relevance in rural SA. In order for SA to address the mental health crisis at rural, primary care level, it requires more innovative strategies and approaches. In the next sections of the chapter, we turn to consider one such innovative approach.

DNA: an innovative digital narrative approach

First advanced as The Digital Narrative Transformation Framework (Grindle, 2014) the DNA to health behaviour change sits at the core of the Wildlife project and could be beneficial in enhancing adolescent mental health. DNA is an innovative, interdisciplinary approach to health behaviour change that is achieved via emotional engagement. The emotional and therapeutic power of storytelling, health behaviour change theory, evidence-based behaviour change techniques, and key messages are used within DNA in order to engage participants of any age across health outcomes within and across local, national, and international boundaries. It is an applied, creative professional approach and has previously engaged parents of children with cystic fibrosis to motivate adherence to chest physiotherapy, patients with acute coronary syndrome to motivate faster responses to acute coronary syndrome symptoms, and adult women to motivate smoking cessation during pregnancy. In a more recent randomised feasibility trial, DNA was used to engage and motivate obese participants from disadvantaged communities in Scotland (within urban and rural areas) over 12 months to help them lose weight (Grindle et al., in press). This digital storytelling approach can bring participants and their stories to the fore. Interventions or services based on this approach will likely engage participants and transform behaviour accordingly.

Wildlife is an MR interactive adventure for adolescents that is currently in development. It is played out in virtual and real-world international locations. Wildlife utilises technology and storytelling to enhance participant-setting and human–animal interaction approaches advocated as conducive to mental health. This approach chimes with Philo and Parr's demonstration in Chapter 3, of the importance of "natural" – rural, scenic countryside – settings as conducive to the recovery of mental wellness and with Gorman's Chapter 7 exploration of human–animal relations in rural settings demonstrates the influence of non-humans in re-shaping the diverse processes of "becoming well".

A Scottish Funding Council grant (Global Challenges Research Fund) was secured to explore the power of DNA to address mental health concerns and promote economic growth in LMICs. SA, Myanmar, and India were selected as cases studies of LMICs with serious socio-economic risk factors for mental illness, where climate change, habitat loss, and the displacement of indigenous communities and biodiversity are key socio-economic concerns. Preliminary findings suggest that one way of innovating, and circumventing, the human resource crisis would be to utilise technology to reach rural communities. Digital technologies provide part of the solution as they can facilitate wider reach and accessibility of relevant treatments in remote and rural contexts. DNA's use of digital storytelling aligns with WHO recommendations (WHO, 2017a) for the treatment and prevention of adolescent mental health disorders in that it can be interactive and participatory in its design and delivery. DNA provides the ability to transport services between the therapist and the patient, across geographical time and place, but also to deepen the nature and quality of emotional engagement.

Taking DNA forward

Direct correlations between a country's adolescent mental health, its socio-economic and political stability, and its level of poverty are well established (Lund et al., 2011). Targeted adolescent mental health interventions are seen as crucial in creating and maintaining a country's good health and wellbeing, and are relevant to the UN's 2030 Agenda for Sustainable Development, as well as South Africa's Health Framework 2017–2020 (Vergunst, 2018).

Investing in adolescent mental health results in a quadruple dividend with benefits for adolescents, their future adult lives, their children, and their societies at large. In LMICs in particular an increase in adolescent mental well-being is postulated to result in declines in both mortality and fertility rates, bringing societal transformation and economic growth with it (Bureau, 2012).

Adolescents in LMICs and areas like rural SA, India, and Myanmar are facing disproportionate challenges keeping them from thriving and contributing positively towards their societies (WHO, 2017a). As evidenced in this chapter, and throughout this book, human resources for mental health remain a major obstacle for achieving health equity in rural and remote settings. The UN's (Kuruvilla et al., 2016) and WHO's (WHO, 2017a) drive towards a paradigm shift in the treatment and care of global adolescent mental health is towards participatory intervention design and delivery. The DNA for health behaviour change is proposed as an intervention that utilises technology to alleviate the mental health workforce shortage in rural settings but one that also incorporates participatory intervention design.

Making use of a DNA for health behaviour change in each of these territories could be beneficial in enhancing adolescent mental health and supporting Indigenous people to tell their story. By exploring the potential for interventions like Wildlife in specific rural contexts internationally, we might help support the development of more relevant and accessible therapeutic services.

Table 7.1 Comparative mental health human resources: selected countries' national averages per 100,000 population[a]

	Population	Psychologists	MHNs	Psychiatrists	Total mental health workers
		Rate	Rate	Rate	Rate
Aus	23,799,556	103.04	90.58	13.53	214.81
Can	35,151,728	48.7	68.7	14.7	285.90
Ind	1,309,053,980	0.07	0.80	0.29	1.93
Mya	52,403,669	0.0	0.32	0.38	1.20
Scot	5 425 686	15.4[b]	122	10[c]	UN
SA	53,291,225	2.6[d]	9.72	1.52	UN
USA	319,929,162	29.86	4.28	10.54	271.28

Aus=Australia, Can=Canada, Ind=India, Mya=Myanmar, Scot=Scotland, SA=South Africa, USA =United States of America. UN=Unknown, MHN=Mental Health Nurse

a World Health Organization. (2017). Mental Health Atlas 2017 World Health Organization, 1–74.

b National Statistics. (2018). Psychology Services Workforce in Scotland. Scotland: NHS, 1–2.

c Kmietowicz, Z. (2017). Access to psychiatrists varies widely across UK, royal college says. *BMJ, 358*, j4211.

d Day, C., & Gray, A. (2014). South African Health Review 2013/2014. In: A. Padarath & R. English (Eds.), SA Health Systems Trust, pp. 201–345.

Table 7.2 SA's mental health workforce compared to that of LMICs and other high MICs per 100,000 population[a,b]

MH Professionals per selected cadre per 100,000 population across healthcare settings				
	LMIC Average (WHO, 2017b)	*High MIC Average[c]*	*SA National Average[d]*	*SA Rural*
Mental Health Professional				
Psychologist	0.26	1.89	2.6	0.47[e]
MHMD	0.21[f]	0.8	0.43	0.37[g]
MHN	1.43	6.83	9.72	0.68[h]
Psychiatrist	0.51	2.03	1.52	0.03

MIC=Middle Income Country, MHMD=MH Medical Doctor (not specialised in psychiatry, but dedicated to MH), MHN=Mental Health Nurse

a World Health Organization. (2011). Mental Health Atlas 2011. World Health Organization, 1–53.

b De Kock, J. H., & Pillay, B. J. (2018). South Africa's rural mental health human resource crisis: A situation analysis and call for innovative task-shifting. *Family Medicine & Primary Care Review*, 124–130.

c World Health Organization. (2017). Mental Health Atlas 2017. World Health Organization, 1–74.

d Day, C., & Gray, A. (2014). South African Health Review 2013/2014. In: A. Padarath & R. English (Eds.). SA Health Systems Trust, pp. 201–345.

e De Kock, J. H., & Pillay, B. J. (2016b). A situation analysis of clinical psychology services in South Africa's public rural primary care settings. *South African Journal of Psychology, 47*, 260–270.

f World Health Organization. (2015). Mental Health Atlas 2014. World Health Organization, 1–82.

g De Kock, J. H., & Pillay, B. J. (2017). A situation analysis of psychiatrists in South Africa's rural primary healthcare settings. *African Journal of Primary Health Care & Family Medicine, 9*, 1–6.

h De Kock, J. H., & Pillay, B. J. (2016a). Mental health nurses in South Africa's public rural primary care settings: A human resource crisis. *Rural Remote Health, 16*, 3865.

Table 7.3 South Africa's rural population sizes, health facilities, and selected mental health human resources and rates per 100,000 population

	*Rural Population reliant on PRPHC health facilities**		*Clinical Psychologists*[a]		*MHMDs*[b]		*MHNs*[c]		*Psychiatrists*[d]		*Total MHC Providers*	
	Population	*Facilities (N)*	*N*	*Rate*	*N*	*Rate*	*N*	*Rate*	*N*	*Rate*	*N*	*Rate*
Total	17,143,872	160	81	0.47	63	0.37	116	0.68	7	0.03	266	1.55

MHMD=Mental Health Medical Doctor (not specialised in psychiatry, but dedicated to Mental Health), MHN=Mental Health Nurse, MHC=Mental Health Care

* The rural population making use of the public health sector was obtained by calculating the health centres included in audit populations, as well as affiliated satellite clinics' population.

a De Kock, J. H., & Pillay, B. J. (2016b). A situation analysis of clinical psychology services in South Africa's public rural primary care settings. *South African Journal of Psychology, 47*, 260–270.

b De Kock, J. H., & Pillay, B. J. (2017). A situation analysis of psychiatrists in South Africa's rural primary healthcare settings. *African Journal of Primary Health Care & Family Medicine, 9*, 1–6.

c De Kock, J. H., & Pillay, B. J. (2016a). Mental health nurses in South Africa's public rural primary care settings: A human resource crisis. *Rural Remote Health, 16*, 3865.

d De Kock, J. H., & Pillay, B. J. (2018). South Africa's rural mental health human resource crisis: A situation analysis and call for innovative task-shifting. *Family Medicine & Primary Care Review, 2*, 124–130.

References

Allwood, C. (1997). Psychiatry in South Africa-yesterday, today and tomorrow. *South African Medical Journal = Suid-Afrikaanse Tydskrif Vir Geneeskunde, 87*, 1728–1731.

Anwar, N., & Thamarangsi, T. (2017). Care for mental disorders and promotion of mental well-being in South-East Asia. *WHO South-East Asia Journal of Public Health, 6*, 1.

Ataguba, J. E., Day, C., & Mcintyre, D. (2015). Explaining the role of the social determinants of health on health inequality in South Africa. *Global Health Action, 8*, 28865.

Bradshaw, D. (2008). Determinants of health and their trends: Primary health care: In context. *South African Health Review, 2008*, 51–69.

Bruckner, T. A., Scheffler, R. M., Shen, G., Yoon, J., Chisholm, D., Morris, J., … Saxena, S. (2011). The mental health workforce gap in low-and middle-income countries: A needs-based approach. *Bulletin of the World Health Organization, 89*, 184–194.

Bureau, P. R. (2012). *The challenge of attaining the demographic dividend. Policy brief.* Washington, DC: Population Reference Bureau, 1.

Burgess, R. A. (2016). Policy, power, stigma and silence: Exploring the complexities of a primary mental health care model in a rural South African setting. *Transcultural Psychiatry, 53*, 719–742.

Burns, J. K. (2011). The mental health gap in South Africa–A human rights issue. *Equal Rights Review, 6*, 99–113.

Burns, J. K., & Tomita, A. (2015). Traditional and religious healers in the pathway to care for people with mental disorders in Africa: A systematic review and meta-analysis. *Social Psychiatry and Psychiatric Epidemiology, 50*, 867–877.

Cooper, S. (2016). *Global mental health and its critics: Moving beyond the impasse*. Oxford: Taylor & Francis.

Council for Medical Schemes (CFMS). (2014). *Public sector dependent population*, Hatfield, Pretoria: Council for Medical Schemes. Retrieved from http://www.medicalschemes.com.

Day, C., & Gray, A. (2014). *South African Health Review 2013/2014*: SA Health Systems Trust, 201–345. Retrieved from http://www.hst.org.za/publications/south-african-health-review-201314.

De Kock, J. H. (2016). *Alleviating the mental health crisis in South Africa's rural primary care areas through task shifting: Non-medical prescribers and the case of clinical psychology*. Ph.D. doctoral, University of KwaZulu-Natal.

De Kock, J. H., & Pillay, B. J. (2016a). Mental health nurses in South Africa's public rural primary care settings: A human resource crisis. *Rural Remote Health*, *16*, 3865.

De Kock, J. H., & Pillay, B. J. (2016b). A situation analysis of clinical psychology services in South Africa's public rural primary care settings. *South African Journal of Psychology*, *47*, 260–270.

De Kock, J. H., & Pillay, B. J. (2017). A situation analysis of psychiatrists in South Africa's rural primary healthcare settings. *African Journal of Primary Health Care & Family Medicine*, *9*, 1–6.

De Kock, J. H., & Pillay, B. J. (2018). South Africa's rural mental health human resource crisis: A situation analysis and call for innovative task-shifting. *Family Medicine & Primary Care Review*, *2*, 124–130.

Degnan, A., Baker, S., Edge, D., Nottidge, W., Noke, M., Press, C. J., … Drake, R. J. (2018). The nature and efficacy of culturally-adapted psychosocial interventions for schizophrenia: A systematic review and meta-analysis. *Psychological Medicine*, *48*, 714–727.

Demyttenaere, K., Bruffaerts, R., Posada-Villa, J., Gasquet, I., Kovess, V., Lepine, J., … Kikkawa, T. (2001). Prevalence, severity, and unmet need for treatment of mental disorders in the World Health Organization World Mental Health Surveys. *JAMA*, *291*, 2581–2590.

Department of Health. (1997a). National health policy guidelines for improved mental health in South Africa, Directorate for mental health and substance abuse. Pretoria: Department of Health.

Department of Health. (1997b). White paper for the transformation of the health system in South Africa. *Government Gazette*, 382.

Dombrowski, S., U., McDonald, M., van der Pol, et al. (2020). Game of stones: Feasibility randomised controlled trial of how to engage men with obesity in narrative text message and incentive interventions for weight loss. *BMJ Open*, 10 (2). 10:e032653. doi: 10.1136/bmjopen-2019-032653.

Emsley, R. (2001). Focus on psychiatry in South Africa. *The British Journal of Psychiatry*, *178*, 382–386.

Forum. (1993). Summary report from the working group on relevance. In: A. Swart (Ed.). *Forum on the role and function of psychology in the New South Africa*, 2–4.

Freeman, M. (1998). Mental health service change. *South African Medical Journal = Suid-Afrikaanse Tydskrif Vir Geneeskunde*, *88*, 742–743.

Grindle, M. (2014). *The power of digital storytelling to influence human behaviour*. Doctoral, Stirling University.

Hanass-Hancock, J. (2009). Disability and HIV/AIDS-a systematic review of literature on Africa. *Journal of the International AIDS Society*, *12*, 34.

Health Professions Council South Africa (HPCSA). (2013). *Registration statistics for psychiatry.* [Accessed on: 13 March 2019].

Karim, S. A., & Karim, Q. A. (2010). *HIV/Aids in South Africa.* Cape Town: Cambridge University Press.

Kautzky, K., & Tollman, S. (2008). A perspective on primary health care in South Africa. *South African Health Review, 20*, 17–30.

Kirmayer, L. J., & Swartz, L. (2013). Culture and global mental health. In V. Patel, H. Minas, A. Cohen, & M. Prince (Eds.), *Global mental health: Principles and practice* (pp. 41–62). Oxford: Oxford University Press.

Kmietowicz, Z. (2017). Access to psychiatrists varies widely across UK, royal college says. *BMJ, 358*, j4211.

Kok, P., & Collinson, M. (2006). *Migration and urbanisation in South Africa.* Pretoria: Statistics South Africa (0621365092).

Kuruvilla, S., Bustreo, F., Kuo, T., Mishra, C. K., Taylor, K., Fogstad, H., ... Rasanathan, K. (2016). The global strategy for women's, children's and adolescents' health (2016–2030): A roadmap based on evidence and country experience. *Bulletin of the World Health Organization, 94*, 398.

Lehohla, P. (2013a). *Census 2011 Census in brief.* Pretoria: Statistics South Africa (03-01-41, 978-0-621–41388-5), 105.

Lehohla, P. (2013b). *Use of health facilities and levels of selected health conditions in South Africa: Findings from the General Household Survey, 2011.* Pretoria: Statistics South Africa (03–00–05 (2011), 978-0-621–41782-1), 1–114.

Lund, C., De Silva, M., Plagerson, S., Cooper, S., Chisholm, D., Das, J., ... Patel, V. (2011). Poverty and mental disorders: Breaking the cycle in low-income and middle-income countries. *The Lancet, 378*, 1502–1514.

Lund, C., Petersen, I., Kleintjes, S., & Bhana, A. (2012). Mental health services in South Africa: Taking stock. *African Journal of Psychiatry, 15*, 402–405.

Massyn, N., Day, C., Peer, N., Padarath, A., Barron, P., English, R. (2014). *District health barometer.* Durban: Health Systems Trust.

Meichenbaum, D. (2014). Evolution of cognitive behavior therapy: Origins, tenets, and clinical examples. In J. Zeig (Ed.), *The evolution of psychotherapy.* London: Routledge, 132–146.

Miller, F. A., & French, M. (2016). Organizing the entrepreneurial hospital: Hybridizing the logics of healthcare and innovation. *Research Policy, 45*, 1534–1544.

Mkhize, N. (2004). Psychology: An African perspective. In Ratele, K., Duncan, N., Hook, D., Mkhize, N., Kiguwa, P., Collins, A., eds., *Self, Community and Psychology*, 4-1 (Cape Town: UCT Press).

Musyimi, C. W., Mutiso, V. N., Nandoya, E. S., & Ndetei, D. M. (2016). Forming a joint dialogue among faith healers, traditional healers and formal health workers in mental health in a Kenyan setting: towards common grounds. *Journal of Ethnobiology and Ethnomedicine, 12*, 4.

National Statistics. (2018). *Psychology services workforce in Scotland.* Scotland: NHS, 49.

Nwoye, A. (2006). A narrative approach to child and family therapy in Africa. *Contemporary Family Therapy, 28*, 1–23.

Patel, V., & Kleinman, A. (2003). Poverty and common mental disorders in developing countries. *Bulletin of the World Health Organization, 81*, 609–615.

Petersen, I., & Lund, C. (2011). Mental health service delivery in South Africa from 2000 to 2010: One step forward, one step back. *South African Medical Journal = Suid-Afrikaanse Tydskrif Vir Geneeskunde, 101*, 751–757.

Petersen, I., Lund, C., Bhana, A., & Flisher, A. J. (2012). A task shifting approach to primary mental health care for adults in South Africa: Human resource requirements and costs for rural settings. *Health Policy and Planning, 27*, 42–51.

Pillay, Y., & Petersen, I. (1996). Current practice patterns of clinical and counselling psychologists and their attitudes to transforming mental health policies in South Africa. *South African Journal of Psychology, 26*, 76–80.

Reid, S. (2006). Rural health and transformation in South Africa: Opinion: SAMJ forum. *South African Medical Journal, 96*, 676–677.

Reid, S., Couper, I., & Nobel, V. (2002). Rural practice in South Africa. *Rural medicine*. New York: McGraw-Hill, 431Á448.

Rock, B., & Hamber, B. (1994). *Psychology in a future South Africa: The need for a national psychology development programme*. Johannesburg: South African Medical and Dental Council, 1–7.

Shah, A. A., & Beinecke, R. H. (2009). Global mental health needs, services, barriers, and challenges. *International Journal of Mental Health, 38*, 14–29.

Skeen, S., Lund, C., Kleintjes, S., Flisher, A., & Consortium, M. R. P. (2010). Meeting the millennium development goals in sub-Saharan Africa: What about mental health? *International Review of Psychiatry, 22*, 624–631.

South African Nursing Council (SANC). (2013). *The national strategic plan for nurse education, training and practice 2012/13–2016/17*. Pretoria: South African Nursing Council, 1–17.

Vergunst, R. (2018). From global-to-local: Rural mental health in South Africa. *Global Health Action, 11*, 1413916.

Versteeg, M., & Couper, I. (2011). *Position paper: Rural health-key to a healthy nation*. Johannesburg: Rural Health Advocacy Project, 1–3.

Vigo, D., Thornicroft, G., & Atun, R. (2016). Estimating the true global burden of mental illness. *The Lancet Psychiatry, 3*, 171–178.

Vlassova, N., Angelino, A. F., & Treisman, G. J. (2009). Update on mental health issues in patients with HIV infection. *Current Infectious Disease Reports, 11*, 163–169.

Whiteford, H. A., Degenhardt, L., Rehm, J., Baxter, A. J., Ferrari, A. J., Erskine, H. E., … Burstein, R. (2013). Global burden of disease attributable to mental and substance use disorders: Findings from the Global Burden of Disease Study 2010. *The Lancet, 382*, 1575–1586.

World Health Organization. (1978). *Alma Ata declaration*. World Health Organization, 1–11.

World Health Organization. (2001). *Broadening the horizon: Balancing protection and risk for adolescents*. World Health Organization, 1–9.

World Health Organization. (2008). *Task shifting: Rational redistribution of tasks among health workforce teams: Global recommendations and guidelines*. World Health Organization (92–4–159631-7, 1–82.

World Health Organization. (2011). *Mental health atlas 2011*. World Health Organization, 82.

World Health Organization. (2012a). *Global burden of mental disorders and the need for a comprehensive, coordinated response from health and social sectors at the country level*. Geneva: WHO, 1–7.

World Health Organization. (2012b). WHO launches the World Health Statistics 2012. *Euro Surveillance: Bulletin Europeen sur les maladies transmissibles = European Communicable Disease Bulletin, 17*, 1–164.

World Health Organization. (2013a). *Mental health action plan 2013–2020.* World Health Organization, 1–48.

World Health Organization. (2013b). *Mental health gap action programme.* Geneva: World Health Organization, 1–37.

World Health Organization. (2013c). Special focus: Launch of the mental health action plan 2013–2020. *Mental Health Gap Action Programme.*

World Health Organization. (2013d). *Strengthening primary care to address mental and neurological disorders.* World Health Organization, 1–80.

World Health Organization. (2015). *Mental health atlas 2014*, 1–82.

World Health Organization. (2017a). *Global accelerated action for the health of adolescents (AA-HA!).* World Health Organization, 1–176.

World Health Organization. (2017b). *Mental health atlas 2017.* World Health Organization, 1–72.

8 Rurality

Social forces, stress, and mental health

Robert Villa and Eva Moya

Introduction

Rural communities face significant challenges, including higher poverty rates and a drastic increase in substance abuse, particularly the manufacture and use of methamphetamines. Chronic poverty is more widespread in rural environments than in urban areas and particularly in more remote rural areas. Characteristically, they are geographically distant from centres of economic or political activity. This includes approximately two-thirds of the rural population of developing countries (Franco, 2008). Exacerbating the challenges faced in rural areas is the fact that social, health, and mental health services are often severely lacking.

As defined earlier in this volume, mental health is a state of wellbeing where the individual realises his/her own potential to cope with normal life stressors and be a productive member of society. Over 90 million individuals live in a mental health professional shortage area (MHPSA). In the United States, one in five adults is affected by mental health issues each year, with rural residents at greater risk of suffering due to the shortage of services in rural areas (Rural Health Information Hub, 2019).

Rural residents attempting to access effective treatment for serious mental health problems face multiple barriers. Firstly, the perceived stigma in small rural towns often leads to shame or embarrassment. Lack of privacy and anonymity results in people feeling uneasy that family or friends may find out or even that the provider could be a relative or acquaintance. A related issue is a shortage of mental health professionals in rural areas, which creates long waiting lists, a lack of provider choice, and increased cost. To low-income and disabled persons, the distance to service and lack of transportation are additional barriers. However, the lack of culturally competent care is one of the most salient issues in rural healthcare. Centralisation of services in urban areas further exacerbates access to equitable services (Rural Health Information Hub, 2019).

The diverse populations who inhabit rural towns, villages, and unincorporated areas in the United States are socially isolated, learn to depend on themselves, and are reluctant to acknowledge mental health issues.

Independence and self-reliance develop into survival values and resiliencies to cope with stress. These values are learned at a young age and are hard to modify, especially for older persons (Slama, 2004). Living in these environments, people are more inclined to use religion, non-traditional healers, and informal support networks as mental health interventions. This avoidance comes from their history of coping with their problems using faith, religion, and spiritual resiliencies/cultural strengths.

Current estimates of the Centers for Disease Control and Prevention show approximately 25% of adults in the United States have a mental illness or diagnosable mental disorder and close to one-half of all US adults at risk to experience at least one mental illness in their lifetime. At least 15 million rural residents struggle with substance abuse dependence, mental illness, and medical-psychiatric problems. The Department of Health and Human Services estimates that 20% of rural residents aged 55 and older have mental disorder and rural environments have significantly higher suicide rates (Wilson, Bangs, & Hatting, 2015).

Mental health is of utmost concern to the social work profession, the perspective from which this chapter's authors write. Evidence exists to support exposure to acute and chronic stressors, such as the effects of economic and social isolation, increases psychological distress. Economic policies affect rural mental health due to the distress associated with poverty, lack of job opportunities, and, more importantly, lack of good political representation. Economic hardship causes psychological stress at the individual level and subsequently affects the family and the community. How can we reach out to people who live in rural environments? One way is to look for strengths and resiliencies associated with attitudes, values, and a rural ideology (Hoyt, Conger, Valde, & Weihs, 1997).

Generalist practice with rural people and their communities is presented along a continuum of services from micro (individual), mezzo (family), and macro (community). Social workers in rural environments must often provide services based on the premise that not all people whose reality is rural live in rural areas. The first step to provide mental health services to rural populations is to define rural. The second step is to address cultural competence issues. Accordingly, a person who is socialised in a rural environment creates a world view that is internalised and remains part of their psychic and goes with them wherever they live (Daley, 2015).

A paradigm shift in cognitive and affective thought processes is needed to incorporate "rurality" and accept that rural people may move out of their rural community to an urban setting, but their rurality goes with them. Daley (2010, 2015) posits that rurality exists in the community and individual systems. Social workers interact with rural people regardless of where they live. To do this, the social worker has to have clinical and activist skills to provide competent services. This means the social worker must have a clear understanding of rurality and how it becomes part of the person regardless of the location at the time of intervention in order to better understand the person and complete a more accurate assessment (Villa, 2020).

Daley (2010, 2015) prefers a socio-cultural understanding of rural, instead of the traditional geographical/population and/or using census data to define rural as what is not urban or to define urban areas and consider what is left to be rural (Ratcliffe, Burd, Holder, & Fields, 2016). Daley's central arguments focus on cultural competence and cross-cultural social work practice using the same skill set regardless of urban and/or rural settings. He posits that the definition is based on how the profession defines and conceptualises rural social work.

Social forces, stress, and mental health

Social workers are clinical activists who understand the structural inequalities inherent in social and economic policies that negatively impact quality of life and wellbeing. Social systems in rural environments can be characterised by poverty, low educational attainment, low employment status, and marginalised social status. The diverse populations living within the world's rural areas are faced with environmental discrimination and political neglect that create stressful situations. In order to cope with the stress created by the intersectionality of social forces, a specialised way of thinking has developed a strong sense of spirituality and resiliencies at the individual, family, group, and communal levels. These resiliencies are part of the rurality ideology that transcends the typical rural/urban geographic boundaries defined by most government agencies (Villa, 2020).

Stress in rural environments can be associated with farming, adverse weather conditions, and financial problems. These rural stresses have been identified across many countries, including, for example, Northern Ireland where changing climate patterns, extreme weather, volatile markets, decline in rural services, increasing isolation, an aging population, and increasing debt levels are present. Increasing pressure in rural Scotland is blamed for breakup of families. Women, children, elderly, disabled, and the young are experiencing the effects of stress. The economic recession and cuts in services added to the stress endured by rural residents (McCann, 2014).

The rurality paradigm focuses on social forces to assess the impact they have on a client's self-image. These forces are in the client's environment and may be perceived as either positive or negative. The intersectionality of the environmental, economic, and political forces that work to shape a person's perspective is addressed. The combined effects of these forces are particularly devastating to populations whose histories are representative of the social injustices and lack of opportunities often present in their communities. The effects of living within these environments has a direct impact on the quality of life and wellbeing of rural individuals, families, and community systems. The effect is particularly critical when addressing the diverse needs of families that are marginalised based on nationality, ethnicity, citizenship status, religion, social class, language, and sexual orientation (Villa, 2020).

Political agendas that influence rurality create public policy in rural environments that are based on power relations that create the stress associated with lack of sustainable social and economic development in the United States and LMICs. A limited tax base results in lack of funding for programs and government expertise. The incapacity to attract outside resources further creates a dependency on limited resources (Morgannoel, 2017).

Globally, poverty has a rural face, with two-thirds of the world's poor defined as rural poor. The more geographically remote from centres of economic and political activity, the higher the prevalence of chronic poverty (Franco, 2008). A related issue that concerns economic and social policy is the association between depressive symptoms and the environment.

A series of interrelated factors create persistent poverty related to lack of resources, infrastructure, and educational systems. Corruption and lack of judicial systems that protect property rights and related social justice issues are prevalent in LMICs. The World Bank estimated that approximately 736 million persons lived in extreme poverty in 2015 (Wadhwa, 2018).

Environmental inequality is an important social justice issue framed as discrimination that often leads to the placing of hazardous industries in rural areas. Increased feelings of powerlessness/helplessness are important predictors of psychological distress. They are also related to industrial activity, perceptions of neighbourhood disorder, and violation of neighbourhood norms. This leads to increased levels of psychological distress caused by constant reminders of living in unsafe and unhealthy environments. Environmental inequality is more prevalent among lower-income people who tend to live close to environmental hazards. Living close to industrial activity is associated with perceptions of neighbourhood disorder, and feelings of personal powerlessness have a negative effect on psychological wellbeing (Downey & Van Willigen, 2005).

Research studies have found an association between depressive symptoms and the structure of the environment. The physical appearance of personal space including neighbourhood and community affects social order and wellbeing. Social disorder and/or substandard neighbourhoods including buildings and housing units may encourage social disorder and crime. These neglected neighbourhoods and the deterioration of social support networks can increase depression associated with feelings of lack of control. Environmental features at the street and housing level are affected by litter in the streets, garbage, graffiti, property in disrepair shanty towns, colonias, or unincorporated areas are all associated with social disorder and are important risk factors for mental illness (Wu et al., 2014).

The social forces that conspire to create stressful circumstances produce a negative effect on quality of life and wellbeing. This is especially true in rural areas that continue to be subjected to economic, political, and environmental policies that impinge on quality of life. Determining the best way to serve ethnically diverse populations who live in non-urban environments is the focus of this chapter. Using a clinical/activist approach to generalist social work practice with vulnerable populations requires a paradigm shift to incorporate the rurality model. To address these mental health issues requires culturally competent social work professionals with the necessary skills to intervene at the micro/individual, mezzo/family/group, and macro/community levels along a continuum of care.

This approach views the individual and their communities in a reciprocal relationship that requires specialised knowledge and skills to implement effective interventions. A holistic and/or a rurality model will best address the economic, political, and environmental forces that can have a negative effect on mental health and quality of life. The rurality paradigm acts as a conceptual representation of rural that transcends geographical locale. It concentrates on self-image as a social construct. The focus is on how people use a combination of resiliency and cultural strengths to cope with stress created by social forces that affect their mental health and wellbeing.

The rurality paradigm illustrates the key concepts that construct self-image and are critical to understanding the sense of self and community. As can be seen from the graphic representation below, environmental forces have a direct impact on the self-image of the individual, family, and community. A good assessment from a clinical/activist perspective must address each of the different concepts depicted in the individual circles surrounding self-image.

Displayed is a paradigm that views the micro, mezzo, and macro systems along a continuum that needs a complete assessment depending on where the presenting problems are located. For example, the clinical/activist social worker comprehends the need to address all three systems as one system in need of assessment and intervention, especially in rural environments. Mental health issues at the micro level may be the result of macro-level stressors related to economic, political, and environmental forces that impinge on perceived quality of life. This is especially salient when working with the inhabitants of the numerous colonias (unincorporated areas) that developed out of the need for land and home ownership on the US-Mexican border. A clinical/activist social worker first completes the micro-level assessment to identify where mental health–related stressors are originating. Poverty is a macro-level stressor that affects the mental health of the individual that in turn stresses the family. The clinical/activist social worker understands the need to first address the micro-level stressors so that an intervention can be aimed at using the person's resiliencies/strengths, spirituality, and religion to cope with macro-level stressors.

Rurality as a paradigm acknowledges the impact of social forces in the rural environment and how they have a direct effect on individuals, families, communities, and social service organisations. Self-image at the micro, mezzo, and macro levels are constructed by language, social interaction, religion, spirituality, values and traditions, locus of control, and time orientation. Rurality sees the individual's self-image along a continuum that unites the family which then forms the foundation of the community self-image. Thus, what happens at either level affects other levels within the rurality environmental context (Figure 8.1).

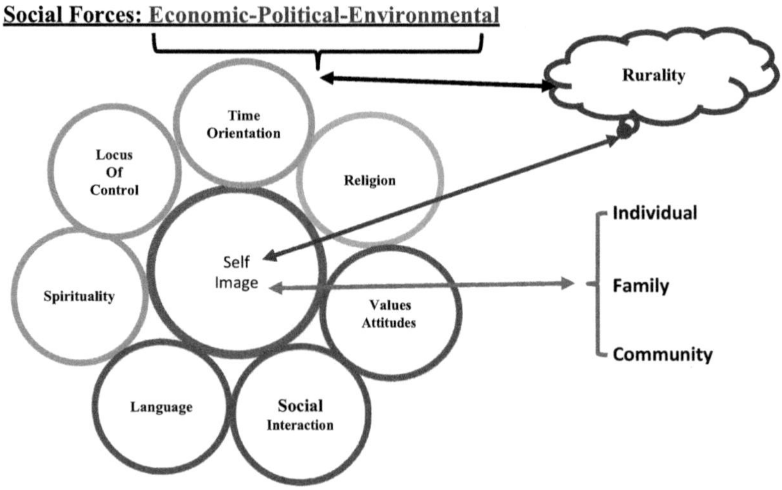

Figure 8.1 Rurality: clinical/activist paradigm.

As can be seen from this model, it takes the generalist ecosystems approach to highlight the interactional effects of each component that come together to form a holistic ideology and/or values system that embraces "rurality" as an internal construct. This infers the internal locus of control that combines with external locus of control into rurality as having symbolic meaning, and, therefore, action can be organised towards the symbols that define it.

Graphically displayed in the rurality paradigm is a generalist ecosystems approach that highlights the interactional effects of environmental forces and their impact on the holistic ideology and/or values systems that embraces "rurality". Rurality as used here replaces the traditional rural concept tied to geography and population size (Daley, 2015). When people move from a rural community to an urban community, they take their rurality with them. A shift in cognitive and affective processes is necessary to work with people who embrace a rurality defined self-image (Daley, 2015).

In rurality, individuals form their self-image according to their construct of reality. What is important to understand is the individual's self-image transcends to the family and therefore to the community. Assessment at one level (micro) requires assessment of the other two (mezzo and macro) depending on the problem or issue. A continuum of assessment beginning at one level transcends to the other two as needed.

The focus of the rurality paradigm is on the diverse families that inhabit the rural border environments of South Texas. This focus provides an opportunity to explore "rurality" within a culturally bound environment in need of culturally competent social workers. In this context, "rurality" becomes a symbol integrated within the cultural values and attitudes of the multicultural rural communities. Rurality as defined by Daley (2010) is a more inclusive perspective that views rural as self-image and not as a geographical location. People who identify with a rural lifestyle are found in urban micro communities. Thus, the" barrio" or neighbourhood can be construed as a rural enclave of people who share rural values, traditions, and a temporal view of time.

Rurality is also taken into consideration from a cultural point of view. Research states rural regions are more at risk of vulnerability but are also at higher possibility of resiliency base coping strategies (Freshwater, 2015).

Social cultural assessment

Social work assessments are critical to the provision of services and/or interventions. A good assessment tool will provide the social worker with important information gathered through use of a socio-cultural-spiritual assessment format that requires culturally competent social workers. The Communist Party of China implemented new directives in cultural development in explaining the ideology and major tasks of cultural reform and development. Yun Shan (2011) did an analysis and review of theory and used the following three concepts: (1) cultural awareness, (2) cultural confidence, and (3) cultural strength.

Cultural awareness is an internal spiritual force and the ideological basis for promoting cultural development. It is also a spiritual fulcrum that unites the hearts of people and is directly connected to perceived happiness and quality of life. People use culture to enlighten their minds, understand society and learn ideological lessons, and gain physical and mental pleasure. If a person does not have a full, rich spiritual and cultural life, their quality of life suffers (Yun Shan, 2011).

In many traditional African belief systems mental health problems can be seen to be caused by ancestors or bewitchment. When issues arise, traditional healers and religious leaders are believed to have the expertise to help relieve the suffering. It could be hypothesised that they are sought out because of their knowledge of the culture and acceptance by the society. Trust is the first step in establishing a working relationship, and they are trusted members of their society with the knowledge to help the healing process (Sorsdahl et al., 2009).

Mental health issues in Latino (Chicano) families and/or communities in the United States are typically kept in secret and/or not spoken of in public. The preference in Latino individuals is to use religion and/or a priest or pastor as their mental health counsellor. Understanding culture and traditional help seeking behaviours is a prerequisite to providing mental health services in rural culturally bound environments. A "curandero" is a traditional folk healer that is often consulted involving issues of physical, emotional, mental, and spiritual self. Lower-income people are more likely to rely on services provided by a curandero or traditional healer than Western medicine due to cost (George, 2013).

Using the rurality paradigm as an assessment tool provides the social worker with opportunities to construct the person's self-image utilising an informal approach to interviewing. This is especially important when the interviewee lives in a culturally defined environment. In addition, the rurality paradigm can allow the social worker to gather information and assess the client's self-image and subsequently the intervention to be implemented. This paradigm stresses that people who have lived in a rural environment for a long time have a culture of their own. The focus is on what is important to rural residents and to gather information on the spiritual context that forms a tight-knit community (Comas-Di´Az, 2006).

Rurality: psycho-socio-spiritual assessment

Rurality as an assessment tool starts at the intersectionality of the social forces that create stress for the individual or micro system. The effects of structural discrimination and other social injustices suffered by the residents of rural environments are seen when the individual's ability to cope is weakened, creating mental health problems that need professional interventions.

Language

In applying the rurality socio-cultural-spiritual assessment, the first phase of assessment needs to begin with language. As applied in this tool, language encompasses not only the person's preferred interview language but also their everyday language, body language, hand/eye movements, jesters, and even silence. The implication is that to use language in assessment requires an in-depth knowledge of the cultural and symbolic meanings ascribed to "La Platica" (informal conversation) as well as the environmental context in which it transpires (Comas-Di´Az, 2006). "Pase a mi humilde casa" (welcome/come into my humble home) conveys the speakers heartfelt welcome to their home and into their world. Much can be learned by the culturally competent social worker who comprehends rurality as a value, as a symbol, and as an ideology. *This is also the first steppingstone to developing trusting relationship.*

Social interaction

Symbolic interaction theory posits that people develop symbolic meaning in the process of social interaction. People interpret their behaviours and these interpretations from their social bond. Social interactions or exchanges are key in applying the clinical/activist method of assessing the person in their environment to identify problems and implement culturally sensitive interventions. In this theoretical premise the individual's family becomes a symbol of unity towards which action can be organised. Extended family is part of the "compradrazco"/parenthood or fictive kin network. Members can be added through religious rituals such as baptism. This system strengthens the family and is favoured among Chicanos (Hopple & Hudson, 2012). The family unit is the basis of society and is subject to the influences of the social environmental forces that dictate behaviours. Patterns of interaction become symbols that hold meaning such as respect for elders, parents, and other authority figures (Stryker, 1987).

When speaking with an elder the clinical/activist social worker is aware of the meanings ascribed to accepted behaviours when conversing with Latinos (Chicanos). Collins (1988) states that social exchange theory concerns the ties that bind people together and the social interactions between persons and systems. The clinical/activist social worker understands the importance of understanding the nature of these interactions. As previously mentioned, "La platica" is equally as important with social interactions because it provides comfort for Latinos. With this understanding, the religious and/or spiritual context of Latino/Chicano ideology is seen as a dance of life that creates a meaningful life, acceptance of hardships, and strengthens resiliency.

Time orientation

Time is a culturally defined concept within the Latino/Chicano world view that requires the clinical/activist social worker to make a shift in their cognitive/affective thought processes to accommodate cultural nuances in time. Case in point is the "Manana" attitude found in the literature on Latinos, particularly people of Mexican heritage. Contrary to the literature, most Latinos' concept of time centres on the present time. This time orientation is prevalent in societies whose history is one of a conquered people who developed coping strategies to survive the social and political injustice they have endured (Evason, 2019).

Don't look to the past for it is over; but also don't look to a future that is uncertain or requires acknowledgement of their present situation which can be depressing. This is a factor in living with "learned helplessness" syndrome; it reflects on the need to survive one day at a time, given their economic status. It is hard to look towards the future when it takes all their FE (faith) and cultural strengths to survive each day. But this does not mean Latinos/Chicanos don't have a sense of the future or a connection to their past "Si Dios quiere" (God Willing) and other culturally constructed symbols which help them cope with their present life's struggle for justice and a good quality of life (Comas-Di´Az, 2006).

Values and attitudes

When assessing values and attitudes of Latinos/Chicanos the need is to shift your cognitive/affective processes to incorporate these concepts within the rurality paradigm. Most of the assumptions and/or perceptions presented here are based on years of ethnographic field research with Chicanos. Case in point here is how do persons of Mexican heritage self-identify? The answers to this question are important in assessing self-image as in the rurality paradigm. Self-image is a social construct based on lived experience and the American experience with discrimination (Comas-Di´Az, 2006). Politically correct labels such as Latino, Hispanic, Mexican American, Mestizo (mixed blood/heritage), and Chicano are some of the labels used when referring to people of Mexican heritage. If I identify with being Mexican, then my values and attitudes are formed in the Mexican culture. But if I identify with Chicano, then I identify with the Mexican Americans or mestizo (mixed blood/heritage) and with the activist movements of the 1960s generation. What is important is to let people tell you how they identify themselves as part of forming their self-image.

What are Chicano values? Not much different than anyone else's; the difference is in how they are communicated and acted upon as in social symbols. Literature documents "familia" (family) as a value but does little to capture the importance of "familia" within the social context of belonging. A glimpse inside the Chicano family reveals the "respeto, dignidad, orgullo, and confianza" (respect, dignity, pride, and confidence) within the culture. Respect among the Chicano population is held highly, especially towards the elders and people of authority. Dignity, pride, and confidence can become barriers at times to seeking mental healthcare. These values are salient in forming the attitudes towards use of social services and healthcare. Attitudes include reliance on natural support networks, indigenous healthcare, and mutual aid societies. For example, a Chicano will first rely on their family and/or priest concerning issues related to mental health (Comas-Di´Az, 2006). Understanding these values is crucial to understanding the person's self-image.

Men especially view mental health problems and inability to cope with them as a weakness in character. Octavio Paz refers to this phenomenon as "rajado" or a crack in the mask that men wear to protect against outside intrusions into their mental state. A man does not allow anyone to see his innermost secret face or consciousness because that would reveal his weaknesses and/or transgressions. To do so would be to appear weak, vulnerable, and unable to control their lives (Octavio, 1961). This is an important cultural value often confused with Machismo but all the same important for the mental health professional to comprehend.

Related to this is the concept of illness and the reliance on curanderos and/or folk medicine as the first line of healthcare. Folk medicine grew out of traditional values and lack of accessible and equitable healthcare. Herbs and prayer are key to healing and often used in combination with traditional Western medicine.

What is important to the clinical/activist social worker is that this knowledge is critical to understanding and adopting a culturally sensitive assessment/intervention. Cultural values and attitudes define the rurality Chicano ideology and world views that dictate healthcare behaviours. These behaviours are tied to locus of control, time orientation, and social interaction patterns, including spirituality.

Spiritual/resiliency assessment

Locus of control

Time orientation and religion are inextricably linked in the spiritual context of the Chicano life and outlook. Most literature portrays the "Latino" as being fatalist because of their belief in Dios/God and that their fates are in God's hand and not in theirs. This is based on theory that Locus of Control is either Inward (I control my destiny) or Outward (God or some other force controls my destiny) to opposing forces that guide our destinies (Joelson, 2017).

In Chicano thought and belief, these two concepts are woven into one view of life and that we control certain things in life but that they are guided by our "destino"/destiny and our ability to control the outcome. Nothing in the Chicano view of life is seen as acceptance of one over the other but as a blending of both into one view that makes life worth living.

Religion

Religion is an organised or institutionalised belief system and is a specific expression of spirituality. Religiosity is the behavioural and cognitive attitudes and values a person places on being a member. It is also known to be an active part of coping or resilience to those who practice their religious beliefs. As such it is often viewed as being part of spirituality (Saad & de Medeiros, 2012). But in the same vein, spirituality operates outside of any religious practice and is based on faith. The important thing for the clinical/activist social worker is to acknowledge the person's religion in forming self-image and their interventions.

Spirituality

Spirituality can be viewed within religion; but it can also be viewed outside of religion as in communing with nature, having a strong relationship with the environment, humility, and having peace or balance with their life circumstances. The strength in being a spiritual person is in the ability to build resilient coping strategies. Resiliency is a process of coping or adapting to adversity, trauma, tragedy, or other sources of stress (https://www.apa.org/helpcenter/road-resilience.aspx).

As such it mirrors the way spirituality is developed throughout a lifetime of struggles that force one to depend on their faith and strength of character to overcome. Chicanos view spirituality as a struggle with life and the lessons that deepens their sense of meaning and purpose in life. To the Chicano, spirituality has a celebratory and festive character because it teaches that despite adversity, life is full of blessings. As life needs to be celebrated, many spiritual and religious activities resemble a fiesta (Comas-Di´Az, 2006). To the culturally competent social worker the task is to draw meaning from the symbolic meanings ascribed to symbols of faith and spirituality that form their outlook on life. The clinical/activist social worker knows not to ask direct questions as to spirituality but within the "platica" (conversation) lets the person talk about their life and the meaning they ascribe to living a good life.

Application of rurality

We focus on the US-Mexico border environment and the diverse Chicano, Mexican, Mexican American, Hispanic, Latino, and/or Latino populations. This population is used to illustrate the need to gain understanding of self-image, culture, traditions, language, beliefs, quality of life, and wellbeing. These concepts are particularly salient when addressing issues of stress and mental health. It is evidenced in the current literature that stress is present in the everyday lives of people in rural areas where limited mental health services are underutilised.

This underutilisation of mental health services comes from a lack of trust in accessing services that are not culturally sensitive. Part of this phenomenon comes from reliance on their spirituality, trusted individuals, and informal support networks in times of crisis.

Self-image is a social construct that creates an ideology and way of life from the experiences in coping with the intersectionality of social forces. These social forces are economic, political, and environmental policies that impact quality of life and wellbeing. Issues of structural discrimination and social injustice are part of political forces that are present in rural environments.

Political forces influence behaviours at the personal level where politicians reach out to the diverse rural populations that include Chicanos. Promises of jobs and better living conditions are used to get out the vote. But in reality, the individual's self-image is affected by the realisation that promises are never kept and the family and community are once again neglected. This neglect creates stressful circumstances and is indirectly responsible for the mental health problems that result from built-up stress in the environment caused by substandard living conditions. Little or no political power is a common stressor in that those without power are at the mercy of those who rule, leaving behind feelings of hopelessness and despair. These feelings translate to added stress and have implications for mental health professionals.

Environmental policies often place the individual, family, and community at risk from the types of industries usually located in rural areas. Colonias are un-incorporated areas that surround urban settings. A typical colonia in South Texas is considered rural, populated by individuals and their families struggling to achieve land ownership, and a sense of pride among the inhabitants. Streets are unpaved roads that flood during rainstorms and further isolate the residents because of bad travel conditions. Along with the lack of roads is the lack of sanitary sewerage systems; most common is a sewerage system that also floods during the rains and leaves sewerage along the roads and the properties that make up a colonia (Barton, Perlmeter, Blum, & Marquez, 2015). Living in these environments is stressful due to the substandard living conditions in a typical colonia. The intersectionality of these social forces is further exacerbated by the economic policies that often neglect rural areas in general. Poverty is the norm and so is the lack of services.

Economic policy and its effects on quality of life are the most salient issue facing rurality-defined colonias. The gaps and barriers established within economic policies create substandard living conditions such as substandard housing, lack of potable water, sewerage systems, paved roads, electricity, and employment opportunities (Barton et al., 2015). Colonias spring up out of a desire to own property on which to build a family home. Land is cheap and sold on instalment plan, making it affordable to low-income families. Houses are constructed using scrap lumber and other discarded materials in order to provide shelter to their families. They usually begin as one room, with other rooms added as materials become available (Barton et al., 2015).

Families in colonias continue to work sometimes two or three jobs just to make ends meet. This is a direct result of little or no economic development in their rural communities. The job market is small and often opportunities are unskilled, low-wage positions without benefits. The work is hard and the hours long, but they do provide much needed income to help support the family. An endless cycle that keeps employers happy and labourers tired without any prospects for improving their circumstances. Living under these circumstances keeps families in a never-ending economic struggle that can last for generations. This struggle with making a good, decent living creates stress that transforms to feelings of powerless that can lead to feelings of hopelessness that have a direct impact on mental health and quality of life (Barton et al., 2015). But Chicanos and other diverse peoples learn to cope with social injustice by using resiliencies and cultural strengths developed within their spiritual context of continuing the struggle with life itself.

Resiliency and cultural strengths

Self-image is socially constructed and develops within the context of the lived experience. Most Chicanos/Latinos see humility as a virtue and the accepted way of keeping a balance between the ego/social status and virtue/"dignidad" (dignity). However, a humble person is one with themselves and their environment; much in the same manner as a spiritual being is at peace with their being. People who live in rural environments give meaning to the symbols that construct their reality and to be a humble being is to have a good self-image. Symbols such as family, community, mutual aid, religion, spirituality, and self-help are internalised in the concept of self-image. This is true of all human behaviour and the social environment in which self-image is developed. Living in environments such as a colonia requires residents to rely on their spirituality as a means of coping with the negative effects of the social forces that impinge on their quality of life and wellbeing.

The spiritual dimension incorporates both inward and outward locus of control that dictates values and attitudes in all social interactions. Spirituality is defined by the way you live your life and not by the religion or social status you may have. It is defined by the day-to-day activities carried out in normal life; the difference comes in the form of social interactions with others and with the environment. It is spiritual resilience that comes from being true to yourself and is a stress-reducing strategy built on faith (http://journalrecord.com/tinkertakeoff/2013/01/24). "Ayudar" (to help) is imbedded deep in the "SOUL" of the spiritual being and the way they give of themselves. Mutual aid and/or help are provided for no other reason than it gives a feeling of self-satisfaction to the person that is giving; and helpful to the person receiving as in a reciprocal relationship that gives meaning to life, thus becoming a symbol towards which action can be organised.

In these environments, the traditional extended family is fast becoming the norm in response to the economic forces that necessitate adult children returning to live in the family home/system. "La familia" (the family) is central to the self-image of the Latino and includes formal and informal relationships. It is a cultural value that puts family in the centre of the persons' spiritual and social world. The family's needs come first, and members are expected to provide support. It is within the "familia" that self-image is born and nurtured throughout the life span, continuing to hold true to the meaning of "mi familia" (my family). Attitudes include reliance on natural support networks, indigenous healthcare, and mutual aid societies. For example, a Chicano will first rely on their family and/or priest concerning issues related to mental health.

What is called for is a paradigm shift from the traditional geographically defined rural environment to a "rurality" paradigm that is socially constructed and defined. Adopting this paradigm shift creates an avenue for exploration of how Chicanos view themselves in relation to their environment. This means that we need to acknowledge differences in how we view the world. Using the rurality social work model provides the means for a more culturally sensitive assessment and interventions with Chicano/Latino people. Equally as important is how the individual and family respond when their emotions and conversations are validated through an accurate assessment. The rurality social work model builds a bridge between the social worker and the cautious individual who has experienced ongoing social injustice and allows for a clearer understanding of the culture that comes with him/her.

The need is not to address each concept identified in the rurality model but to respect and acknowledge that these concepts construct a way of life that dictates the preferred method of social interactions. Because the concepts are symbols internalised within the Chicano/Latino world view, the social worker can organise actions (assessment/interventions) towards them. Care must be taken in addressing familial issues in the traditional dominant Western mannerisms that often can be offensive.

Social workers need to be cognisant of the prerequisite to be culturally sensitive in working with Chicano populations. A famous saying by Benito Juarez "Entre los individuos, como entre las naciones, el respeto al derecho ajeno es la paz", meaning "Among individuals, as among nations, respect for the rights of others is peace", forms the basis for *respeto* among Mexican and Latino/Chicano *gente* (people) (https://www.significados.com/el-respeto-al-derecho-ajeno-es-la-paz/) and provides the framework for rurality social work practice with Latino individuals, families, groups, communities, and organisations.

Although the *Platica* method of interviewing will take considerably more time, the social worker will be rewarded with a plethora of in-depth information concerning the individual's quality of life and issues that may be important for them to voice. A home visit can set the stage for future interactions that include mental health and wellbeing. Trust is the key to accessing people who have developed a self-reliant, independent self-image to cope with social injustice. The social worker who is sensitive to the culture will acknowledge the person's reluctance to reveal personal information or issues of poverty, education, and especially their homes. But once trust is obtained (with patience and *respeto*), the information can be gathered in a non-threatening or offensive manner that respects the person's *dignidad* and sense of self.

The clinical/activist trained social worker acknowledges the distrust that exists in colonias whose history is one of neglect and false political promises. This is the point where the micro-level mental health issues are investigated to include a macro-level social and economic development agenda. If the hypothesised cause and effect relationship among social forces and psychological distress is accepted, then it becomes a political issue. Clinical/activist master of social work professional should bring more attention to the economic and environmental problems that exist in rural environments.

References

Barton, J., Perlmeter, E. R., Blum, E. S., & Marquez, R. R. (2015). Las Colonias in the 21st Century: Progress along the Texas–Mexico border. Retrieved from https://www.dallasfed.org/~/media/documents/cd/pubs/lascolonias.pdf.

Collins, R., (1988). *Theoretical Sociology*. San Diego: Harcourt, Brace, Jovanovich.

Comas-Di´Az, L. (2006). Latino Healing: The integration of ethnic psychology into psychotherapy: Theory, research, practice, training copyright 2006 by the American Psychological Association, *43*(4), 436–453 0033–3204/06/$12.00 doi:10.1037/0033–3204.43.4.436. Retrieved from https://pdfs.semanticscholar.org/881c/ef8b3fdde8d13f0a7edad0ebd98aac89f815.pdf

Daley, M. (2010). A conceptual model for rural social work. *Contemporary Rural Social Work*, Vol. 2. Retrieved from file:///C:/Users/kurfv000/Downloads/392–1087-1-PB%20(9).pdf.

Daley, M. (2015). *Rural social work in the 21st century (1st Edition).* Oxford University Press.

Defining mental health in rural communities (2019). *Rural Health Information Hub*, Mental health in rural communities toolkit. Retrieved from https://www.ruralhealthinfo.org/toolkits/mental-health/1/definition

Downey, L., & Van Willigen, M. (2005). Environmental stressors: The mental health impacts of living near industrial activity. *Journal of Health and Social Behavior, 46*(3), 289–305. Retrieved from https://www.ncbi.nlm.nih.gov/pmc/articles/PMC3162363/.

Evason, N. (2019). Mexican culture. Retrieved from https://culturalatlas.sbs.com.au/mexican-culture/core-concepts-832ad8e8-b637-4291-9209-ce0aec07c6a5

Franco, J. (2008). *Rural democratisation: (Re)framing rural poor political action. Transnational Institute.* Retrieved from https://www.tni.org/en/publication/rural-democratisation-reframing-rural-poor-political-action

Freshwater, D. (2015). Vulnerability and resilience: Two dimensions of rurality. *Sociologia Ruralis, 55*(4), 497–515. doi:10.1111/soru.12090

George, M. P. (2013). The Mexican American health paradox: The collective influence of sociocultural factors on Latino health outcomes. *Discussions, 9*(2). Retrieved from http://www.inquiriesjournal.com/a?id=663

Hoyt, D. R., Conger, R. D., Valde, G., & Weihs, K. (1997). Psychological distress and help seeking in rural America. *American Journal of Community Psychology, 25*(4), 449–470. Retrieved from https://onlinelibrary.wiley.com/doi/abs/10.1023/A:1024655521619.

Joelson, R. B. (2017). Locus of control how do we determine our successes and failures? *Psychology Today.* Retrieved from https://www.psychologytoday.com/us/blog/moments-matter/201708/locus-control.

McCann, J. (2014). Combatting stress and suicide in rural communities: Issues identified and recommendations for rural support in Northern Ireland. Winston Churchill Memorial Trust Fellowship Research Paper. Rural Support. Retrieved from https://www.wcmt.org.uk/sites/default/files/migrated-reports/1122_1.pdf

Morgannoel18 (2017). Rural policy. Federalism in America 10/28/2017. Retrieved from http://encyclopedia.federalism.org/index.php?title=Rural_Policy&oldid=1418.

Octavio, P. (1961). The labyrinth of solitude. New York: Grove Press. Hermitary: Resources and reflections on hermits and solitude. Book reviews: House of solitude. Retrieved from https://www.hermitary.com/bookreviews/paz.html.

Ratcliffe, M., Burd, C., Holder, K., & Fields, A. (2016). "Defining rural at the U.S. Census Bureau," ACSGEO-1, U.S. Census Bureau, Washington, DC. Retrieved from https://www.census.gov/content/dam/Census/library/publications/2016/acs/acsgeo-1.pdf.

Rural Health Information Hub (2019). Defining mental health in rural communities. Mental health in rural communities toolkit. Retrieved from https://www.ruralhealthinfo.org/toolkits/mental-health/1/definition.

Shun, Y., (2011). 'Cultural Awareness, Cultural Confidence, Cultural Strength', *Qiushi, 3*(1), http://english.qstheory.cn/magazine/201101/201109/t20110920_111442.htm accessed 20/07/2020

Slama, K. (2004). Rural culture is a diversity issue. Dimensions of diversity Minnesota psychologist. Retrieved from https://www.apa.org/practice/programs/rural/rural-culture.pdf.

Sorsdahl, K., Stein, D. J., Grimsrud, A., Seedat, S., Flisher, A. J., Williams, D. R., & Myer, L. (2009). Traditional healers in the treatment of common mental disorders in South Africa. *The Journal of Nervous and Mental Disease*, Jun, *197*(6), 434–441. doi: 10.1097/NMD.0b013e3181a61dbc. Erratum in: J Nerv Ment Dis. 2010 Sep, *198*(9), 695. PubMed PMID: 19525744; PubMed Central PMCID: PMC3233225. Retrieved from https://www.ncbi.nlm.nih.gov/pmc/articles/PMC3233225/

Stryker, S. (1987). The vitalization of symbolic interactionism. *Social Psychology Quarterly*, *50*(1), 83–94. Retrieved from http://www.csun.edu/~snk1966/Stryker%20The%20Vitalization%20of%20Symbolic%20Interactionism.pdf.

Villa, R. (2020). *Rural social work on U.S./Mexico Border*. Manuscript submitted for publication.

Wadhwa|, D. (2018). Number of extremely poor people continues to rise in Sub-Saharan Africa, while falling rapidly in all other regions. World Bank Blogs. Retrieved from https://www.worldbank.org/en/understanding-poverty.

Wilson, W., Bangs, A., & Hatting, T. (2015). The future of rural behavioral health. Retrieved from https://www.ruralhealthweb.org/NRHA/media/Emerge_NRHA/Advocacy/Policy%20documents/The-Future-of-Rural-Behavioral-Health_Feb-2015.pdf.

Wu, Yu-Tzu, Nash, P., Barnes, L. E., Minett, T., Matthews, F. E., Jones, A., & Brayne, C. (2014). Assessing environmental features related to mental health: A reliability study of visual streetscape images. BioMed Central; BMC Public Health 201414:1094. Published online 10/22/2014. PMCID: MMC4219017; PMID: 25335922. doi:10.1186/1471-2458-14-1094. Retrieved from https://www.ncbi.nlm.nih.gov/pmc/articles/PMC4219017/

9 Rural mental health and global ethical perspectives

Steve F. Bain and Sarah-Anne Munoz

Introduction

In the not-too-distant future, a manned rocket will blast off from the gravitational confines of earth with the sole mission of travelling to another planet. Even before that rocket ship has left on its daunting and unprecedented mission, the crew (and those who sent them) will be faced with a variety of ethical issues. Should people from earth inhabit another planet and disrupt whatever life system is on that sphere? Should society subject the crew itself to a mission that carries with it no promise of returning? What are the ethical codes to guide astronauts on this interstellar journey? They have been trained and told what they can and what they must do, yet have they been educated on what they *should* do?

Although the similarities may not be immediately apparent, this scenario echoes the experience of rural mental health professionals and residents across the globe. Those who work within a rural community or with a remote population also will be called upon to face extraordinary ethical dilemmas as surely as if they were being sent to a remote planet! And, like their imaginary astronautical counterparts, rural mental health professionals worldwide will likely be challenged to make ethical decisions in potentially unique and extraordinary situations. Isolated rural communities (along with their inimitable challenges) task the mental health professional with making ethical judgements and solving ethical dilemmas without a strong support group or the luxury of people who have heretofore faced those exact issues.

As professionals committed to meeting the mental health needs of rural communities, the challenge is how to make a difference in a rural and/or remote context. Professionals must be ready to respond, react, decide, behave, think, and practice in ways designed to ensure maximum benefit to their clients, to stay true to their professional convictions, and to honour the professions in which they serve. This chapter proposes a number of fundamental ethical principles through which a global mental health profession may align in order to foster a standard of expectation from which all clients and patients may benefit. This will be particularly helpful as an ever-growing number of people travel throughout the world, thus increasing the likelihood of needing some level of mental health services. Moreover, because there are many similarities in regard to the ethical challenges faced across borders, oceans, and beliefs, mental health professionals will be working with a growing number of international connections and populations within rural and remote areas. Hence, it seems logical for countries to develop an international organisation designed for global collaboration. Such an inclusive organisation would help de-stigmatise the subject of mental health, foster contemporary research into common psychoses, develop effective intervention strategies, help unique and marginalised populations, and identify a global ethical standard at the heart of the mental health profession regardless of one's native origin. The potential benefits of a global ethics code would include:

1 A globally recognised, and shared, definition of rural mental health and the rural mental health profession. This description will serve to help remove the stigma and misunderstanding surrounding mental health so prevalent throughout a variety of cultures and countries.
2 An ethical standard that would allow participating countries and international entities to formulate the basics of what is to be expected of all mental health professionals and which would mesh with their own country's ethical guidelines. This standard would likely necessitate the formation of a global organisation of rural mental health professionals.
3 Facilitates the identification of a global aspirational code of professional conduct that would support country-specific codes of conduct. This would theoretically provide an expectation of quality rural mental health services regardless of the world or region in which professionals may find themselves serving. For the global rural mental health professional, such a standard would ensure that they understand what comprehensive ethical conduct is and how it can be fostered. Ethical standards at this level would ensure collective calibration of ethical principles, provide a global accountability perspective, and serve as a foundational support of the mental health profession in rural regions.

Before addressing the international issues related to ethics and rural mental health, it is paramount to understand the challenges related to rural mental health in general. Some of these challenges have been detailed in the introduction to this book (Chapter 1). Here, it is pertinent to highlight again some of the challenges related to a lack of consensus on definitions of "mental health" and of "rural". The greatest obstacle to defining a global set of ethical standards for rural mental health may be the denotation of the very definition of mental health itself. As Lane (2016) avowed, "Mental health is an integral and essential component of health, but it is also notoriously difficult to define narrowly or universally" (para. 2). In the United States, distinction continues to be made between "health" and "mental health" in terms of healthcare, legislation, treatment, and social education. Erroneously, the terms "mental health" and "mental illness" have been used interchangeably as if they mean the same. Defining mental health is both a critical need and a seemingly illusive venture, particularly as it relates to legislation. At the time of this writing, for example, the US Congress is grappling with a strategy to thwart the plague of mass shootings and gun violence. At the centre of the discussion is mental health. Historically, mental health has been given a type of Hippocratic nuance focusing on the absence of pain, sadness, hurt, and personal discomfort. Even the WHO's definition of mental health as "a state of well-being" (World Health Organization, 2004, p. 10) is fraught with difficulty. This definition overly emphasises positivity and an absence of abnormality (Lane, 2016). Mental health is not the equivalent of mental illness. In addition, mental health does not mean the absence of sadness and the constancy of happiness. Because of this universal misunderstanding of mental health, prescription-based interventions have abounded. Lane (2016) cited "overly broad definitions of mental disorders" as contributing to "over-diagnosis, overmedication, and overtreatment" related to the excessive and addictive use of antidepressants and opioids (para. 5). Galderisi, Heinz, Kastrup, Beezhold, and Sartorius (2015) quoted a proposed re-definition of mental health put forth by a group of European psychiatrists:

> Mental health is a dynamic state of internal equilibrium which enables individuals to use their abilities in harmony with universal values of society. Basic cognitive and social skills; ability to recognize, express and modulate one's own emotions, as well as empathize with others; flexibility and ability to cope with adverse life events and function in social roles; and harmonious relationship between body and mind represent important components of mental health which contribute, to varying degrees, to the state of internal equilibrium.
>
> (pp. 231–232)

This definition allows for an understanding that mentally healthy people undergo crises, personal setbacks, life changes, grief, and emotional upheavals. Mentally healthy people have the internal resources to achieve a state of equilibrium and homeostasis through the good times and the bad.

Defining rural can also be problematic to say the least. Smalley, Warren, and Rainer (2012) emphasise the difficulties and inconsistencies associated with adequately identifying "rural" in the United States. And like America, most countries define rural as it relates to physical geography or population densities. However, the lack of consensus on this type of definition is obvious. Rather than elucidate on the multiplicities of worldwide definitions related to rural, it might be more prudent to address what is needed is a definition which would promote mental wellness for rural and remote populations. Bain, Rueda, Mata-Villarreal, and Mundy (2011) concluded that we need ta new definition of rural:

> Perhaps "neo-rustico" would better define rural districts in regards to their community resource needs, particularly mental health resource

> needs. This new rural definition would help comprehend the scope of the problem. In fact, while families, schools, and communities may be within 30 minutes of a major city or population area, specific mental health resources may still not be available or accessible. This creates a new paradigm for understanding "rural."
>
> (p. 7)

Galderisi et al. (2015) argued for a definition designed to "overcome perspectives based on ideal norms or hedonic and eudemonic theoretical traditions, in favor of an inclusive approach, as free as possible of restrictive and culture-bound statements" (p. 232). This type of definition would also consider remoteness, access to services and specialist professionals, and lack of financial resources, and would be inclusive in its recognition of life experiences. Because each rural community or population is socially and culturally distinct, with its own unique challenges related to mental health, it is both unfair and unwise to thrust each rural community and population into a general category and under an all-encompassing title such as "rural". Defining rural (as it relates to mental health) must include factors such as the lack of accessibility, available resources, and policy reform initiatives worldwide.

International perspectives

The WHO's analysis of the mental health disparities worldwide is sobering. According to their Health Action Plan 2013–2020, "only 36% of people living in low-income countries are covered by mental health legislation compared to 92% in high-income countries" (World Health Organization, 2013, p. 8). Couple this with the fact that 46% of the world's population is considered rural and the significance of rural mental health as a global issue is instantly obvious (Pendse & Nugent, 2017). Addressing the global perspective, Hann, Pearson, Campbell, Sesay, and Eaton (2015) stated, "it is estimated that 30% of countries do not have mental health programmes, whereas 40% do not have mental health policies to inform service delivery" (Hann et al., 2015, p. 2). It is important to note that when we talk about mental health programmes, we refer to those countries who have an identifiable and intentional system of mental health care supported by both governmental policy and funding. These programmes ideally should include delivery and availability of services that prioritise the individual, connect to some legislation, and advocate for all that country's citizens with mental health conditions. Sobering statistics such as these should elicit a societal concern and commitment to rural populations on an international scale. By understanding and appreciating the need to address the rural mental health needs of all countries, the impetus to effect global awareness, collaboration, and change may then be expected to strengthen. Mental health professionals around the globe constantly face ethical challenges as they seek to serve rural populations. Ethical issues related to treatment, the avoidance of dual or multiple relationships, lack of professional support, practicing beyond one's areas of competency, and confidentiality are among the many challenges related to the provision of mental health services within rural areas. Having a generic ethics code related to rural mental health is fundamental if the nations of the world are resolved to reaching rural communities with their mental health resources. A number of international publications which relate to ethical behaviour among the health and care professions exist, but most fail to address the specific needs related to mental health or rural populations. The 2015 WHO's publication on Global Health Ethics addressed bioethical issues related to medicine, physical health, and healthcare but fell short in terms of also speaking to mental health (World Health Organization, 2015). The International Commission on Occupational Health stated within its own code of ethics: "The purpose of occupational health is to serve the protection and promotion of the physical and mental health and social well-being of the workers individually and collectively" (International Commission on Occupational Health, Code of Ethics, 2014, p. 16). But the issue of mental health is not addressed any further. Even the World Medical Association's International Code of Medical Ethics mentions mental illness once and that is in relation only to the physician: "A physician shall seek appropriate care and attention if he/she suffers from mental or physical illness" (World Medical Association, 2018).

So, the question may be asked: Is it possible to conceive of and implement an international commitment to mental health ethics on a global scale, particularly as it relates to rural regions of the world? One might argue against a global standard for rural mental health ethics because of the immense diversity among countries, populations, cultures, and communities. Yet, an international code would bring a global focus on mental health issues and professionalism within rural communities. This would clearly construct a larger social stage on which to address major issues such as mental health stigma and lack of professional mental health resources worldwide. An international code would also offer an opportunity for all countries to rally around a global cause related to rural mental health.

Overview of international ethical guidelines

Before there is any substantive attempt at formulating a global ethics guideline for rural mental health, questions must be addressed as to the aims, goals, and purposes of such a code. There must be a foundation for any ethics code that is based on a core purpose or series of purposes. By providing a basic review of the professional counselling and mental health ethics codes of selected countries, some generalities start to emerge. These are outlined below.

United Kingdom

The UK's Council for Psychotherapy's Ethical Principles and Code of Professional Conduct identifies the purpose of their code as being "to define generic UKCP ethical principles which UKCP registrants commit to and maintain" (United Kingdom Council for Psychotherapy, 2009, p. 2). In this instance, the ethical guideline is meant to safeguard ethical practice among psychotherapists. The UKCP code addresses the general ethical principles related to the best interests of clients, diversity and equality, confidentiality, conduct, professional knowledge and skills, communication, consent, records, physical or mental health issues related to the professional, professional integrity, advertising, insurance, and complaints.

Australia

For the Australian Counselling Association, the Code of Ethics and Practice is bound within the framework of the ACA (INC) itself, which serves to "monitor, maintain, set and improve professional standards in counsellor education and practice" (Australian Counselling Association INC, 2015, p. 3). This ethics guideline serves as a monitoring and regulatory force for all its members. The code emphasises the counsellors' responsibilities to their clients and to the profession. It also addresses anti-discriminatory practise, confidentiality, boundaries, professional competence, and the counselling environment.

United States of America

The American Counseling Association's 2014 Code of Ethics (p. 3) lists six primary purposes:

1 The Code sets forth the ethical obligations of ACA members and provides guidance intended to inform the ethical practice of professional counsellors.
2 The Code identifies ethical considerations relevant to professional counsellors and counsellors-in-training.
3 The Code enables the association to clarify for current and prospective members, and for those served by members, the nature of the ethical responsibilities held in common by its members.
4 The Code serves as an ethical guide designed to assist members in constructing a course of action that best serves those utilising counselling services and establishes expectations of conduct with a primary emphasis on the role of the professional counsellor.
5 The Code helps to support the mission of ACA.
6 The standards contained in this Code serve as the basis for processing enquiries and ethics complaints concerning ACA members.

Canada

The Canadian Code of Ethics of the Canadian Counselling and Psychotherapy Association (CCPA, 2007) recognises the code as invaluable in its ability to express "the ethical principles and values of the Canadian Counselling and Psychotherapy Association and serves as a guide to the professional conduct of all its members" (p. 1). The code emphasises the accountability of the CCPA's members, the focus of integrity and accountability, the essentiality of an ethical decision-making process, and the need to revise the code as a result of ever-changing ethical knowledge and unique ethical situations (CCPA, 2007).

China

The Chinese Psychological Society (CPS) finalised their code of ethics in January 2007. The preamble declares the goal of this code is to "promote the mental health status and enhance the welfare and wellbeing of the general public" (CPS, 2007, p. 1). This document, addressing counselling and clinical practice, divides the code into general principles and ethical standards. It concludes by providing a glossary of terms designed to further clarify key concepts and definitions. The general principles address beneficence, responsibility, integrity, justice, and respect. There are seven ethical standards which clearly identify the counselling/psychological professional's responsibilities. These include the professional relationship, privacy and confidentiality, professional responsibility, assessment and evaluation, teaching, training, and supervision, and resolving ethical issues. These ethical standards are especially important as research in rural areas of China show dramatic increases in various types of mental health illnesses (Ran et al., 2017). The socio-economic development of China over the past two decades has potentially affected the mental health of rural residents. Findings such as this suggest that "mental health policy and services should be improved and adjusted according to the prevalence change of mental disorders" (Ran, et al., 2017, p. 37). Changes in those policies and services should be guided by strong ethical codes to ensure the mental wellbeing and welfare of rural peoples.

By reviewing these current professional codes, two major aspects of purpose seem to emerge: reflection and regulation. By reflection, we are referring to the indispensable concept of helping professionals pause and ponder their actions, interventions, and decision-making. It also refers to helping clients and patients understand more clearly what they can expect from their mental health professional. Reflection carries with it the understanding that professionals will carefully consider their obligations to make person-centred decisions related to their practice and delivery of services. Reflection serves as the driving opportunity to implement an ethical decision-making strategy and act in accordance to ethical standards. Regulation, on the other hand, refers to legal-based standards and requirements, which can result in substantial penalties if violated. Those who study the complicated subject of ethics warn that law and ethics are not always the same. To be clear, the law must have some level of morality to its base. Yet law and the values related to ethics may not always be similar. In its purest form, "law is insufficient as an ethical system" (Iacovino, 2002, p. 58). Law is often represented as being the minimum standards by a government and ethics having to do with more lofty or ideal standards (Corey, Corey, Corey, & Callanan, 2015).

Framing an international ethical standard for rural mental health professionals

It is important for the international community of rural mental health professionals to have some form of ethical standard in order to assure adherence to a professional code and a quality of service to rural populations. This ethical framework would serve as a starting point for those countries whose mental health professionals may not have a clear ethics code. It would also serve as a connected framework on which existing ethics codes could be supported. By comparing a number of international codes of ethics related to mental health, some basic principles are either specifically delineated or thematically referenced. These typically include beneficence, nonmaleficence, autonomy, fidelity, justice, and societal interest. These principles address the ethical outlook related to the people, the professional, the profession, and the practise connected to rural mental health services.

The people

There is a basic understanding for the rights and dignity of all people across the board by healthcare professionals. Mental health professionals are an integral part of that group. A strong framework of international ethics would affirm the dignity and worth of rural peoples worldwide. Rural mental health professionals must be committed to the people whom they serve. Any rural mental health professional code of ethics must address the dignity of the people served through the encouragement of self-strength and independence, the commitment of beneficence and non-maleficence, the support of human rights, and promise of authentic, genuine, and honest services. Throughout the course of history, the issue of mental health has been treated with negative reaction, stigmatisation, and abuse. In many countries, even today, the mentally ill experience forced institutionalisation, incarceration, and sub-standard treatment. The WHO fact sheet reported, "In low- and middle-income countries, between 76% and 85% of people with mental disorders receive no treatment for their disorder. In high-income countries, between 35% and 50% of people with mental disorders are in the same situation" (WHO, *Mental Disorders*, April 9, 2019, para. 22).

Regardless of the economic status of a country, mental health is largely denied the significant importance, contextualisation, and prioritisation in the vast majority of nations across the globe. Thus, as this critical aspect of international health is neglected, the issue continues to be more about people and their basic human rights. Such neglect is never more pronounced than in rural and remote communities and populations. Compared to urban populaces, rural peoples consistently are challenged by the lack of mental health professionals, lower quality of services (when available), inflated costs, inaccessibility issues, shorter lifespans, poorer states of overall health, and deficient government provisions related to policy development, funding, education, and research (Strasser, Kam, & Regalado, 2016). Every country is *culpabilis* when addressing the international crisis of rural mental health because rural cultures, communities, and populations are consistently being neglected and intentionally denied essential services and support. This is why the mental health professional working with rural and remote places is so very vital. Rural peoples often have no voice and no advocate. The ethical responsibility of rural mental health professionals is to give a voice for the people whom they seek to serve.

The professional

In many countries, the concept of a mental health professional is seen as something new and uncertain, particularly in the eyes of rural people. Even in more developed countries, such as the United States, mental health professionals are often met by scepticism and a lack of trust in rural communities (who are often not accustomed to a professional listening to their deepest and darkest secrets). It is of utmost importance that rural mental health professionals keep a keen eye on professional conduct. Serving in a rural environment is fraught with professional challenges, most of which are directly or indirectly correlated to ethical considerations. In this fast-paced world, even rural communities feel the impact of social, economic, political, cultural, and industrial changes. The mental health professional who works with these populations must be able to swiftly address ethical dilemmas that arise all too frequently and expectantly. Perhaps one of the greatest challenges lies within the soul of each person who seeks to be a mental health professional and who wishes to serve in a rural community. Some essential questions must be answered in order to discover one's fundamental purpose in this profession:

- Why do I want to be a mental health professional?
- Why would I want to serve in rural communities?
- How knowledgeable am I about rural communities?
- How strong are my collaborative skills?
- Do I exhibit strong problems solving skills?
- Am I comfortable asking for help or advice?
- How open am I to building relationships within the community?
- How strong are my advocacy skills?
- How comfortable am I in initiating a collaboration with potential community leaders/organisations?

Many counsellors never envisioned being employed to serve a rural community or population, yet there they are. As mental health professionals actively monitor their own unresolved personal issues, they must carefully consider their professional suitability and sustainability within a rural context. Adapting to the changing rural landscape is a continual challenge for the rural mental health professional. While there is generally only a slight difference in the prevalence of different types of mental health issues in urban compared to rural areas, the greatest dissimilarity is related to accessibility and the challenges associated with living and working in a rural neighbourhood. This can take an emotional toll on the professional who seeks to help these disenfranchised populations.

In terms of developing a professional rural counselling identity, it is essential to understand that both personal and professional aspects of this identity are important. Each counsellor must recognise his or her own humanity. In fact, our personal self will reflect what our professional self will be. We all come with our own biases, values, life experiences, and core beliefs. However, we must not allow these to interfere with the therapeutic process of our clients. A counsellor can have a set of values and still be able to affirm the client's own personal beliefs and values. In fact, it is important for counsellors to gauge their own capacity to affirm personal values and beliefs while simultaneously supporting their clients' values and beliefs. An important concept element in therapy is the ability to know oneself as a counsellor while at the same time affirming the dignity of the person one is counselling. The capacity of a mental health professional to differentiate and separate his or her own personal values from the therapeutic process is known as *bracketing*. Kocet and Herlihy (2014) described this process as:

> The intentional separating of a counselor's personal values from his or her professional values or the intentional setting aside of the counselor's personal values in order to provide ethical and appropriate counseling to all clients, especially those whose worldviews, values, belief systems, and decisions differ significantly from those of the counselor.
>
> (p. 182)

Bracketing focuses on the needs of the client rather than a value-difference between the counsellor and counselee. This ability to set one's beliefs and values aside in order to help a client can be a win-win situation for both client and counsellor. With such a potential diversity within rural and remote areas, the rural mental health professional must be able to master this skilled capacity.

An unyielding attitude towards this level of professionalism could be an indication of personal needs or problems within the counsellor. This could lead to a burnout or a type of career failure. Lent and Schwartz (2012) conducted research related to burnout among counsellors in the United States using, among other instruments, the *International Personality Item Pool-Big Five*. Their findings supported previous research regarding professional burnout among mental health professionals and demonstrated that neuroticism was the predominant internal factor connected with burnout. From this research perspective, neuroticism refers to the tendency for one to have a negative perspective on life. Their conclusion was "increased neuroticism predicted more emotional exhaustion and depersonalization, and less sense of personal accomplishment" (Lent & Schwartz, 2012, p. 365). From a professional standpoint, this study also found burnout seemed to occur more often in community mental health settings (Lent & Schwartz, 2012). In the United States, community mental health centres are often found in rural areas. Those who are given an opportunity to serve as a mental health provider for rural and remote populations must carefully consider the personal and professional dynamics which may make that decision a monumental task.

The profession

Each country will have its own definition of what a rural mental health professional is. At the core of this profession is a commitment to helping those who are served reach a higher standard of life. A crucial element within the development of the rural mental health professional is education. Foundational courses in professional identity are essential in helping potential counsellors connect their personal strengths with the demands of the mental health profession. An international standard for education would be immensely helpful to ensure appropriate, effective, and professional care is given to all rural people. In fact, the professional's own identity starts with formal education and training. This accentuates the vital role of mental health programs in the development of the modern professional. Corey et al. (2015) emphasised the importance of faculty (university academic staff) and their program requirements to serve as gatekeepers for the counselling profession. They concluded: "a key role of clinical training faculty is to promote and facilitate students' competence and professional behavior" (Corey et al., 2015, p. 321). Nevertheless, a formal education is just the beginning. The rural mental health professional must be a continual lifelong learner. In addition to the normal requirements for continuing education that most mental health professionals must complete, the natural tendency of the counsellor must be to maintain skill sets and acquire new information related to the profession. Dynamically changing forces related to multiculturalism, contemporary research, counselling techniques, and working with diverse clientele necessitate a continual need to hone one's professional competence.

The practice

Developing an ethics-based practice must be intentional with a clear design. But what does that look like throughout the global landscape? While each country will have its own perspective of rural mental health, a general consensus of what constitutes an ethical practice should be acknowledged. The WHO's understanding of health ethics is a good place to start (WHO, "*Global*

Health Ethics", 2015). In the WHO's elaboration of health ethics, they concluded: "Health ethics has a broad focus, taking in ethical issues faced by health professionals, health policy-makers and health researchers" (WHO, "*Global Health Ethics*", 2015, p. 10). Obviously, this focus encompasses a much wider audience including patients and stakeholders engaged in either the provision or receiving of health services. This definition also affirms all questions and input that is value-based which indicates a strong commitment to the welfare of those constituents who are provided with health services. Hence, the global mental health profession must be committed to a client-centred mindset. This will inevitably foster trust and respect from the international community and sustain a clear definition for the rural mental health profession.

The successful rural mental health counselling practice must be known for respecting each human being, appreciating diversity and multiculturalism, promoting social justice, and providing competent and ethical services for those rural communities and populations served. An ethical decision-making plan must be in place in order to foster a proactive approach to any ethical dilemma which may arise. There are many ethical decision-making models, but most will include some basic reference to the model put forth by Corey et al. (2015, pp. 21–24). These steps are suggestions to encourage the counsellor to carefully consider ethical problems which may arise:

1 Identify the problem.
2 Identify the potential issues involved.
3 Review the relevant ethics code.
4 Know the applicable laws and regulations.
5 Obtain consultation.
6 Consider possible and probable courses of action.
7 Enumerate the consequences of various decisions.
8 Choose what appears to be the best course of action.

The American Counseling Association supports a similar model based on the work of Forester-Miller and Davis (2016, pp. 2–5):

1 Identify the problem.
2 Apply the ACA Code of Ethics.
3 Determine the nature and dimensions of the dilemma.
4 Generate potential courses of action.
5 Consider the potential consequences of all options and determine a course of action.
6 Evaluate the selected course of action.
7 Implement the course of action.

Regardless of which model is chosen or adapted for ethical decision-making, the process should include the following components: (1) clarify the problem,

(2) consider the Code of Ethics one is bound to, (3) consult professional/legal experts if necessary, and (4) choose the best course of action that will benefit all concerned.

Conclusions

This chapter has served to raise some important issues around the subject of ethics related to global rural mental health. First, by examining country-specific codes of conduct for mental health professionals, it is hoped that a global approach to the conduct of mental health professional working in rural areas can be articulated. Second, such a global code of ethics would serve to emphasise the worth of individuals worldwide by sanctioning personal freedom and choice. This type of code would resonate with the world community as it promotes social justice and professional integrity for rural and remote populations. These populations are all too often underserved or never-served and represent a significant global at-risk populace. It would be presumptuous to call for a unilateral ethics code that would replace country-specific codes, and it is certainly not the intent of this chapter to suggest such. Nevertheless, a global ethical code related to rural mental health and committed to the people, the professional, the profession, and the practise could be the catalyst for mental health advocacy in every region of the world. Third, the bold effort to advocate for underserved peoples in rural and remote areas will undoubtedly reverberate to the urban populations as well. Rural communities must be viewed as microcosmic representations of both mental health challenges and solutions for national and global populations. Rural areas have identifiable social factors, which contribute to overall positive health outcomes. These include "dense social networks, social ties of long duration, shared life experiences, high quality of life, and norms of neighborliness, self-help, and reciprocity" (Phillips & McLeroy, 2004, p. 1663). Finally, a global rural mental health ethics code potentially opens the door for global research initiatives, cross-disciplinary collaborations, initiative-driven policy reforms, evidence-based intervention research, and implementation, adaptation, and assessment of effective rural mental health models garnered from collaborative entities across the globe.

References

American Counseling Association. (2014). *ACA code of ethics*. Alexandria, VA: Author. Retrieved from https://www.counseling.org/resources/aca-code-of-ethics.pdf.

Australian Counselling Association. (2015). *Code of ethics and practice of the Association for Counsellors in Australia*. Retrieved from https://www.theaca.net.au/documents/ACA%20Code%20of%20Ethics%20and%20Practice%20Ver%2013.pdf.

Bain, S., Rueda, B., Villarreal, J., & Mundy, M. A. (2011). Assessing mental health needs of rural schools in South Texas: Counselors' perspectives. *Research in Higher Education Journal, 14*. Retrieved from https://files.eric.ed.gov/fulltext/EJ1068820.pdf.

Canadian Counselling and Psychotherapy Association. (2007). *Code of ethics*. Ottawa: Author. Retrieved from https://www.ccpa-accp.ca/wp-content/uploads/2014/10/CodeofEthics_en.pdf.

Chinese Psychological Society. (2007). *Code of ethics for counseling and clinical practice*. Beijing: Author. Retrieved from https://proyectoeticablog.files.wordpress.com/2016/03/cc3b3digo-de-c3a9tica-china1.pdf.

Corey, G., Corey, M., Corey, C., & Callanan, P. (2015). *Issues and ethics in the helping professions* (9th ed.). Stamford, CT: Cengage Learning. (ISBN: 9781305389458).

Forester-Miller, H., & Davis, T. E. (2016). Practitioner's guide to ethical decision making (Rev. ed.). Retrieved from http://www.counseling.org/docs/default-source/ethics/practioner's-guide-to-ethical-decision-making.pdf.

Galderisi, S., Heinz, A., Kastrup, M., Beezhold, J., & Sartorius, N. (2015). Toward a new definition of mental health. *World Psychiatry*, *14*(2), 231–233. doi:10.1002/wps.20231.

Hann, K., Pearson, H., Campbell, D., Sesay, D., & Eaton, J. (2015). Factors for success in mental health advocacy. *Global Health Action*, *8*. doi:10.3402/gha.v8.28791.

Iacovino, L. (2002). Ethical principles and information professionals: Theory, practice and education. *Australian Academic & Research Libraries*, *33*(2), 57–74. doi:10.1080/00048623.2002.10755183.

International Commission on Occupational Health. (2014). *International code of ethics for occupational health professionals*. Retrieved from http://www.icohWeb.org/site/multimedia/code_of_ethics/code-of-ethics-en.pdf.

Kocet, M. M., & Herlihy, B. J. (2014). Addressing value-based conflicts within the counseling relationship: A decision-making model. *Journal of Counseling and Development*, *92*(2), 180–186. doi:10.1002/j.1556–6676.2014.00146.x.

Lane, C. (2016). Why is mental health so difficult to define? *Psychology Today*. Retrieved from https://www.psychologytoday.com/blog/side-effects/201606/why-is-mental-health-so-difficult-define.

Lent, J., & Schwartz, R. C. (2012). The impact of work setting, demographic characteristics, and personality factors related to burnout among professional counselors. *Journal of Mental Health Counseling*, *34*(4), 355–372.

Pendse, S. R., & Nugent, N. R. (2017). Mental health challenges and opportunities in rural communities. *The Brown University Child and Adolescent Behavior Letter*, *33*(6), 1–7. doi:10.1002/cbl.30216.

Phillips, C. D., & McLeroy, K. R. (2004). Health in rural America: Remembering the importance of place [Editorial]. *American Journal of Public Health*, *94*(10), 1661–1663.

Ran, M. S., Weng, X., Liu, Y. J., Zhang, T. M., Thornicroft, G., Davidson, L., … CMHP Study Group (2017). Severe mental disorders in rural China: A longitudinal survey. *Lancet*, *390*, S37. Poster abstract. Retrieved from https://www.thelancet.com/action/showPdf?pii=S0140-6736%2817%2933175-6.

Smalley, K. B., Warren, J. C., & Rainer, J. P. (2012). *Rural mental health: Issues, policies, and practices*. New York: Springer Publishing Company. ISBN-13:9780826107992.

Strasser, R., Kam, S. M., & Regalado, S. M. (2016). Rural health care access and policy in developing countries. *Annual Review of Public Health*, *37*(1), 395–412. doi:10.1146/annurev-publhealth-032315-021507.

United Kingdom Council for Psychotherapy. (2009). *Ethical principles and code of professional conduct*. London: Author. Retrieved from https://www.psychotherapy.org.uk/wp-content/uploads/2017/11/UKCP-Ethical-Principles-and-Code-of-Professional-Conduct.pdf.

World Health Organization (2004). *Promoting mental health: Concepts, emerging evidence, practice* (Summary Report). Retrieved from http://www.who.int/mental_health/evidence/en/promoting_mhh.pdf.

World Health Organization (2013). *Mental health action plan: 2013–2020.* Retrieved from https://apps.who.int/iris/bitstream/handle/10665/89966/9789241506021_eng.pdf;jsessionid=DADAB455AC871EA0C922A64BFF889E52?sequence=1.

World Health Organization (2015). *Global health ethics: Key issues.* Retrieved from https://apps.who.int/iris/bitstream/handle/10665/164576/9789240694033_eng.pdf?sequence=1.

World Health Organization (November 28, 2019). *Mental disorders.* Retrieved from https://www. who.int/news-room/fact-sheets/detail/mental-disorders.

World Medical Association (July 9, 2018). *WMA international code of medical ethics.* Retrieved from https://www.wma.net/policies-post/wma-international-code-of-medical-ethics/.

10 Towards a research agenda for global rural mental health

Sarah-Anne Munoz and Steve F. Bain

Introduction

This volume has considered mental health, ill health, and wellbeing within remote and rural contexts, predominately within the Global North. We have taken a holistic view of mental health, drawing on the definition from the World Health Organisation. We have attempted, through our constituent chapters, to present a picture of the contextual factors that both influence mental health and promote wellbeing within rural regions. We believe there are some underlying themes which have emerged that present a research agenda for global rural mental health. In this concluding chapter, we first summarise the main themes to have emerged within this volume and secondly reflect on what these themes suggest for a future research agenda for global, rural mental health.

Conclusions: mental health and the rural context

Each of the individual chapters within this volume has engaged with the concept of mental health within rural regions. The diversity of scales considered ranges from the individual to the regional, national, and international comparison. This illustrates that it is possible to think about how rurality and mental health interact on many levels. Our chapters illustrate the intersectionality of various factors that can be considered "rural" with the mental health and wellbeing of individuals and communities.

At the national level, Dalton and Perkins (Chapter 1) consider the case of Australia. The authors highlight how rural Australia is characterised by economies that depend to a much higher degree than Australian urban areas do on primary industries such as mining, farming, fishing, forestry, and other land-based activities, as well as tourism. This is a situation that is paralleled in the rural areas of many other countries of the Global North. It follows, therefore, that changes and challenges that affect these land-based industries have ripple effects that impact on the mental health and wellbeing of rural dwellers, workers, and wider communities. In Australia, and other industrialised nations, rural areas are experiencing changes in population structure, economic sustainability, and environmental conditions. A stark example of this is given in the form of the drought and bushfire conditions experienced by rural Australia. Similar increases in the frequency of bushfire and drought have been experienced elsewhere, such as in California and the Southern United States. Equally impactful can be flooding and climactic changes that bring monsoon and hurricane conditions. Ikonomopoulos, Yi-Lang and Furgerson (Chapter 6) illustrate the severe impact of such environmental conditions on survivors. Jean-Pierre and Compos-Flores (Chapter 2) remind us that these affect not only permanent rural residents but also itinerant and migrant workers who, especially seasonal workers within land-based industries, can face limited or no access to healthcare and can feel acutely the negative impacts of economic and environmental change.

Although such climatic conditions and impacts on rural areas can be considered stressors that contribute negatively to the mental health and wellbeing of individuals and communities, there are other aspects of rurality that are associated with therapy, recovery, and positive mental health. Therapeutic landscapes literature has pointed towards positive mental wellbeing and restorative effects of, for example, natural landscapes, woodlands, beaches, seascapes, lakes, and a connection with the seasons. Philo and Parr (Chapter 3) illustrate, through their case study of the New and Old Craigs hospitals in the Highlands of Scotland, that such connections with nature are not only therapeutic for people coming from urban environments to experience them – the people from across the Highlands connected with features such as the trees and the duck pond as key therapeutic spaces. They illustrate that for many patients (and staff) aspects of the natural landscape become associated with the therapeutic experience and what might be called hope for recovery. As Philo and Parr note, the notion of nature as therapeutic is not new but one that was enshrined in, for example, the design of the Victorian asylum. The contrasting of the "natural" Old Craigs with the "sterile" New Craigs brings into focus how a medicalisation of mental (ill)health and recovery may have systematically excluded potentially therapeutic elements of nature. Attitudes may be shifting, however, back towards a recognition of the role that nature and rural spaces can play in fostering and maintaining good mental health.

Gorman (Chapter 4) illustrates how this theme is played out in the context of care farming and the consumption of the countryside. His work highlights how particular imaginings of, and elements of, rurality and rural landscape become imbued with meanings of therapy and recovery that are consumed by those coming into rural spaces in order to enact these anticipated becomings of mental wellness. Morton and Bradley (Chapter 5) consider one aspect of engagement with nature (woodland therapy) as it is experienced by rural residents themselves. This is an important contribution to the literature that is lacking in examination of the relationship between rural residents themselves, natural and rural landscapes, and the therapeutic experience. They illustrate how being outside and interacting with nature are key elements in the generation of positive mental health outcomes for the participants within their case studies. However, both Gorman's (Chapter 4) and Morton and Bradley's (Chapter 5) work reminds us that no matter how "idyllic" societal discourses of rurality may be, they are experienced as "real" spaces that can evoke a gambit of human emotion.

It is erroneous to consider rural populations to be homogeneous. Although our chapters show common threads of "rurality" that span regional and national borders, they also reinforce the need to pay heed to the diversity of experience. Dalton and Perkins (Chapter 1), for example, illustrate this with reference to the Aboriginal people of Australia who, like many other indigenous and minority ethnic populations in the Global North, have poorer physical and mental health outcomes in comparison to the population average. This can be seen to be due, at least in part, to their experience of being subject to non-Indigenous rule that is often accompanied by a loss of their ancestral lands and, by association, their sense of connection to the land, leading to reductions in self-esteem and increases in anxiety and depression. This can lead to feelings of hopelessness, loss of control, and pessimism in relation to the future. Jean-Pierre and Compos-Flores (Chapter 2) illustrate that this diversity also needs to be taken into consideration within the study of rural migrants. They highlight that most rural migration literature focuses on agricultural seasonal workers, who often move on temporary working visas. As Jean-Pierre and Campos-Flores reflect, their experiences do not necessarily equate with those of international students moving to rural places of further or higher education, those moving to rural areas on permanent work visas, or asylum seekers who are all under-studied within rural migration literature.

We need to understand local cultural context – and historical – if we are going to work with such minority rural groups to improve health and well-being. The writings of Ikonomopoulos, Yi-Lang, and Furgerson (Chapter 6) and of Villa and Moya (Chapter 8) particularly highlight this. They illustrate that it may be that Indigenous people themselves are the ones best placed to be mental health advocates and to be trained to deliver at least immediate and emergency mental health support. While Ikonomopoulos et. al. (Chapter 6) use Maslow's hierarchy of needs to examine this in the Taiwanese context, Villa and Moya (Chapter 8) illustrate this with relation to the *colonias* of rural South Texas. In doing so, Villa and Moya make a particularly important contribution to progressing thinking on rural mental health – that rural may not only be viewed as a geographical entity but as a set of characteristics – social, cultural, and historical – that can be carried with an individual or a community as they move through other rural and urban spaces. This is one factor that is important for rural mental health care professionals to understand when working with rural populations. This is reinforced by the writings of Bain and Munoz (Chapter 10), who illustrate the benefits that could be achieved from a global approach to rural mental health care professional working ethics.

Mental health services in rural areas can be sparse. Mental health care professionals can be few and far between. This is highlighted, in the South African context in particular, by Grindle and De Kock (Chapter 7). When professionals are present, they may not be from the same cultural, ethnic, or religious background as rural residents and, therefore, lack social, cultural, and historical understanding of rural communities and individual circumstances (see, in particular, Chapters 6 and 8). Our chapters have illustrated that rural areas tend to be underserved by mental health services providers. We have also seen that providing services to remote and rural areas can be challenging and costly for many reasons, not least the large geographical distances between communities and low population densities. Rural residents often experience a long drive time to access mental health services providers – this may even serve to mitigate the positive impact of receiving treatment by further entrenching the disconnect between rural resident and their ancestral land/landscape/homescape (see Chapter 6) – a disconnect that is echoed in Philo and Parr's (Chapter 3) recognition that patients seem more at home with an "aged" and "weathered" mental health facility that is very much part of the local landscape. Turning to interventions that use cultural appropriateness, digital mechanisms of connection, and actively seek to reinforce connections between people, nature, and land (such as the Wildlife programme highlighted in Chapter 7 by Grindle and De Kock) may go some way towards providing more appropriate and efficacious treatments for rural residents.

The response by rural residents, healthcare professionals, and communities to a sparsity of mental health (and other) services is often to initiate activities of their own to help combat, for example, stress, depression, and anxiety. We have seen in this volume that this can take the form of local initiatives based within primary care as in Australia (Chapter 1), South Africa (Chapter 7), Scotland (Chapter 5), the Southern United States (Chapter 8), and Taiwan (Chapter 6). This plays out in different ways in different countries and regions but in some cases may go so far as to constitute a "parallel" primary care system adapted to the needs of indigenous rural residents as highlighted by Dalton and Perkins (Chapter 1) for rural Aboriginal and Torres Strait Islander peoples in Australia or through the WHO Mental Health Gap Action Programme (Chapter 6). Increasingly, the interventions promoted to facilitate and maintain good mental wellbeing are non-clinical and non-pharmaceutical in nature. Morton and Bradley's work (Chapter 5) illustrates the positive outcomes that can be achieved for rural residents from such interventions. Through their case studies, they illustrate how non-pharmaceutical interventions can produce outcomes such as increases in physical activity, reductions in anxiety, and increases in self-confidence. They also illustrate how, for many people, the social aspect of undertaking such interventions in a peer group is one of the ways in which positive outcomes are generated.

However, several of our chapters have touched on the issue of stigma. We have seen that living in a remote and/or rural community can be a doubled-edged sword. It can bring a close-knit support network to buffer the effects of mental ill health, but it can also produce a "goldfish bowl" effect in which it can feel like everyone knows everyone else's business. Several of our chapter authors have commented on how an increased notion of the visibility of an individual's mental ill health within such small, rural populations can impact upon people's help-seeking (or lack of help-seeking behaviour). Jean-Pierre and Campos-Flores, for example (Chapter 2), note that visible stigma can be a factor that dissuades rural migrants from seeking formal mental health support.

Towards a research agenda for global rural mental health

This volume has considered how rurality interacts with mental health and wellbeing at different geographical scales. Through each of the chapters, we have demonstrated that mental health and wellbeing in rural areas have social determinants – how the conditions in which people are born, grow, live, work, and age influence and interact with mental health. It is possible to reflect on the gaps in knowledge and new avenues for research that have been highlighted by the work presented in this volume. The chapters shave considered rural populations in different forms – those currently residing in rural areas, migrants arriving to rural areas, Indigenous and ethnic minority populations with traditional rural lands, those who carry characteristics and cultures developed in rural areas as they move. This has highlighted several avenues for future rural mental health research.

Firstly, research and scholarship around rural mental health has tended to view rural as a fixed geographical construct, formed in opposition to the urban. We argue for a research agenda for global rural mental health that recognises rurality as more than geographical location – a recognition that the populations of rural areas are changing and subject to flows of movement. Thus, more research that takes a longitudinal or life-course approach is needed. Rural populations across the globe tend to be categorised, marginalised, and generalised apart from their uniqueness and inimitability. For mental health providers, researchers, community leaders, and legislators, seeing rural populations as distinct cultures rather than geographical categories would positively impact rural mental health literature, identification of scalable interventions, and global policy change.

Secondly, we argue that a research agenda for global rural mental health would include consideration of connections to land, landscape, and nature – not only in terms of the potential for rural areas to act as therapeutic space for recovery but of how various processes of disconnection from land and nature can impact negatively on mental wellbeing. Further research is needed to understand the potential for nature therapy for those coming in to rural landscapes from urban areas in comparison to those already living within rural landscapes, with mental ill health. More work is also needed to explore the links between rural mental health, notions of belonging, and environmental trauma.

Thirdly, a global rural mental health research agenda needs to engage with new and innovative ways of supporting wellbeing, and delivering mental health services within, rural areas. Greater evidence is required on the use of non-clinical, non-pharmaceutical, and community-based interventions. Broad collaborations must be had as to how to support mental health professionals as they provide the most appropriate and efficacious services possible to rural areas.

In closing, we must emphasise that this work in no way purports to be an end-all treatise of the global aspects of rural mental health. In fact, it serves as a reminder of the epic amount of work that still needs to be done. But it does have as a main goal the determination to engage in greater and more in-depth conversations related to the wellbeing of rural peoples worldwide. In a very tangible way, the book serves as an intentional form of advocacy as it relates to underserved rural populations wherever they may be found. For in addressing the needs of rural and remote peoples, we find our way to helping other marginalised populations within our global family and resonating the fundamental truth that everyone everywhere matters.

Index

Note: *Italic* page numbers refer to figures; **bold** page numbers refer to tables and page numbers followed by "n" denote endnotes.

AAI *see* animal-assisted interventions (AAI)
abolitionist views 54n7
Aboriginal Community Controlled Health Services 15
Aboriginal Medical Services 15, 16
Aboriginal people 5, 8, 21, 167; health service system 15–16; mental health problems 10; principles of social and emotional wellbeing 10, *11*; suicide rates 12
Accessibility and Remoteness Index of Australia (ARIA) 8
adolescent mental health disorders 124
adolescent mental wellbeing 126
adversity 13
affective (mood) disorders 10
Africa, mental illness in 119
Agricola, H. J. 61
agricultural migrant workers 32, 34
American Counseling Association 161; Code of Ethics 155
animal-assisted interventions (AAI) 78
anti-depressants 2, 96
anti-stigma initiatives 2
anxiety 10
Aonach Mor 89
Argyll and Bute Branching Out service 83–85
ARIA *see* Accessibility and Remoteness Index of Australia (ARIA)
ART *see* attention restoration theory (ART)
assessment of mental health 95
asylum 53n3–54n3; afterlives of 41; farms 70; fit localities for 43; lunatic 41, 42; and mental healthcare 40–42; nineteenth-century 43, 53n3; therapeutic landscapes 42, 43
asylum seekers 30, 31, 33
Atkins, G. 77, 78
attention restoration theory (ART) 78
attitudes 146; of Latinos/Chicanos 141–143; Manana 141
Australian Bureau of Statistics 10
Australian Counselling Association (ACA): Code of Ethics and Practice 155
Australian healthcare system 14, 21; issues for *14*
Australian Rural Mental Health Study 19
Australian rural population 8–9; *see also* Aboriginal people; Torres Strait Islander people
Australia, rural mental health 5, 21, 165–167; bushfires and drought-related worry/distress 12–13, 166; national surveys 10; natural disasters 13; principles of social and emotional wellbeing 10, *11*; service models (*see* rural mental health service models, in Australia); solastalgia 13; suicide rates 10–12, *12*; traumas 12

Bain, Steve F. 7, 152, 167
Beezhold, J. 152
behavioral activation 96
biophilia hypothesis 78
Birchwood Recovery Centre 89
Bowen, M. 1
bracketing 159–160
Bradley, Sara 6, 166–168
Bragg, R. 77, 78

Branching Out for Mental Health 79, 81; Argyll and Bute 83–85; Highland 81–83
British tabloids 1
Browne, W.A.F. 44
Bryant, L. 64, 67
Burns, N. 45, 54n5
bushfires 13

Cacciatore, J. 68
Campbell, D. 153
Campos-Flores, Linamar 5, 166, 167, 169
Canadian Counselling and Psychotherapy Association (CCPA) 155–156
Canberra bushfires 13
care farming 57, 59–61, 68–70, 78, 166
Carter, T. 75
CBT *see* cognitive behavioural treatment (CBT)
CCPA *see* Canadian Counselling and Psychotherapy Association (CCPA)
Centers for Disease Control and Prevention 134
Chao, S. F. 102, 103
Chicanos (Latinos): locus of control 143; mental health issues 139; resiliency and cultural strengths 145–147; social interaction 141; spirituality 143–144; time orientation 141; values and attitudes 141–143
Chile, PTDPHC program in 99–100
China, ethical standards in 156
Chinese Psychological Society (CPS) 156
clinical/activist paradigm of rurality 135, 137–138, *138*, 140; generalist ecosystems approach 138; language 140; locus of control 143; paradigm shift 146; psycho-socio-spiritual assessment 140; religion 143; resiliency 145–17; self-image 135, 137–139, 142, 144; social forces 135–139; social interaction 140–141; socio-cultural assessment 139–140; spirituality 143–144; time orientation 141; values and attitudes 141–143
Code of Professional Conduct 154
cognitive behavioural therapy (CBT) 96, 123
collaborative care programs 99, 100
Collins 141
Collins, D. 58
colonias 145
Community Wellbeing Collaboratives (CWC) 19
Conradson, D. 61
conservation on prescription
Cooke, A. 1
Cosgrave, C. 18
counselling strategy 104–106, 109, 110, 112
counsellors 104–106, 109–112
CPS *see* Chinese Psychological Society (CPS)
Craig Dunain Hospital 5–6, 44–48, 166; *vs.* New Craigs 51–53
crisis interventions services 101
cultural awareness 139
cultural competence 135
cultural strengths 145–147
cultural values 108
"curandero" 139
Curtis, Sarah 42, 62
CWC *see* Community Wellbeing Collaboratives (CWC)
Cycle to Health programme 86
cycling 85–88

Daley, M. 134, 135, 139
Dalton, Hazel 5, 165, 167, 168
DALYs *see* disability-adjusted life-years (DALYs)
Davis, T. E. 161
DBT *see* dialectical behaviour therapy (DBT)
deinstitutionalisation 41
De Kock, Johannes H. 4, 6, 168
Deloitte Access Economics 13
Department of Health and Human Services 134
depression 1, 2, 6; assessment 95; concept of 98; group IPT 97–98; mental health Gap Action Programme 96–97, 111; natural disasters and 103; PM+ program 97; remote collaborative care programs 99, 100; in rural India 98–99; and suicide 94–96; symptoms of 95–96; treatment for 96–97; types of 95
"Design in Mental Health Conference" 51
Diagnostic and Statistical Manual of Mental Disorders (DSM-5) 110
dialectical behaviour therapy (DBT) 123
DIDO model *see* drive in-drive out (DIDO) model
digital narrative approach (DNA) 6, 116, 125–126; for health behaviour change 126
Digital Narrative Transformation Framework 125

digital technologies 126
Di Iacovo, F. P. 69
disability-adjusted life-years (DALYs) 117, 124
discrimination 33, 34
DNA *see* digital narrative approach (DNA)
domestic violence 12, 106–107, 112; approaching survivors 110; effects of 108–110; mental health consequences 109; perceptions of 107–108
drive in-drive out (DIDO) model 17
drought-related worry/distress 12–13, 166

Earth for Life 77
Eaton, J. 153
Ecominds scheme 77
Economic and Social Research Council (ESRC) 45
ecotherapy, mind 77–78
Elings, M. 61
environmental conservation 78
environmental inequality 136
Equally Well movement 10
ESRC *see* Economic and Social Research Council (ESRC)
esteem needs, Maslow's theory 105, 111
ethical decision-making models 161–162
ethical standards 151

FIFO model *see* fly in-fly out (FIFO) model
Fifth National Mental Health and Suicide Prevention Plan 14, 15
financial and business worries 12
floods, and mental health 13
fly in-fly out (FIFO) model 17
Forester-Miller, H. 161
Forum for the Future 9
Furgerson, Karen 6, 166, 167

Gairing, M. 68
Galderisi, S. 152
GAMH *see* Glasgow Association of Mental health (GAMH)
Gartnavel Royal Hospital 53n2, 54n4
Garza, Kristopher 6
Gayaa Dhuwi (Proud Spirit) declaration 10
Georges, C. M. 110
Gesler, Wil 62, 65; 'therapeutic landscapes' 42
Glasgow Association of Mental health (GAMH) 77
global burden of mental illness 116–117
global ethics, benefits of 151
Global Strategy for Women's, Children's and Adolescents' Health 124
"goldfish bowl" effect 168
Gorman, Richard 6, 68, 166, 167
green exercise 78, 90
Green Exercise Programme 91
Greenleaf, A. T. 60
greenspace and health 76–77
greenspace interventions for mental health 79–90; barriers 91–92; benefits 90; Branching Out for Mental Health 79, 81–85; factors for success 90–91; Nature Walks for Wellbeing 88–90; in Scotland 77–78; Velocity – Cycle to Health 85–88
Grindle, Mark 4, 6, 168
group interpersonal therapy (group IPT) 97–98, 101, 111

Halfacree, K. H. 58
Hann, K. 153
Hassink, J. 61
health ethics 160
healthy migrant effect 30
Heinz, A. 152
Herlihy, B. J. 159
high-income countries (HICs) 116, 117; mental illness in 117–124
Highland Branching Out service 81–83
Highland Users Group (HUG) 46
Hine, R. 60
Humphreys, J. S. 9
Hussain, R. 18
Hynds, H. 91

ICA *see* Inverness City Advertiser (ICA)
Ikonomopoulos, James 6, 166, 167
India (rural areas): adolescent mental wellbeing 126; alleviating symptoms in 98–99; depression concept in 98; mental health nurses in 119
Indigenous cultures and norms 105–106, 112
indirect tangible costs 13
Individual, Social, Material (ISM) model 79, **80**
information and communications technology (ICT) 20, 100, 101
intangible costs 13
International Code of Medical Ethics 154
International Commission on Occupational Health 154

international ethical guidelines 7, 154; Australia 155; Canada 155–156; China 156–157; United Kingdom 154–155; United States of America 155
international ethical standard for rural mental health professionals 157; people 157–158; practice 160–162; profession 160; professional 158–160
International Personality Item Pool-Big Five 159
international perspectives 153–154
international students 33
interpersonal psychotherapy (IPT) 96; group IPT 97–98, 101, 111
intimate partner violence 106–107, 112; approaching survivors 110; effects of 108–110; mental health consequences 109; perceptions of 107–108
Inverness City Advertiser (ICA) 86
Inverness District Lunatic Asylum 44–45
IPT *see* interpersonal psychotherapy (IPT)
irregular migrants 31
ISM model *see* Individual, Social, Material (ISM) model

Jean-Pierre, Johanne 5, 166, 167, 169
Jegede, S. 107
Journal of Rural Studies 61
Juarez, Benito 147

Kadianaki, I. 1
Kastrup, M. 152
Kearns, R. 58, 65
Kelly, B. J. 10
Kenez, S. 1
Kinderman, P. 1
Klerman, Gerald L. 97
Kocet, M. M. 159

labour migration: agricultural, and mental health issues 32
Lane, C. 151, 152
language, rurality paradigm 140
Latinos (Chicanos): locus of control 143; mental health issues 139; resiliency and cultural strengths 145–147; social interaction 141; spirituality 143–144; time orientation 141; values and attitudes 141–143
Lent, J. 159
LHNs *see* Local Health Networks (LHNs)
Liamputtong, P. 1
Liang, Ya-Wen Melissa 6
Lin, J. 102
Lin, W. 102
literature review 5, 26–27; agricultural labour migration and mental health issues 32; gaps and future directions 33–34; methodological approach 27, **28–29**, 30; migrant mental health in rural contexts 31–32; thematic analysis 30–34; wellbeing, mental health, and migration 30–31
Little, J. 63
Local Health Networks (LHNs) 14–15
love and belonging needs, Maslow's theory 104–105, 111
low- and middle-income countries (LMICs) 116, 117; adolescent mental wellbeing 126; mental illness in 117–124, *118*
Luginaah, I. 68
lunatic asylums 41, 42

MacKian, S. C. 59
McLaughlin, H. 62
Maple, M. 18
Maslow's hierarchy of needs 104, 111, 167; esteem needs 105; love and belonging needs 104–105; physiological needs 104; safety needs 104; self-actualisation 105
Mason-Renton, S. 68
Ma, Z. 1
media, perceptions of mental illness 1–2
medical-psychiatric gaze 47
mental health 2–4; definition of 2, 151–152; and rural context 165–169
mental healthcare 33; ruralising and de-ruralising 42–44
Mental Health Emergency Care-Rural Access Program (MHEC-RAP) 18
mental health Gap Action Programme (mh GAP) 96–97, 111
mental health human resources, comparative analysis **127**
mental health nurses, in South Africa 122–123
mental health professional 158–160
mental health professional shortage area (MHPSA) 133
mental health programmes 153
mental health workforce crisis, in South Africa 120, 121, **127, 128**; clinical

psychologists 122; mental health nurses 122–123; psychiatrists 121; task-shifting approach 123
mental illness/ill health: global burden of 116–117; in LMICs and HICs 117–124, 118; media portrayals of 1–2
mental wellbeing, in rural regions 2–4
MHEC-RAP *see* Mental Health Emergency Care-Rural Access Program (MHEC-RAP)
mh GAP *see* mental health Gap Action Programme (mh GAP)
migrants 26–27; social determinants of health 27; stressors 30, 31
migration studies 26
Millennium Drought 12
Milligan, C. 58
mind ecotherapy 77–78
mixed reality (MR) 116
modified Monash approach 8
Moon, G. 58
Morton, Sarah 6, 166–168
Moving On service 84
Moya, Eva 7, 167
Mundy, M. A. 152
Munoz, Sarah-Anne 7, 167
Muswellbrook Healthy and Well 20
Myanmar: mental health nurses in 119

NACCHO *see* National Aboriginal Community Controlled Health Organisation (NACCHO)
NAHSWP *see* National Aboriginal Health Strategy (NAHSWP)
National Aboriginal and Torres Strait Islander Leadership and Mental Health (NATSILMH) 10
National Aboriginal Community Controlled Health Organisation (NACCHO) 16
National Aboriginal Health Strategy (NAHSWP) 10
National Health Policy Guidelines 120
National Mental Health Commission 14
NATSILMH *see* National Aboriginal and Torres Strait Islander Leadership and Mental Health (NATSILMH)
natural disasters: criteria 101; dealing with the aftermath 104–106; flooding 101; mental health effects 102–103; in rural Taiwan 101–102; Typhoon Morakot 102
nature-based interventions 77–78
"nature cure" 51; *see also* therapeutic landscapes
Nature Walks for Wellbeing 88–90
neuroticism 160
New Craigs 5–6, 48–51, 166; *vs.* old Craig Dunain 51–53
non-clinical interventions 75
Northern Ireland, rural stresses 135

O'Connor, D. 69
O'Halloran, P. 1
Ohlsson, R. 1
Ojo, R. C. 107
online therapies 116
Open Aye 77
Orphanidou, M. 1
Osborne, Terry 52–53; *Sightlines: The View of a Valley through the Voice of Depression* 40, *52*
Our Healthy Clarence 19
"Our Natural Health Service" 78
Oyefara, O. O. 107

"paradox of proximity" 32
Parr, Hester 5, 6, 45, 54n5, 58, 166, 168
Peacock, J. 60
Pearson, H. 153
Perkins, David 5, 17, 165, 167, 168
permanent residents 33
personal identity 108
Philo, Christopher 5, 6, 45, 53n3, 54n5, 166, 168
PHNs *see* Primary Health Networks (PHNs)
physical activity 76, 91
physiological needs, Maslow's theory 104, 111
Pini, B. 64, 67
PM+ *see* Problem Management Plus (PM+)
post-asylum geographies 41
post-traumatic stress disorder (PTSD) 103
poverty, psychosocial difficulties 120
Pretty, J. N. 60
primary healthcare (PHC) system 120–122
Primary Health Networks (PHNs) 14–15; stepped care approach 15
Problem Management Plus (PM+) 97, 101, 111
Productivity Commission 14, 15

Program of treatment for depression in primary healthcare (PTDPHC) 99–100
psychiatric survivors 54n7
psychiatrists, in South Africa 121
psycho-evolutionary stress reduction theory (PET) 78
psychosis 31
psycho-socio-spiritual assessment 140
PTDPHC *see* Program of treatment for depression in primary healthcare (PTDPHC)
PTSD *see* post-traumatic stress disorder (PTSD)

racism 33
Rainer, J. P. 152
refugees 31, 33
regional imagination 45
religion, rurality paradigm 143
relocation of people 41
remote collaborative care programs 99, 100
Repper, J. 75
research agenda 169–170
resiliency 135, 143, 145–147
RFDS *see* Royal Flying Doctors Service (RFDS)
risk governance 54n4
Rivera, M. J. 59
Roberts, R. 17
Roessger, K. M. 60
Rosen, A. 17
Royal College of Nursing (RCN) 91
Royal Flying Doctors Service (RFDS) 9, 17
Rueda, B. 152
Rural Adversity Mental Health Program (RAMHP) 19
rural affect 59
rural deficits approach 9
rurality 70, 133–135; application of 144–145; cultural constructions of 68, 69; definition of 139; discourses of 64, 70; healthification of 68; ideology 135; methods for exploring 61–63; paradigm (*see* clinical/activist paradigm of rurality); poverty 133, 136; social work model 146; therapeutic landscapes and 57–59
rural mental health 2–4; professional code of ethics 157–162
rural mental health service models, in Australia 5, 13, 21; annual mental health plan 15; DIDO and FIFO models 17; digital apps 15; Fifth National Mental Health and Suicide Prevention Plan 14, 15; integrated specialist services 17; Local Health Networks 14–15; MHEC-RAP 18; Muswellbrook Healthy and Well 20; National Mental Health Commission 14; non-emergency services 15; Primary Health Networks 14–15; Productivity Commission 14, 15; RFDS 17; telepsychiatry service 18–19
rural suicidality 100–101
rural–therapeutic landscapes 6, 57–59; care farming and 59–61, 68–70; contesting and disrupting 66–70; entanglements of 63; ethnographic observation 62; interview research 62; producing and recruiting 63–66

safety needs, Maslow's theory 104, 111
SAMH *see* Scottish Association for Mental Health (SAMH)
Sanders, T. 17
Sartorius, N. 152
schizophrenia 31
Schwartz, R. C. 159
Scotland, greenspace interventions in 77–78
Scottish Association for Mental Health (SAMH) 77, 91
Scottish Government Mental Health Strategy 91
Scottish Index of Multiple Deprivation 83
Scottish Natural Heritage 78
selective serotonin reuptake inhibitors (SSRIs) 96
self-actualisation, Maslow's theory 105, 111, 112
self-harm 10
self-image 135, 137–139, 142, 144
Serenity Café project 77
Sesay, D. 153
"Shifting the Dial" (2017) 14
Sightlines: The View of a Valley through the Voice of Depression (Osborne) 40, *52*, 52–53
Smalley, K. B. 152
Smarter Choices, Smarter Places (SCSP) Open Fund 85
Smith, G. 62
Smith, K. B. 9
social and therapeutic horticulture (STH) 78

social determinants of health 27
social exchange theory 141
social exclusion 33
social forces 135–139
social interaction 140–141
social prescribing 75, 76
social work assessments 139
social workers: in rural environments 134
socio-cultural assessment 139–140
solastalgia 13, 49
South Africa (SA): clinical psychologists 122; democracy 121, 122; HIV/AIDS 119; innovative strategies 123–124; mental health nurses 122–123; mental health workforce 120, 121, **127, 128**; mental illness in 119; PHC system 120–122; psychiatrists 121
South-East Asia: mental health care professionals in 118
spiritual fulcrum 139
spirituality 143–144
STH *see* social and therapeutic horticulture (STH)
stigma/stigmatization 2, 19, 30, 32–34, 168
stress 30; psychological 31; in rural environments 135; work-related 32
stressors 30, 31, 166
substance use disorders 10
suicidal ideation 96
suicide 2; Aboriginal and Torres Strait Islanders 10–12; depression and 94–96; family and community support 101; protective factors 100–101, 111; in rural areas 96
symbolic interaction theory 140

TAG unit *see* Training and Guidance (TAG) unit
Taiwan (rural areas), natural disasters in 101–102; connecting professional volunteers 106; counselling strategy 104–106; dealing with the aftermath 104–106; Indigenous cultures and norms 105–106, 112; Maslow's hierarchy of needs 104–105; mental health effects 102–103; Typhoon Morakot 102
tangible costs 13
task-shifting approach 123, 125
temporary workers 33
therapeutic carescapes 43
therapeutic landscapes 42, 57, 166; Craig Dunain Hospital 44–48; New Craigs 48–51; and rurality 57–59 (*see also* rural–therapeutic landscapes)
Thissen, J. T. 61
time orientation 141
Tomlinson-Clarke, S. M. 110
Tonsing, J. C. 107, 108
Torres Strait Islander people 8, 21; mental health problems 10; principles of social and emotional wellbeing 10, *11*; suicide rates 12
Training and Guidance (TAG) unit 54n5
traumas 12
tricyclic antidepressants (TCAs) 96
Typhoon Morakot 102, 104

undocumented migrants 30, 31
United Kingdom Council for Psychotherapy (UKCP): Ethical Principles and Code of Professional Conduct 154–155
United States: mental illness 133, 134
utilitarian 26

values: of Latinos/Chicanos 141–143
Velocity – Cycle to Health 85–88
Villa, Robert 7, 167
Villarreal, J. 152
violence against women 107; perceptions of 107–108

walking 88–90
Warren, J. C. 152
Warwick-Edinburgh Mental Well-Being Scale (WEMWBS) 86
Washburn, S. 62
Weissman, Myrna M. 97
What Research Matters for Mental Health Policy in Scotland 75
White Paper for the Transformation of the Health System 120
wilderness therapy 78
wildlife, and DNA 125
Wilkins, R. 9
Wilson, M. G. 9
Wood, Angela 43
Woods, M. 63, 67
World Bank Hazard Management 101
World Health Assembly 95
World Health Organization (WHO) 26, 117; domestic/intimate partner violence 107; Global Health Ethics

154; Global Strategy for Women's, Children's and Adolescents' Health 124; Health Action Plan (2013–2020) 153; health, definition of 27; health ethics 160–161; mental health, definition of 152; mental health Gap Action Programme 96–97, 111; PM+ program 97
World Medical Association 154
Wu, H. C. 102
Wydler, H. 68

years lived with disabilities (YLDs) 117
Yun Shan 139

Zwartbol, C. 61

For Product Safety Concerns and Information please contact our EU representative GPSR@taylorandfrancis.com Taylor & Francis Verlag GmbH, Kaufingerstraße 24, 80331 München, Germany

Batch number: 10725798

Printed by Printforce, the Netherlands